The Dilemma of Drug Policy in the United States

The HarperCollins Public Policy Series

The Dilemma of Drug Policy in the United States

Elaine B. Sharp
The University of Kansas

HarperCollins*College*Publishers

Acquisitions Editor: Leo Wiegman
Project Editor: Janet Frick
Design Supervisor: Mary Archondes
Cover Design: Kay Petronio
Production Manager: Laura Chavoen
Compositor: R.R. Donnelley & Sons Company
Printer and Binder: Malloy Lithographing, Inc.
Cover Printer: Malloy Lithographing, Inc.

THE DILEMMA OF DRUG POLICY IN THE UNITED STATES

Library of Congress Cataloging-in-Publication Data

Sharp, Elaine B.
    The dilemma of drug policy in the United States / Elaine B. Sharp.
      p.   cm.
    Includes bibliographical references and index.
    ISBN 0-06-500973-8
    1. Drug abuse—Government policy—United States. 2. Drug abuse and crime—United States. 3. Drug abuse—United States—Prevention. 4. Drug abuse—Treatment—United States. I. Title.
HV5825.S4497 1994
362.29'0973—dc20   93-44564
                                                   CIP

93 94 95 96 9 8 7 6 5 4 3 2 1

Contents

Foreword

This volume is the first in the HarperCollins Public Policy Series, studies of significant domestic policy issues facing the American people as we move into the twenty-first century. Designed both to complement public policy textbooks for advanced undergraduates and graduate students and to provide a resource for specialists, each of these brief works provides a comprehensive, coherent, scholarly account of the development of a particular substantive policy domain. In doing so these books offer an historical review of policy development in a given domain as well as an analysis and evaluation of current efforts to deal with key problems.

Unlike much of the writing in the field of policy studies, the books in this series are more concerned with the ideas that lie behind policy and their implementation than with issues of political process. Providing an account of the drama of Congressional give-and-take in passing the Food Stamp program, for example, or of interest group strategic considerations in tax reform politics is less important here than the exploration of the sources and substance of competing definitions of problems and the resulting programs that emerge. These books, in short, immerse us more in the substance of public policy than the politics that surround its creation.

Thus, the meat of public policy in this series is conceived as a set of government objectives and programmatic initiatives that evolve over time. Rest assured this series does not and cannot ignore politics. Any public policy undergoes an evolution driven by shifting definitions of the problem which programs or government positions attempt to address, by changing political and economic considerations, and by the learning experiences gained through the implementation process. These elements, of course, are all contested in the political arena. It is clearly essential to understand the array of actors and interests involved in this competition. Furthermore, it is important to take account of the structure of public opinion, which provides a matrix in which contests over problem definitions and solutions occur. Thus, although the books in this series are principally concerned with definitions, programs, and implementation, they are at the same time attentive to the need to establish the political context in which substantive policy initiatives are developed and later modified or abandoned.

Public problems are, of course, rarely solved. Drug use, poverty, environmental degradation, and inadequate housing are perennial issues. Not only is our social technology often inadequate to eliminate social and economic problems (in contrast, say, to our ability to eliminate polio with scientific technology), but we must make choices about how to allocate our resources. There is always a question, then, of what remains to be done. Each book in this series not only looks backward, examining history as a way of understanding where we are at the present, but also forward to the policy challenges that face us at the beginning of the twenty-first century. What advances in knowledge must we make to address a particular public problem more successfully? Must we shift our definition of what the problem is? Are our approaches to problem solution evolving in ways different from the past? What changes in the political and social landscape will bear on the policy domain in question in the future? To confront these questions armed with the benefits of historical perspective is perhaps to be as well prepared for what lies ahead as we can be.

Peter Eisinger
La Follette Institute of Public Affairs
University of Wisconsin

Preface

Drugs constitute an important policy problem in American society because the abuse of illicit substances yields a variety of social pathologies and because governmental efforts to control drug distribution and use have been less than successful and sometimes yield undesirable side consequences. For these reasons, the topic of drug policy has been the focus of much discussion and commentary and the subject of an ever-growing number of books. Much of the discussion and most of the books begin with a critique of existing drug policy and proceed to wrestle with the question of what should be done about drugs. While this is an important question, it is not the only question that can be asked about drug policy. From the viewpoint of a political scientist interested in public policy processes, there are other, equally compelling questions. In particular: Why do we do what we do with respect to drugs? That is, what political dynamics have led us to the constellation of drug policies that characterizes the U.S. approach to the drug problem? Furthermore, to the extent that existing drug policy is flawed, why is there nevertheless so much continuity over time in the U.S. drug policy?

This book focuses on these sorts of questions. It is premised on the notion that calls for change in U.S. drug policy cannot be properly evaluated without a clear sense of the history of U.S. drug policy and the political dynamics that are a part of the history, along with the lessons that history offers about the opportunities for and constraints on policy change. Compared with other treatments, it assumes that the political feasibility of policy change is the central issue in the quest for a better response to the drug problem in the United States. In short, it is intended to explicitly focus the theoretical lenses of political science on a topic that has been largely dominated by the prescriptive assessments of economists; criminal justice, mental health, and legal experts; and journalists.

The book is intended for a diverse set of audiences, ranging from professional scholars to interested citizens, and including both undergraduates and graduate students in public policy-oriented courses. Most important, the book is intended to be worthwhile to those who are interested in drug policy only insofar as it illuminates more general phenomena of politics and policy change as well as those who are interested in drug policy per se. The challenge of meeting the needs of all these audiences, of course, is to find the right mix between background and conceptual discussion as well as the right mix between descriptive detail unique to this policy realm and analytical conclusions that might transcend the case of drug policy.

Chapter 1 sets the stage by outlining important concepts about policy failure, the policy cycle, agenda setting, and evaluation that place the drug problem in a policy learning context. In the process of introducing these themes, basic information about the scope of the drug problem and the methods for making that assessment is provided. Chapters 2 through 4 constitute a thematic policy history, outlining the content of drug policy as it has evolved from the Progressive Era through the Bush administration while highlighting how important aspects of agenda setting are reflected in this history. These chapters are organized around three defining episodes of drug policy formation in the contemporary era—President Nixon's high-profile "war on drugs," President Carter's efforts to decriminalize marijuana, and the Reagan-Bush "war on drugs." Chapters 5 through 7 outline the drug treatment, prevention, and enforcement programs that have been implemented as a result of this policy history, as well as documenting what is known about the effectiveness of the various programs. These chapters offer crucial information that the reader needs to make sense of widespread arguments that existing drug policy is flawed. Chapter 8 takes up the task of accounting for the continuity in drug policy, despite evidence of failure. It returns the discussion to general questions of political accountability, policy learning, and the political feasibility of change. With this discussion as the foundation, Chapter 9 concludes with a discussion and assessment of legalization and other suggestions for drug policy reform that have become so prominent in recent years.

Credit and many thanks are due to many individuals who have, in one way or another, been a part of the creation of this book. Bob Lineberry turned a conversation over coffee at the APSA meetings into an occasion for encouragement of this work. Marybeth Sughrue and Marissa Kelly made important contributions to the data collection process. A number of my colleagues, most especially Burdett Loomis and Allan Cigler, offered helpful comments on early portions of the work. I have also benefited from the perceptive comments and suggestions of the following reviewers:

James Anderson, Texas A&M University; Leonard Champney, University of Scranton; David Dabelko, Ohio University; Alan Shank, SUNY, Genesco; Carolyn Thompson, University of North Carolina, Charlotte; Frank Thompson, SUNY, Albany; and Norman Zucker, University of Rhode Island. I am grateful to the University of Kansas for the funding support provided through the General Research Fund. And through it all, Bob Adams was understanding, encouraging, and patient.

Elaine B. Sharp

The Dilemma of Drug Policy in the United States

Policy, Politics, and Learning: The Case of Illicit Drugs

INTRODUCTION

The setting is somber, as the U.S. president, a Republican in his first term of office, begins his public statement on a new drug policy initiative:

> America's public enemy number one in the United States is drug abuse. In order to fight and defeat this enemy, it is necessary to wage a new, all-out offensive. I have asked Congress to provide the legislative authority and the funds to fuel this kind of an offensive. . . . It will be governmentwide, pulling together the nine different fragmented areas within the government in which this problem is now being handled, and it will be nationwide in terms of a new educational program that we trust will result from the discussions that we have had.[1]

The setting is still somber as the Republican president explains his drug policy initiative in a nationally televised address to the nation. In that address, the president says:

> All of us agree that the gravest domestic threat facing our nation today is drugs. Drugs have strained our faith in our system of justice. . . . The social costs of drugs are mounting. In short, drugs are sapping our strength as a nation. . . . Earlier today, I sent this document, our first such national strategy, to the Congress. . . . Tonight, I'm announcing a strategy that reflects the coordinated, cooperative commitment of all our Federal agencies. In short, this plan is as comprehensive as the problem.[2]

The elapsed time between these two sets of comments is *not* the few hours that separate a morning news conference from a televised address in the evening. The elapsed time between the two is 18 years. The latter comments are those of George Bush in September 1989. The first statement, virtually identical in tone and themes, was given by Richard M. Nixon in June 1971. Similar comments were made by important government officials in the 1950s and the 1930s.

These examples indicate that drugs have long been a source of concern and the subject of government attention and public policy in the United States. However, the continuing rhetoric about the drug crisis in America suggests that despite a lengthy history of public policy interventions, the drug problem has not been "solved"—or at least that drugs continue to be definable as a problem by politicians, bureaucrats, and private individuals.

Drugs are a problem to individuals whose lives are ravaged by drug addiction and to families that suffer the tragedy of losing loved ones to drug overdoses or the difficulties of dealing with drug-abusing family members. But these are personal forms of the drug problem. From a policy perspective, drugs are also a social problem. Drugs impose costs on employers (and indirectly on society) in the form of absenteeism, medical costs, and lessened productivity. For example, General Motors Corporation estimates that substance abuse among its workers or their families "cost the company $600 million in 1987."[3] Drugs are also defined as a social problem because of their connection to crime, and especially violent crime. The precise nature of the drugs-crime connection remains controversial. However, when innocent children are killed on their way to school in drive-by shootings between rival drug-selling gangs, as occurred in several cities in 1992, or more generally when urban neighborhoods are transformed into combat zones because of drug-related violence, a strong link between drugs and violent crime is forged in the public's mind.

Drugs have also been implicated in other frightening public health problems. Intravenous drug use is one of the most important avenues for spread of the virus that causes acquired immunodeficiency syndrome (AIDS), for example. And babies born to mothers who are addicted to crack cocaine constitute individual tragedies and bring other costs as well—at least $100,000 per baby in neonatal hospital care alone.[4] Drugs are also a social problem in the same sense that drinking and driving is a social problem. Later in this chapter, we will see that alcohol use is much more widespread than the use of illicit drugs such as cocaine and heroin; therefore, drunk driving is presumably more widespread than driving while under the influence of drugs. But when it occurs, the latter can be just as deadly. Similarly, the use of illicit drugs by even very small numbers of airline pilots, police officers, railway engineers, or individuals in many other occupations can present substantial problems of public safety.

In short, even though illicit drug use is viewed as a voluntary behavior and a harmless life-style choice made by some individuals, it imposes costs on others. It remains, then, an important social problem.

DRUGS AND THE POLICY CYCLE

Why has public policy failed to resolve the drug problem, despite dramatic "wars on drugs" and the expenditure of billions of dollars at the federal, state, and local levels?

In an effort to find insights about this question, Chapters 2 through 4 present a policy history of drugs; Chapters 5 through 7 carefully examine drug enforcement, treatment, and prevention programs and evaluative information available about them; and Chapter 8 explores why drug policy has exhibited so much continuity despite evidence of failure. Chapter 9 examines the implications for the future of drug policy, including attention to the issue of drug legalization. At least implicitly, then, this book follows a familiar pattern—the policy cycle. That is, policy develops through a series of stages or phases, beginning with agenda setting, problem definition, and their effect on the politics of enactment (Chapters 2–4). After enactment, public policies are implemented in the form of detailed programs; and on the basis of the results of these programs in action, evaluative information is developed (Chapters 5–7).

But what is most important is not merely the identification of these various stages. Rather, the policy cycle is best understood as a normative conception of policy as a learning process. The key feature of the cycle, from this point of view, is the feedback loop that carries evaluative information about the impact of implemented policy back to the agenda-setting phase. In the case of drug policy, for example, information about the intended and unintended impacts of drug-law enforcement programs, treatment programs, and prevention programs should be derived from the experiences of program administrators, from systematic studies like those reported in Chapters 5 through 7, and from the interpretation of such evidence by various experts inside and outside of government. This complex set of information should then be instrumental in bringing the drug issue back onto the agenda, if existing programs are ineffective, and in redefining the problem in terms of what has been learned from the first cycle.

The policy cycle model suggests two important sources of policy failure: disjunctures between stages, and a mistracking of policy at the earliest stage. The first of these points to the problems that can ensue when a particular stage is not appropriately constrained by the preceding stage, or when there is a lack of fidelity between the stages. The policy cycle conception implies that the results of each stage should shape the ensuing stages. For example, the definitions of the problem that attain legitimacy in the agenda-setting stage help to determine what set of policies are discussed in the enactment stage; policy implementation needs to be directed by some consciousness of the intent of policymakers as expressed in the enactment stage; and policy evaluation relies heavily upon evidence gleaned from program implementors. But sometimes there is substantial slippage between stages, leading to problems that can derail a policy. This has been most pointedly noted with respect to policy implementation, which some scholars have found to be jeopardized by poor directions from the enactment stage, in the form of vague legislation, overly complex or contradictory program mandates, unresolved conflicts, or any number of other factors that interfere with the credibility of the policy message.[5]

Although much literature explores the disjunction between policy enactment and implementation, disjunction also causes problems at another link in the policy cycle: the policy evaluation–agenda setting feedback loop. As Chapters 5 through 7 show, the implementation of drug programs generates a substantial amount of evaluative information. However, this information is not necessarily influential in defining continuing drug problems and bringing the issue back onto the agenda. Rather, agenda setting and problem definition for the drug issue appear to be driven by political imperatives and crisis events that direct attention away from what we have learned from previous policy episodes. The result is that policy development with respect to drugs has a disjointed, spasmodic character, not the evidence of policy learning that is implied by the policy cycle model.

The history of drug policy thus exemplifies how policy failure can result from disjunction between two key stages of the policy process—evaluation and agenda setting. This would not be so damaging to policy development if the agenda setting stage were fluid enough to allow for innovative problem definitions that could carry drug policy in more productive directions. Unfortunately, the history of drug policy also exemplifies a second source of policy failure, one that interferes with remedial policy change every bit as much as does the failure to use evaluative information. This second source of policy failure is the dominance of a policy's initial problem definition, which channels policy more or less permanently in a particular direction. If the earliest episodes of attention to a particular issue involve mistaken, overly narrow, or otherwise inadequate conceptions of the problem, policy can be tracked toward failure.

Margaret Weir has given particular emphasis to this interpretation of policy failure, and to the importance of studying policy as a sequence of development in which future change is constrained by initial presumptions.[6] She demonstrates that employment policy in the United States initially was based on a narrow definition of the problem, one that restricted attention to aggregate unemployment figures and to economic policies that might influence those figures. Social programs, such as job training, were viewed as separate and unrelated to the economic aspects of employment policy. The result, according to Weir, was a sequence of development that "systematically bounded employment policy and narrowed the possibilities for adapting policy to new political and economic conditions."[7] Similarly, drug policy in the United States has been crucially constrained by the way the problem was defined in the earliest period of attention to the issue. That definition treats the problem as a criminal matter rather than a medical one, and it focuses attention on the suppliers of drugs rather than the users who sustain the demand for drugs.

Just as job training and other social programs were eventually added to the repertoire of U.S. employment policy despite the dominance of a macroeconomic definition of the problem, so also have treatment, prevention, and other demand-side programs been added to supply-side programs of drug-law enforcement. Because of the dominance of the initial definition of the employment problem, social programs to influence the labor market were added only under extraordinary circumstances (i.e., the civil rights movement and the urban riots of the 1960s); these programs were never integrated with the economic sphere of employment policy, and they never attained the political legitimacy that traditional employment policy approaches had.[8] Similarly, drug treatment and prevention programs were added to the traditional law enforcement repertoire under extraordinary circumstances, such as the special reelection imperatives of the Nixon administration in 1971–1972 (see Chapter 2) and the dramatic emergence of crack cocaine in the mid-1980s (see Chapter 4). Treatment and prevention programs have been much less generously funded than drug-law enforcement, and these demand-side programs have never attained the legitimacy of supply-side programs, as evidenced by the substantial amount of program evaluation directed at treatment and prevention programs (see Chapters 5 and 6) and the relative scarcity of evaluation of drug-law enforcement (see Chapter 7).

In short, failures of drug policy can be attributed to two different points at which the ideal model of the policy cycle was not realized. On the one hand, results from the policy evaluation stage have not been influential in agenda setting. And on the other hand, policy development has been constrained by a relatively narrow problem definition that has dominated since the earliest cycle of attention to the issue. Both of these features of drug policy development mean that policy learning has been limited rather than maximized.

These critiques of drug policy development may seem to suggest that there is no rationality to policy-making with respect to this problem. That is not necessarily the case. The policy cycle model suggests one kind of rationality—a rationality that features orderly movement from one stage to another and action driven by the results of experience. But there are other models of rationality, models that highlight the political rationality of policy development processes that would otherwise seem disorderly and irrational.

DRUG POLICY-MAKING AND KINGDON'S ANALYSIS

One of the most important of these models is Kingdon's[9] reformulation of the "garbage-can" model of decision making. In this reformulation, three *separate* streams contribute to policy development. The *problem stream* consists of a variety of events and indicators highlighting matters that might be defined as worthy of government attention. The *policy stream* incorporates a variety of ideas and policy proposals that might serve as solutions to some matter in the problem stream. Finally, the *political stream* includes the balance of partisan and ideological forces in Congress, the organization of relevant interest groups, the timing and results of elections, and similar political dynamics. In Kingdon's formulation, innovation and policy development result from those brief and sometimes unexpected moments when the three streams come together, producing windows of opportunity for policy change. The following sections outline the contents of Kingdon's three streams from the perspective of the drug issue.

The Problem Stream

Kingdon identifies two important sources of problem definition: official indicators, such as unemployment and inflation figures, which permit government to engage in routine monitoring of some phenomena; and "focusing events," such as natural disasters or crises, which galvanize attention to a problem.[10] Both sources of problem definition are evident with respect to the drug issue, though focusing events have been more influential than official indicators.

Official indicators of the extent of drug abuse and trafficking include surveys of drug use and medical and law enforcement sources. Two different national surveys by the National Institute on Drug Abuse (NIDA) provide at least some consistent information on drug use in America over time. A survey of high school seniors has been conducted annually since the early 1970s. The survey asks a representative sample of these seniors about their use of a variety of different drugs and about their attitudes toward drug use. The other survey, of a representative sample of households, has been conducted every two or three years since 1972. Respondents to this survey can be either "youth" (ages 12–17), "young adults" (ages 18–25), or "older adults" (age 26 or older). This survey covers both legal and illegal drugs, ranging from alcohol and cigarettes to heroin and cocaine. For each drug, respondents are asked whether they are currently using the drug and whether they have used it during the past month, during the past year, or at any other time.[11]

Figure 1.1, based upon the survey of high school seniors, shows that there has been a notable decline in reported use of marijuana—the illicit drug most commonly used among youth. In 1978, about half of high

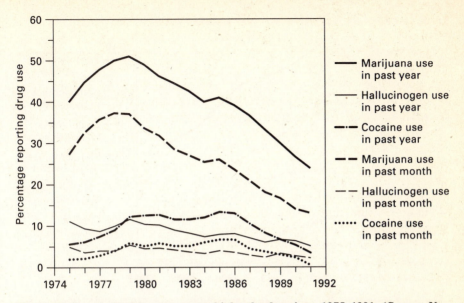

Figure 1.1 **Trends in drug use among high school seniors, 1975–1991. (*Source:* National Institute on Drug Abuse, 1991, *Drug Use Among American High School Seniors, College Students and Young Adults, 1975–1990.*)**

school seniors had used marijuana in the preceding year and over one-third had used it in the preceding month; by 1991, fewer than one-third of high school seniors had used marijuana within the past year and about 14 percent reported using the drug within the past month. Hallucinogens, never used as widely as marijuana, also appear to be less frequently used by high school seniors than they once were. Cocaine, which was used by no more than 13 percent of seniors in any given year, reveals a somewhat different trend than marijuana. Cocaine use increased in the 1970s, just as marijuana use did; however, while the rates of reported marijuana use were dropping sharply throughout the 1980s, the rate of cocaine use held steady or slightly increased. Only after 1986 is there evidence for the beginning of a similar decline in cocaine use. Reported heroin use among high school seniors is very rare—it is not charted in Figure 1.1. Reported use of heroin or other opiates has never exceeded 0.2 percent throughout the nearly two decades of the survey's existence. By contrast, reported alcohol use, not charted in Figure 1.1, is relatively high. Throughout the life of the survey, about 5 percent of the high school seniors have reported daily use of alcohol, and over one-third report they have recently taken five or more drinks in a row.[12]

The data from the survey of high school seniors have been criticized because they do not reveal patterns of use among young people who have dropped out of school. Furthermore, they focus on a narrowly age-specific segment of the population. An examination of results from NIDA's

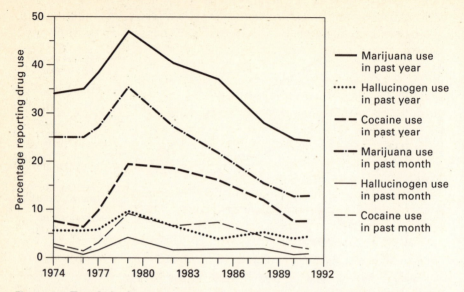

Figure 1.2 **Trends in drug use among 18- to 25-year-olds, 1974–1991. (***Source:* **Na-tional Institute on Drug Abuse, 1991,** *National Household Survey on Drug Abuse: Main Findings 1990,* **pp. 25, 29.)**

household survey provides additional information about drug use trends. Figure 1.2 presents household survey data for those in the 18-to-25 age group. The relative prevalence of marijuana use and the sharp decline in marijuana use after 1979 are once again evident. Similarly, the decreas-ing use of hallucinogens after 1979 is also evident. Compared to the sur-vey of high school seniors, however, the household survey data reveal a much more dramatic pattern in the rise and subsequent decline of co-caine use. In the mid-1970s, fewer than 10 percent of younger Americans reported use of cocaine in the preceding year and only about 3 percent re-ported use within the last month. By 1979, nearly one-fifth of 18- to 25-year-olds reported some use of cocaine within the past year, and almost 10 percent reported use within the past month. After this high point, however, reported use of cocaine declined steadily. In 1991, fewer than 10 percent reported using cocaine in the past year, and fewer than 5 per-cent reported using cocaine within the past month. Like the survey of high school seniors, the household survey detects negligible levels of heroin use.

Survey-based indicators of the scope of the drug problem have been criticized on a number of grounds. Respondents may not answer truth-fully about their use of drugs, and national-sample survey research does not adequately represent a number of relevant populations, such as homeless individuals. Alternative indicators of the scope of the drug problem include, for example, the federally created Drug Abuse Warning Network (DAWN), which gathers information on drug-related deaths and medical emergencies from more than 700 hospitals, which include two-thirds of all hospitals in 27 of the nation's cities, along with 75 medical examiners' offices.[13] Changes in the DAWN network over the years have made comparisons over time difficult; however, its data are often suggestive of problems. For example, DAWN data show that drug-related hospital emergency cases increased from a little over 7,000 in 1984 to almost 16,000 in 1986 and to over 26,000 in 1987. Marijuana-related hospital emergencies increased dramatically during this period, from 2,887 in 1984 to over 5,000 in 1987. Data from all institutions in the DAWN network *except* those in New York City show an increase in cocaine-related deaths from 666 in 1984 to 1,253 in 1986.[14]

Drug testing, using urinalysis or other chemical testing techniques, is increasingly being conducted by private and public employers to screen and reject drug users from among job applicants, to create a deterrent for employees, and to identify workers with drug problems for referral to employee assistance programs.[15] Since such testing is not randomly applied to all employees or applicants, drug-testing results cannot be treated as accurate estimates of the extent of drug abuse in America's working or working-age population. However, the results of various employee drug-testing programs have inevitably made their way into the ongoing public discussion about the character and scope of the drug problem. Such results may be viewed as illustrative of the scope of the drug problem in America, especially if they show nontrivial levels of drug use in occupations (such as the transportation industry) in which drug-impaired performance implies safety issues for the general public.

For example, Southern Pacific Railroad began urinalysis testing of its employees in 1984. In that year, nearly one-quarter (23 percent) tested positive for either alcohol or drugs. A little over half of these positive tests were findings of marijuana; one-fifth were findings of cocaine. Positive urinalysis tests among Southern Pacific employees dropped to 13 percent in 1985 and to 5 percent in 1988.[16] In 1988, 37 of 3,946 New York City police officers tested for drugs showed positive results (a rate of about 1 percent); about 2 percent of the police department's recruits tested positive.[17] In addition to these organization-specific results, there have been some studies of particular categories of workers, based on drug testing of blood and urine samples. One study of a random sample of truck drivers in 1986 determined that 16 percent tested positive for marijuana, 3 percent tested positive for cocaine, and 2 percent tested positive for stimulants not available in over-the-counter medications (i.e., amphetamines, methamphetamine)—this despite the fact that participation in the study was voluntary, with 12 percent of the sampled drivers not participating in the drug testing.[18]

Yet another method of assessing the magnitude of the drug problem relies upon data regularly collected by law enforcement authorities. For example, the Federal Bureau of Investigation (FBI) collects data from local police departments across the country, including numbers of arrests

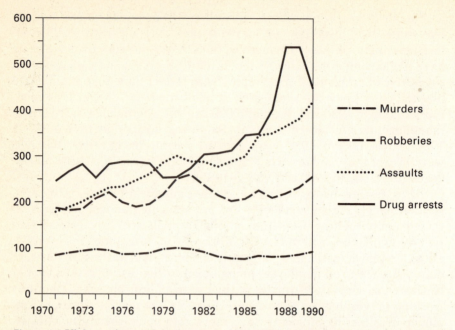

Figure 1.3 **Violent crime and drug arrests, 1971–1990. Murders are shown in rate per 10,000 population; other crimes are shown in rate per 100,000 population.** (*Sources:* **Relevant years of FBI's** *Crime in the United States* **and the Census Bureau,** *Statistical Abstract of the United States.*)

for drug abuse violations. On the basis of Figure 1.3, which shows local arrest data, we might be tempted to conclude that the drug problem increased or at least held steady for most of the 1970s, declined briefly in 1979 and 1980, and then resumed an upward trend. But arrests were growing while levels of drug use, as reported in national surveys, were decreasing (see Figures 1.1 and 1.2). The reason for this apparent contradiction is that arrests and other enforcement activities are driven by the availability of agency resources and by political pressure for agencies to make substantial drug enforcement efforts.[19] There is no direct correspondence between the magnitude of drug abuse and the magnitude of the law enforcement response to drugs.

In addition to arrests for drug possession or trafficking, drugs have often been linked to other types of crime. The nature of that connection is complex and has been studied extensively.[20] However, regardless of the complexities, politicians point to crime rates, and particularly violent crime, as manifestations of the drug problem. In the 1970s, for example, heroin use was linked to various forms of predatory street crime, such as robbery, because addicts were alleged to find it necessary to prey upon others in order to finance their drug habits. In the contemporary war on drugs, violent competition between various individuals and groups trafficking in cocaine has been blamed for skyrocketing homicide rates.

As Figure 1.3 shows, however, the nation's homicide rate has held remarkably steady over the past twenty years. Neither the peaking of marijuana and hallucinogen use in 1979 nor the emergence of cocaine as a notable drug in the 1980s had an obvious impact on the national homicide rate. The robbery rate increased noticeably in the late 1970s, in roughly the same period that reported drug use was on the increase nationally; and the aggravated assault rate has increased in each of the past twenty years except the first half of the 1980s. Because of the differences between these crime trends, and the inconsistencies between them and reported drug use data, their value as indicators of the magnitude of America's drug problem is suspect, despite the tendency of politicians, law enforcement officials, and the media to superficially link the drug problem with the crime problem.

The National Narcotics Intelligence Consumers Committee (NNICC) also relies on law enforcement data as indicators of the magnitude of the drug problem. These data have not been compiled as consistently or for as long a period as crime and arrest data, but the NNICC data represent the best evidence on the drug problem that is available to the Coast Guard, the Central Intelligence Agency (CIA), the Drug Enforcement Administration (DEA), the Immigration and Naturalization Service, the Departments of State and Treasury, NIDA, and the White House Drug Abuse Policy Office. For example, the NNICC reports on the price and purity of illegal drugs in this country. Increased purity suggests greater drug availability—that is, dealers presumably are less likely to dilute drugs by mixing them with other substances when the supply of drugs to be sold is more plentiful. Likewise, lower prices for illegal drugs suggest greater availability, just as a comparatively large supply of any commodity or service relative to demand means lower asking prices in a market exchange. Since agents regularly engage in staged "buys" of drugs as a preliminary to drug arrests, data on the street price and purity of drugs are known to law enforcement authorities. In the mid-1980s these data, as reported by the NNICC, suggested an alarming increase in the availability of cocaine. The purity of street cocaine increased from 35 percent by weight in 1984 to between 55 and 65 percent in 1986 and remained at over 50 percent purity in 1987. During this same period wholesale prices declined from $40,000 to $50,000 per kilogram in 1984 to $12,000 to $40,000 in 1987.[21]

In short, there are many official indicators of the scope of the drug problem. But they have not been as influential in the problem stream as are official indicators of economic problems, because they do not have the legitimacy of economic indicators. They have not been collected over as long a time; their validity is more subject to question; and their collection has not been firmly institutionalized in an agency trusted for its professional, politically neutral treatment of the data, as is the Bureau of Labor Statistics. Nevertheless, like economic indicators, results of the regularly released NIDA surveys of households and high school seniors attract media attention. To the extent that they do, their potential impact as agenda-setting devices is enhanced.

Focusing events, in contrast, have been enormously important in the problem stream. A focusing, or triggering, event is an incident "that brings the issue vividly before the public"[22] and consequently onto the decision-making agenda of government officials. One commonly cited example was the cocaine-related death of basketball player Len Bias in June 1986. Another was the kidnapping and killing of U.S. drug enforcement agent Enrique Camarena in 1985 by drug-trafficking figures in Mexico. In Kansas City, Missouri, a highly publicized report in September 1989 that a woman had traded her baby for crack cocaine served as one of several focusing events that set the agenda for a successful campaign to enact a quarter-cent sales tax designated for antidrug programming.[23] As these examples show, individual tragedies and human interest stories have been crucial focusing events for the drug issue.

The Policy Stream

In Kingdon's formulation, the problem stream is paralleled by a quite separate stream of potential solutions and policy proposals. These policy ideas are developed by "policy communities" composed of experts and specialists both inside and outside of government. Through their interaction with each other, such experts continuously exchange ideas, refine policy proposals, and develop innovative program initiatives and recycle old ones. The result is a "primeval soup" of diverse ideas in a constant state of recombination.[24]

One of the most significant features of the policy history described in this book is the changing character of the policy stream. Early episodes of attention to the drug issue featured relatively few policy-making leaders, and their ideas appeared to be derived from relatively small and undeveloped networks of experts and specialists. By the 1980s, however, the drug issue had attracted the professional attention of experts and specialists in various niches of a very diverse and highly fragmented policy community. The policy stream for drugs now contains the ideas of specialized professionals in medicine and psychotherapy; the ideas of specialists in education, training, and public relations; and the ideas of law enforcement professionals, military leaders, foreign policy experts, and many others.

Embedded in this policy community are policy entrepreneurs, or individuals with the motivation, political skills, and opportunity to invest some of their own energy and political resources in the shaping of a political issue.[25] Members of Congress, congressional staff, bureaucrats, interest group leaders, and various experts such as scientists can serve as policy entrepreneurs. The motivations, skill, and resources of such people vary considerably, and these differences are presumably related to the individuals' level of success. As we will see in Chapter 2, for example,

Harry Anslinger, as director of the Federal Bureau of Narcotics (FBN) from 1930 to 1962, was successful in repeatedly getting the drug issue on the congressional agenda, partly because of his leadership skills and political aggressiveness and partly because of his ability to manipulate popular opinion.[26]

The drug policy stream includes a number of entrepreneurs with substantial political clout, along with a wide array of organized interests. But, consistent with Kingdon's formulation, the drug policy stream is best understood as a source of ideas, not simply political pressure.[27] The history of drug policy in the United States shows that despite the availability of competing ideas about the drug problem, drug policy has by and large adhered closely to the same approach—one dominated by a law enforcement model of the problem and an emphasis on the interruption of drug supplies. The many reasons for this consistency despite policy failure are the subject of Chapter 8. Here, it is important to note that Kingdon's third stream—the political stream—has a great deal to do with this continuity in policy.

The Political Stream

The political stream consists of "swings of national mood, election results, changes of administration, changes of ideological or partisan distributions in Congress, and interest group pressure campaigns."[28] These many factors condition whether and when government attention will turn to a particular problem, and which proposed solutions from the policy stream will be persuasive.

Although the political stream is always instrumental in policy development, it is possible to imagine situations in which the imperatives of politics are muted relative to the dynamics of the problem stream and the policy stream. In drug policy, however, political imperatives have been a dominant factor. The drug issue has been propelled onto the agenda by politicians seeking dramatic raw material for their election campaigns; drug legislation has often featured blatant posturing for political credit; and drug policy-making has been skewed by partisan skirmishing.

In the case of drugs, then, policy entrepreneurs have typically been political entrepreneurs as well. This should perhaps not be surprising, because the drug issue has important characteristics that appeal to political entrepreneurs—characteristics that make it easier to propel this issue onto the agenda when it is politically convenient to do so, and characteristics that make it harder to evaluate the potentially embarrassing results (or lack thereof) of public policy.

In particular, the drug issue has dramatic elements that "fit closely with broad cultural concerns,"[29] which can be described in terms of personified threats such as enemies or deviants[30] or more generally portrayed as problems with intentional causes,[31] such as the greed of drug traffickers or the conspiracies of international drug cartels. Drugs provide many dramatic situations—tragic stories of lives lost and children harmed, juicy tidbits about celebrities teetering on the edge of drug-induced catastrophe, tales of intrigue concerning the enforcement of laws against drugs and the corruption of those in and around drug-law enforcement. Meanwhile, drugs are readily defined as a social problem and a political issue because they fit so closely with several core cultural concerns, including concerns about health and about the controllability of youth. Furthermore, drugs are readily portrayed in terms of personified threats, most notably drug lords in foreign lands and predatory drug dealers within the community.

Novelty is yet another important aspect of issue definition and agenda setting. Even the most dramatic events and symbols lose power as raw material for agenda setting if they are too familiar or repetitive. "Especially in dealing with familiar social problems, operatives and interest groups constantly look for new images and new ways to capitalize on current events to inject urgency into their presentations."[32] Here again, the drug problem has advantages as a potential issue, because it is so readily transformed into new and yet more alarming images. The drug issue has long been defined largely in terms of a link between drugs and crime. This basic link was embellished with some potent new symbols, however, in the 1980s. For example, the drug problem is now also an AIDS transmission problem, a problem of "crack babies," and a problem of gangs and of innocent victims of drive-by shootings. In this regard, Robert Morgenthau, district attorney for New York, has argued that "drugs are the very core of virtually every problem that plagues society—crime, child abuse, homelessness, AIDS."[33] In short, the drug issue is particularly potent because it can be attached to related problem symbols.

With dramatic elements and links to deep-seated cultural concerns, drug policy captures the attention of the media and the American public. As Figure 1.4 shows, popular and media attention to drugs were notably high during President Nixon's administration, surged in President Reagan's second term, and escalated still further during the Bush administration.

The very characteristics that make the drug issue so politically manipulable, however, also keep drug policy from straying too far from a law enforcement solution *and* make drug policy less amenable to hard-nosed evaluation. As Chapters 2 through 4 show, drug policy is often grounded in public fears, and sometimes in outright hysteria. Under these circumstances, the tough rhetoric of increased criminal penalties and enhanced resources for law enforcement is more politically potent than ideas for substance abuse treatment or prevention programs. Politicians who might be inclined to challenge the utility of further investments in drug-law enforcement run a substantial risk of being painted by their opponents as lacking in firmness on this explosive issue.[34] And the symbolic reassurance that continuing drug-law enforcement provides

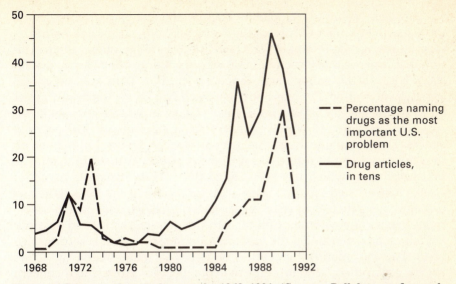

Figure 1.4 **Drugs on the popular agenda, 1968–1991. (*Sources:* Poll data are from relevant years of *The Gallup Poll* or, after 1979, *Gallup Report;* data on drug articles are from the author's original coding of relevant years of the *Reader's Guide to Periodical Literature.*)**

combines with data limitations and other challenges to militate against much assessment of policy results.

BEYOND THE KINGDON MODEL

Kingdon's conceptualization is useful in highlighting important aspects of the development of drug policy, and in offering a political rationality that may be more relevant to drug policy than the rationality of the policy cycle model. However, Kingdon's approach has an important limitation. Consistent with the garbage-can model from which it is derived, it leaves us with an amorphous portrait of policy development. Windows of opportunity for government attention to issues are said to occur when the three streams are aligned, and a variety of mechanisms for coupling the streams are suggested (e.g., the activity of policy entrepreneurs, or spillover of policy activity from one subject to a closely related one).[35] In general, however, Kingdon's formulation is so comprehensive and leaves so much room for random elements that a comparative analysis of policy-making processes is impossible. One is left with a conclusion that there are countless forms of policy development. Although this model may be more sophisticated than the unitary model of the policy cycle, it does not provide a useful framework to help us to understand how the case of drug policy differs from the case of agriculture policy or employment policy or health policy, or indeed how contemporary episodes of drug policy-making differ from earlier episodes.

However, policy development may be thought of as falling into a more limited number of interestingly different types, especially with respect to the agenda-setting stage. Cobb, Ross, and Ross offer a categorization that is particularly useful in the analysis of drug policy because it focuses both on the policy entrepreneurs within (or with easy access to) government and on the mass public, which can be an important target for symbolic appeals in this issue area.[36] Cobb, Ross, and Ross acknowledge that escalation in popular concern about an issue, like the peaks of popular concern about drugs that are portrayed in Figure 1.4, may be either the cause or the result of government attention to a problem. The first possibility, which has been called the *outside initiative model* of agenda setting, suggests that issue areas emerge from the grass roots and that the appearance of an issue on the government agenda reflects the responsiveness of government officials to the public. The second possibility, which has been called the *mobilization model* of agenda setting, suggests that the public's perception of issues is manipulated by actors within government who attempt to evoke popular interest and concern in order to build support for an agenda of their own.

There is yet a third possibility—that an issue can quietly move onto the government agenda without ever having evoked substantial interest or concern from the mass public. In this *inside-access model* of agenda setting, an issue is developed inside a government bureau or within an interest group that has regular access to the government agenda. In contrast to the mobilization model, policy entrepreneurs do not need to evoke widespread public concern in order to capture the attention of government officials; in fact, entrepreneurs wish to limit issue expansion and to keep control of the issue by confining it to the relevant participants on the formal agenda.

As Chapters 2 through 5 show, the United States has experienced at least two forms of agenda setting with respect to the drug issue. Chapter 2 shows that the "war on drugs" during the Nixon administration is an excellent example of the mobilization model of agenda setting. By contrast, during the Carter administration, the drug issue was handled primarily through an inside-access model of agenda setting (see Chapter 3). Chapter 4 shows that the contemporary war on drugs began as an instance of the mobilization model of agenda setting; however, as the episode unfolded, a sequence of dramatic triggering events and symbolic reformulations of the issue forced politicians into the mode of responding to outside pressures rather than simply mobilizing those outside pressures.

CONCLUSIONS

Do these differences at the agenda-setting stage lead to differences in policy that is enacted? The following chapters show that there are some differences. They also show that the importance of the political stream relative to the other streams and the limited role of policy evaluation are more characteristic of episodes initiated through a mobilization form of agenda setting than of an episode initiated through inside access. But most drug policy has, in fact, been enacted during mobilization-style episodes; the inside-access episode that is described in Chapter 3 generated little in the way of new drug laws or programs. Herein may lie the ultimate lesson of the history of drug policy in the United States. The conditions that make drugs an explosive and timely issue are not the conditions that lend themselves to analysis, evaluation, and learning from past efforts.

NOTES

1. *Public Papers of the Presidents of the United States. Richard Nixon, 1971* (Washington, DC: U.S. Government Printing Office, 1972), p. 738.
2. *Public Papers of the Presidents of the United States. George Bush, Book II, 1989* (Washington, DC: U.S. Government Printing Office, 1990), pp. 1136–1137.
3. Mathea Falco, *Winning the Drug War: A National Strategy* (New York: Priority Press, 1989), p. 6.
4. U.S. House of Representatives, Select Committee on Narcotics Abuse and Control, *Cocaine Babies* (Washington, DC: U.S. Government Printing Office, 1988b), p. 6.
5. Malcolm Goggin, Ann O'M. Bowman, James P. Lester, and Laurence J. O'Toole, Jr., *Implementation Theory and Practice* (Glenview, IL: Scott, Foresman, 1990).
6. Margaret Weir, *Politics and Jobs: The Boundaries of Employment Policy in the United States* (Princeton, NJ: Princeton University Press, 1992).
7. Weir, 1992, p. 5.
8. Weir, 1992, pp. 165–166.
9. John Kingdon, *Agendas, Alternatives, and Public Policies* (New York: HarperCollins, 1984).
10. Kingdon, 1984, pp. 95–101.
11. Erich Goode, *Drugs in American Society*, 3rd ed. (New York: McGraw-Hill, 1989).
12. National Institute on Drug Abuse, *National Household Survey on Drug Abuse: Main Findings 1990* (Washington, DC: U.S. Government Printing Office, 1991), pp. 25, 29.
13. Goode, 1989, p. 102.
14. National Narcotics Intelligence Consumers Committee (NNICC), *The NNICC Report 1987: The Supply of Illicit Drugs to the United States* (Washington, DC: National Narcotics Intelligence Consumers Committee, 1988), pp. 7, 27.
15. Royer F. Cook, "Drug Use Among Working Adults: Prevalence Rates and Estimation Methods," in Steven Gust and J. Michael Walsh, eds., *Drugs in the Workplace: Research and Evaluation Data* (Washington, DC: U.S. Government Printing Office, 1989), p. 29.
16. Robert Taggart, "Results of the Drug Testing Program at Southern Pacific Railroad," in Steven Gust and J. Michael Walsh, eds., *Drugs in the Work-*

place: Research and Evaluation Data (Washington, DC: U.S. Government Printing Office, 1989), pp. 101, 104.

17. James McKinley, "In New York, New Drug Tests Set for Police," *New York Times*, September 6, 1989, p. 16.

18. Adrian Lund, David Preusser, and Allan Williams, "Drug Use by Tractor-Trailer Drivers," in Steven Gust and J. Michael Walsh, eds., *Drugs in the Workplace: Research and Evaluation Data* (Washington, DC: U.S. Government Printing Office, 1989), pp. 47–67.

19. Kenneth Meier, "Political Institutions and the Control of U.S. Drug Enforcement Policies," paper presented at the Annual Meeting of the Midwest Political Science Association, Chicago, April 18–20, 1991.

20. Michael Tonry and James Q. Wilson, eds., *Drugs and Crime* (Chicago: University of Chicago Press, 1990).

21. NNICC, 1988, p. 26.

22. Dennis Palumbo, *Public Policy in America* (New York: Harcourt Brace Jovanovich, 1988), p. 40.

23. Lynn Horsley, "Case of Alleged Sale of Baby Cited as Proof of Drug Crisis," *Kansas City Times*, September 30, 1989, p. B4.

24. Kingdon, 1984, pp. 122–124.

25. Kingdon, 1984, pp. 129–130.

26. John C. McWilliams, *The Protectors: Harry J. Anslinger and the Federal Bureau of Narcotics, 1930–1962* (Newark, University of Delaware, 1990).

27. Kingdon, 1984, p. 131.

28. Kingdon, 1984, p. 170.

29. Stephen Hillgartner and Charles L. Bosk, "The Rise and Fall of Social Problems: A Public Arenas Model," *American Journal of Sociology* 94 (July 1988), pp. 61–64.

30. Murray Edelman, *Political Language: Words That Succeed and Policies That Fail* (New York: Academic Press, 1977).

31. Deborah Stone, "Causal Stories and the Formation of Policy Agendas," *Political Science Quarterly* 104 (1989), pp. 281–300.

32. Hillgartner and Bosk, 1988, p. 62.

33. U.S. House of Representatives, Select Committee on Narcotics Abuse and Control, *The Drug Enforcement Crisis at the Local Level* (Washington, DC: U.S. Government Printing Office, 1989b), p. 40.

34. Kenneth J. Meier, "The Politics of Drug Abuse: Laws, Implementation, and Consequences," *Western Political Quarterly* 45 (March 1992), p. 43.

35. Kingdon, 1984, pp. 173–204.

36. Roger Cobb, Jennie-Keith Ross, and Marc Ross, "Agenda Building as a Comparative Political Process," *American Political Science Review* 70 (March 1976), pp. 126–138.

2

The History of U.S. Drug Policy: The Early Years and Nixon's War on Drugs

INTRODUCTION

Chapters 2 through 4 describe three significant episodes in U.S. drug policy history: during the Nixon administration, a brief but dramatic war on drugs focused primarily on heroin; during the Carter administration, a disappointing effort failed to reorient drug policy involving marijuana (see Chapter 3); and during the Reagan and Bush administrations, a surge of attention hit the drug issue in general and cocaine in particular (see Chapter 4).

Before turning to these three post–World War II drug policy episodes, however, we need to consider the longer-term roots of drug policy in American history. This chapter provides an overview of these roots, beginning with the nation's first drug legislation in 1914. These and other early public policy responses are important for two reasons. First, they created a legal and organizational environment that shaped subsequent drug policy development. In particular, the institutionalization of a law enforcement–oriented approach to drug policy strongly overshadowed the treatment and rehabilitation approach. Second, the character of the debate surrounding drug policy and certain key features of agenda setting and policy formulation constitute common themes, to be echoed again and again in more recent drug policy episodes.

HISTORY OF DRUG POLICY:
THE FOUNDATION YEARS

Federal drug-control policy in the United States dates from the *Harrison Narcotics Act*, passed in 1914. Prior to the Harrison Act, the only federal drug legislation was a 1909 law prohibiting opium importation except for medical purposes. The 1909 law, quickly enacted in the same year the United States had convened an international commission on opium trafficking, was largely a gesture to show that the country was not neglecting its responsibilities to control opium. Because much of the opium in use was in the form of various patent medicines, the 1909 law amounted only to a ban on opium for smoking.[1]

To those accustomed to the full panoply of contemporary drug law, complete with federal drug police to enforce laws against possession and trafficking of a broad variety of illicit substances, the Harrison Narcotics Act seems quaint indeed. Perhaps because the constitutional legitimacy of the federal government's use of police powers in intrastate commerce was not accepted then as it has been since, the Harrison Act was in the form of a taxation and registration policy, to be administered by agents within the Treasury Department.[2] Basically, the act created a special tax on producers, importers, and manufacturers of opium and coca products, which include heroin, morphine, and cocaine; it required that all who sold these products had to register with the local internal revenue office and pay the tax, set at $1 per year. In addition, sales of these drugs had to be recorded on special forms, indicating the use of the drug for a legitimate medical purpose. Records of drug sales had to be maintained for two years for possible federal inspection.[3]

If it had been administered in a low-key fashion, the Harrison Narcotics Act would be relatively uninteresting from the contemporary vantage point. Instead, it was aggressively enforced, particularly with respect to physicians who were dispensing heroin or other drugs to addicts. There is some evidence that between 1915 and 1938, more than 25,000 physicians came under the scrutiny of federal agents enforcing the Harrison Act and about 5,000 were convicted and fined or jailed.[4] Many may have been irresponsibly dispensing drugs to addicts. But aggressive enforcement also caught up those who may have been attempting to humanely treat addicts with dosages of drugs adequate to keep them comfortable. As we will see later in this chapter, such a "maintenance" approach to the treatment of addicts, using the synthetic drug methadone, is a widely accepted practice today. But the regulations developed by the Treasury Department as it implemented and enforced the Harrison Act effectively quashed the maintenance approach to treatment of drug addicts in America.

In the case *Webb et al. v. United States*, 1919, the Supreme Court ruled against the maintenance of addicts as a legitimate form of treatment. Webb, a physician, had been charged with conspiracy to violate the Harrison Narcotics Act by giving morphine to an addict for purposes of responding to his usual need for morphine and with no intention to cure. The court held that this was a subversion of the meaning of a physician's prescription.[5]

It may seem odd and ironic, from the vantage point of the 1990s, that the targets of the nation's first drug war were physicians and druggists. The transformation of a relatively simple revenue and registration law into a potent weapon for drug enforcement may seem surprising as well, especially given the relatively casual handling of many drugs at the turn of the century. Many patent medicines contained morphine, cocaine, laudanum, or heroin; cocaine was used as an ingredient in Coca-Cola (until 1903) and was also marketed in cigarettes, alcohol, and wine drinks. However, a combination of problems, real and imagined, led to an antidrug movement. A nontrivial number of drug addicts had developed, and both elites and some of the attentive public were aware of the medical problems that drug addiction involved. At the same time, a series of frightening beliefs and myths had developed, linking drugs with socially outcast groups. For example, opium smoking was associated with the Chinese, and this linked drugs to a group already viewed with disdain; there were also fears that cocaine use would energize blacks to rebel against white society's restrictions on them.[6]

In 1930, treasury agents' drug-law enforcement responsibilities were institutionalized with the creation of the Federal Bureau of Narcotics (FBN) within the Treasury Department. Harry J. Anslinger took the helm of this new agency from the outset and served as U.S. commissioner of narcotics until 1962.[7] Anslinger's long tenure as narcotics commissioner is significant because of his particularly visible and effective role as a drug policy entrepreneur. During his tenure in office, several new pieces of antidrug legislation were passed—all reflecting increasing intolerance of drug use and all strongly influenced by the active leadership of Anslinger.

In 1937, for example, the *Marihuana Tax Act* was passed, effectively prohibiting legal use of the drug by imposing extremely high taxes on marijuana sales. Anslinger was instrumental in the passage of this legislation, using his position as head of the FBN to authoritatively promote myths that helped feed a marijuana scare. In hearings on the issue in 1937, for example, Anslinger claimed that use of marijuana caused some people to "fly into a delirious rage and many commit violent crimes"; Anslinger also offered lurid cases of insanity, murder, and sex crimes alleged to result from marijuana use.[8] Although Anslinger is best known for his skillful practice of symbolic politics through the manipulation of myths and horror stories, he was also a skilled legal, political, and bureaucratic tactician. For example, the development and wording of the Marihuana Tax Act as a control measure separate from the Harrison Narcotics Act was based upon his concerns over the repeated constitutional challenges to the Harrison Act; and his policy impact was heightened by the army of organized groups, ranging from the General Federation of Women's Clubs and the Women's Christian Temperance Union to the World Narcotic Defense Association and the American Drug Manufacturers, that Anslinger could regularly mobilize to support his cause.[9]

Anslinger's influence was also evident in the passage of two notable pieces of drug legislation in the 1950s. In 1951 the *Boggs Act* made penalties for marijuana use identical to those for narcotics and imposed more severe penalties for drug-law violation. The act mandated a combination of fines of up to $2,000 and a minimum sentence of two to five years for first offenders and five to ten years for second offenders, with no possibility for probation or a suspended sentence.[10] This act was sponsored by Congressman Hale Boggs, a longtime supporter of Anslinger's, who was at the time positioning himself to develop a law-and-order reputation that would enhance his prospects against Earl Long's political faction in his home state of Louisiana. Testifying in support of the bill, Anslinger attributed narcotics dealing to "underworld" forces, criticized judges for being too easy on drug dealers, and pleaded for longer minimum sentences.[11]

The *Narcotics Control Act of 1956* grew out of hearings held in 1955 that were chaired by Senator Price Daniel, a Texas Democrat who "needed name recognition to establish himself as a front-runner in the 1956 Texas gubernatorial campaign."[12] Hearings were held in cities throughout the United States, with Anslinger and other officials of the FBN playing key roles as witnesses to supply dramatic information about the prevalence of drug activity. The resulting act did not include the mandatory death sentence for narcotics smuggling that had been urged by Senator Daniel and some other members of Congress. But its provisions were "the most punitive and repressive anti-narcotics legislation ever adopted by Congress. All discretion to suspend sentences or permit probation was eliminated. Parole was allowed only for first offenders convicted of possession, and the death penalty could be invoked for anyone who sold heroin to a minor."[13]

As many observers have noted, some consistent themes were established in this early period of antidrug policy—themes that echo in more contemporary drug policy. First, the development of American drug policy heavily emphasized a punitive, law enforcement–oriented approach, with little concern for treatment or rehabilitation of addicts. Second, antidrug legislation was typically accompanied by characterizations of drug use as the purview of alien, dangerous elements—Chinese opium smokers, Mexican marijuana traffickers, and so forth. It is also notable that escalating attention to the drug problem was frequently linked with political necessities. Politicians were not slow to see the possibilities of the drug issue for enhanced name recognition and for claiming credit.

Perhaps the most important and distinctive aspect of this early period of drug policy was the fact that policy leadership was focused within the bureaucracy, in the influential hands of Harry Anslinger. Although bureaucratic leaders are still important figures in the development of drug policy, congressional and, more especially, presidential leadership have come to be more important in the development of the drug issue. As the following section shows, the skillful manipulation of public concerns about drugs, which had once been the purview of Anslinger in the FBN, was stemming from the White House by 1971.

THE NIXON ADMINISTRATION'S WAR ON DRUGS

One of the most dramatic episodes of drug policy-making in American history occurred during the Nixon administration. In the early 1970s there were incredibly high levels of public concern about drugs, and several major pieces of drug legislation were passed. As this chapter will show, however, drug policy-making was not so much responsive to public concern as it was instrumental in fueling public concern over drugs. In other words, drug policy-making in this episode approximates the mobilization model described in Chapter 1. But perhaps most remarkable of all is the character of drug policy that was attempted in this period. Although Nixon-era drug policy included controversial new developments in law enforcement, this era is most interesting because it was the single period in American history in which the federal government devoted more funding to the treatment side of the drug problem than to the law enforcement side. The character of that treatment program, the ways in which public opinion was mobilized behind Nixon's war on drugs, and the interaction of politics and drug policy in this period are the subjects of the remainder of this chapter.

The Context for Nixon's War on Drugs

As the first section of this chapter shows, an important theme in the early history of drug control was the way in which the drug issue emerged at times when the nation was convulsed with anxieties about perceived threats from lower-social-class elements and racial minorities, as in the concerns about opium use by Chinese laborers and cocaine use by Southern blacks in the first decade of the twentieth century. More generally, it might be argued that the drug issue typically involves the symbolic manipulation of national fears and is therefore most potent at historical moments when threats to mainstream values upset national stability.

If this thesis is correct, then there could have been no more likely occasion for a major drug policy episode than the early 1970s. The preceding decade had brought waves of social and political disruption and controversy, including massive protests over civil rights and the Vietnam War; the rise of a youth counterculture that eschewed middle-class values in favor of new forms of dress, music, and behavior, including un-abashed drug use; race riots in a number of cities; the emergence of black militant organizations; and the deaths by assassination of John Kennedy, Robert Kennedy, and Martin Luther King, Jr.

Not surprisingly, then, social disorder in general and drugs in partic-ular were matters of some public concern as the 1960s ended. But as Fig-ure 1.4 shows, drugs were quickly to escalate to much greater levels of public concern: the number of articles on drug topics in popular maga-zines more than doubled between 1966 and 1971, and the percentage of Gallup poll respondents who named drugs as the most important prob-lem facing the country increased from 1 or 2 percent in the late 1960s to 11 percent in 1971 and to 20 percent in 1973.

Examination of the *New York Times Index* for 1971 shows that many of the drug-related news stories at this time had precisely the sort of dramatic quality that it takes to engender public interest. Drugs were already on the government agenda, and it was largely the activity of gov-ernment itself that was fueling story after story about drugs and hence directing public attention to the issue.[14] For example, in January 1971, President Nixon announced the appointment of a former governor of Pennsylvania to chair a special commission investigating marijuana abuse. Meanwhile, the National Institute of Mental Health (NIMH) in the same month released the largest-ever study of marijuana use on col-lege campuses—which showed that one out of three students had tried marijuana. An NIMH director estimated that severe psychotic episodes were experienced by a nontrivial number of marijuana users. In February, Senator Walter Mondale and Congressman Charles Rangel announced the creation of a national commission to determine ways to stop heroin importation and to deal with what they referred to as a narcotics crisis in the United States. In March, the Federal Communications Commission made the splashy announcement that commercial broadcasters must not air any song with lyrics that "tend to promote or glorify use of illegal drugs." In the same month, high-level meetings between officials of the U.S. Justice Department and the Mexican government resulted in an-nouncements that increasing numbers of individuals had been arrested for trafficking in heroin, cocaine, and marijuana.

And so it went, month after month, in 1971. Americans were regu-larly being treated to news stories about government pronouncements, studies, actions, and disclosures—all tending to underscore the serious-ness of the drug problem. The drug issue was highlighted in an especially dramatic fashion by the discussion of heavy drug use in the military, which by the end of the 1960s was bogged down in a long and controver-sial war in Vietnam. The House of Representatives in 1970 created a spe-cial Subcommittee on Alleged Drug Abuse in the Services. In his opening comments as chairman of this subcommittee, Congressman G. Elliot Hagan recounted alarming stories that had been swirling for months around Capitol Hill. These included vague reports that 90 percent of the soldiers in Vietnam used marijuana, stories about military pilots using "pep pills" in combat, and rumors that the deliberate massacre of Vietnamese civilians at My Lai by American soldiers under Lieutenant William Calley was somehow attributable to widespread drug use prior to the incident.[15]

Richard Nixon had been elected to the presidency in 1968, at the height of the social and political convulsions of that tumultuous decade. Coming to office on a rhetorical platform stressing "law and order," Nixon attached the symbol of crime to the general disruption, social dislocation, and challenges to authority that characterized the period; he evoked expectations that things could be brought back under control. Before long a link between disorder, crime, and drugs had been politically forged. The surprising twist, however, was to be the innovative manner in which drug treatment was also incorporated into this symbolic equation.

Criminal Justice Policy Developments

The first drug policy initiative to emerge in the Nixon administration gave little hint of the dramatic treatment-oriented emphasis that would shortly emerge. Instead, the *Comprehensive Drug Abuse and Control Act*, passed by Congress in 1970, was primarily a law enforcement housekeeping measure, consolidating and clarifying the means by which drugs could be brought under legal controls. Title II of the act established five categories (or schedules) of drugs, based upon their "degree of abuse potential" as well as their known level of harmfulness and their potential for legitimate medical use. Heroin, LSD, mescaline, peyote, and marijuana were included among the most dangerous drugs in Schedule I. The act gave authority over the control of dangerous drugs to the attorney general, who also had the authority to "add, remove, or transfer substances to, from, or between" categories (schedules), subject to consultation with the secretary of Health, Education, and Welfare.[16]

As in contemporary drug policy debates, there was conflict in Congress between proponents of an exclusively criminal justice orientation and those interested in a treatment- and prevention-oriented approach. As a result, the final legislation included some gestures toward drug treatment. For example, Title I authorized $85 million for drug treatment project grants and $39 million for drug abuse education projects, along with increases in the existing Mental Health Centers Act funding authorization to enable those community facilities to deal with addicts.

However, the Comprehensive Drug Abuse and Control Act was landmark legislation primarily because of its contribution to the criminal justice side of drug policy. The act set a mandatory minimum sentence of ten years and a maximum fine of $100,000 for first-time drug trafficking convicts, with still harsher penalties for second-time offenders. In addition to establishing a comprehensive legal mechanism for drug control, it authorized substantial new funding for drug-law enforcement—

$220 million over a three-year period—and its "no-knock" provision gave police agencies a crucial new enforcement power. This provision allowed law enforcement officers to enter private premises without giving notice if there was a likelihood that illegal property would be destroyed or if announcing themselves would endanger life or safety.[17] As a result of this provision, drug traffickers would presumably no longer have time to flush away or burn incriminating evidence while police officers awaited admission at the door, nor would they have the time to get weapons in hand and in place to "shoot it out" with police officers. Unfortunately, the no-knock provision also meant that any innocent citizen whose residence was mistakenly identified by law enforcement authorities would be subject to the traumatic and potentially lethal experience of having armed police unexpectedly break down the door.

From the perspective of drug-law enforcement policy history, another important piece of legislation passed in 1970 was the *Organized Crime Control Act,* Title IX of which is called the Racketeer Influenced and Corrupt Organizations (RICO) statute. This legislation not only instituted relatively severe penalties for drug law violators but also gave enforcement agencies the power to seize property gained through organized criminal activity.[18] Under the RICO statute, creation of an enterprise to commit illegal acts (including drug trafficking), or conspiracy to create such an enterprise, constitutes racketeering. Upon proof of two prior such acts, a violator of the RICO statute can be stripped of all property or other assets so amassed. While the RICO statute was not heavily used in the initial years after its passage, its forfeiture provisions constituted a sleeping giant, which was awakened to heavy use in the 1980s (see Chapter 4).[19]

Finally, drug-law enforcement was escalated in 1971 through the creation, by executive order, of a new drug control agency—the Office of Drug Abuse Law Enforcement (ODALE). ODALE was the first of two drug agencies created by President Nixon to function directly under White House control, thus short-circuiting or overpowering the existing permanent bureaucracy. The other agency, which had drug treatment functions, is described in the following section. Both new drug agencies were created because the existing bureaucracy was resistant to particular new initiatives that the Nixon administration wished to pursue. In the case of ODALE, the new initiative was simply the escalation of arrests against street-level dealers. As we will see in Chapter 7, a strategy of massive arrests of relatively low-level street dealers can be criticized on several grounds: it puts enormous pressures on the rest of the criminal justice system (e.g., courts and prisons); it does not really disrupt drug trafficking because the major figures remain in place and can easily replace lower-level dealers; and the stresses placed on courts and prisons lead to coping devices such as plea bargaining, dropped charges, and early release from prison, thus turning the massive-arrest strategy into meaningless "revolving-door" justice. Perhaps for these reasons, the existing federal drug enforcement agency—the Bureau of Narcotics and Dangerous Drugs (BNDD)—had seen its proper mission as the pursuit of higher-level drug dealers and therefore was recalcitrant when the Nixon administration pushed for an escalation in arrests of street dealers.[20] The creation of ODALE was an end run around this recalcitrant bureaucracy.

The Emergence of a Treatment Emphasis: Methadone

If the Nixon administration's war on drugs had included nothing more than the law enforcement measures just outlined, it would not have been nearly so historically important. After all, those drug-law enforcement developments are fully consistent with the approach to the drug issue that had prevailed from the passage of the Harrison Narcotics Act through the Anslinger era at the FBN. What made the Nixon war on drugs especially interesting was its introduction of a new emphasis, linked to the crime issue but focused on drug treatment. In the period from 1971 to 1972, the Nixon administration promoted a treatment-oriented drug initiative, relying on what was then an experimental method using the synthetic drug methadone.

President Nixon's message to Congress on June 17, 1971, signaled this new emphasis on drug treatment. In that message, Nixon argued that "as long as there is a demand, there will be those willing to take the risks of meeting the demand." He called for $105 million, in addition to the funding already in the 1972 budget, for treatment and rehabilitation of drug addicts.[21] Echoing the frightening scenario of drug-addicted service personnel returning to society, Nixon ordered the immediate creation of drug testing and rehabilitation programs in Vietnam, and he indicated that legislation would be requested that would empower the military to prevent discharged addicts from returning to civilian life without first undergoing mandatory drug treatment.

Nixon appointed a special consultant to spearhead the new emphasis on drug treatment: Dr. Jerome Jaffe, a psychiatrist who had worked in the Illinois drug abuse program and who was a committed proponent of treatment of addicts with methadone. Nixon also persuaded Congress to create a new drug agency, the Special Action Office for Drug Abuse Prevention (SAODAP), located within the Executive Office of the President. SAODAP was intended to play a strong coordinating and leadership role, with powers to direct funding for treatment and rehabilitation to the programs and activities that were most promising. The need for coordination and central leadership in this area was undeniable. While funding on the drug treatment side had been limited, a host of different federal agencies, including the Veterans Administration, the Office of Economic Opportunity, and NIMH, were involved in drug treatment in one fashion or another. The lack of any "big picture" or central focus with respect to drug treatment made the argument for SAODAP compelling.

But there was yet another reason for the creation of a special drug treatment organization within the White House itself. The Nixon administration was at this time interested in methadone maintenance as a form of drug treatment. Federal agencies such as NIMH were resisting this initiative, because methadone treatment involved a relatively new and experimental drug, treating drug addicts with another drug raised philosophical concerns among many in the established agencies, and use of such a drug-based approach undermined the counseling approach central to the professions represented in agencies such as NIMH.[22]

Though it was being used in a number of state programs by 1971, methadone maintenance treatment was controversial. As described in more detail in Chapter 5, this form of treatment involves the regular administration of controlled doses of the synthetic drug methadone. Drs. Vincent P. Dole and Marie Nyswander of the Rockefeller Institute had demonstrated in their clinical research that regular maintenance doses of this synthetic drug did not induce euphoria in the patient but did prevent the addict's craving for heroin. As a result, they argued, the heroin addict could, through the use of methadone, lead a relatively normal life. Without the recurring need for a heroin fix, for example, methadone patients could hold regular jobs and would not be drawn into a life of crime to support a heroin habit.

But methadone is, like heroin, a powerful drug, and some critical voices argued that long-term administration of such a drug simply substituted one addiction for another. Furthermore, because heroin addicts in publicly funded programs were disproportionately poor and black, methadone treatment raised the specter of deliberate, permanent drugging of the ghetto underclass, perhaps as a response to the racial uprising that had occurred in the 1960s. David Bellis provides a powerful description of this potentially explosive objection to methadone, including the following charges made by a minority group at a 1971 conference on methadone treatment:

> The white "power structure" encourages methadone maintenance because it affects mainly those who have the most to gain from "revolution," weakening their will to resist "illegitimate authority." . . . Methadone maintenance programs expose clients to constant surveillance. Since methadone is highly addictive, addicts on the programs remain under "life-long government supervision."[23]

In the light of these difficult and sensitive issues, bureaucratic agencies such as NIMH were inclined to move slowly and cautiously with respect to methadone maintenance. The Nixon administration's efforts to forge ahead with aggressive initiatives in the drug treatment field were in danger of being mired down by this bureaucratic reticence. Hence, the creation of SAODAP was an organizational strategy to ramrod change in the drug treatment field. More generally, Nixon has often been portrayed as being at odds with the existing permanent bureaucracy and as responding with attempts to circumvent it by creating units within the White House that would be more readily controllable.[24] In

this respect, the creation of SAODAP was simply the drug policy equivalent of a more general pattern in the Nixon presidency.

SAODAP, created in 1971 with Jerome Jaffe as its head, had responsibilities for formulating overall policy with respect to drug demand reduction and for coordinating federal programs involving drug research, rehabilitation, treatment, and prevention. In 1972, SAODAP and the new
orientation toward drug treatment that it represented were legislatively
institutionalized with the passage of the Drug Abuse Office and Treatment Act of 1972.

With organizational arrangements and legislative authorization in
place, there was a dramatic move toward a treatment response to the
drug problem. Funding for drug treatment and rehabilitation increased
from $33.5 million in 1970 to $196.1 million in 1972 and $350.3 million
in 1973—more than a tenfold increase in three years! Funding for other
demand-side approaches to the drug problem, including drug education,
prevention, and training, increased from $8.5 million in 1970 to $45.7
million in 1973—a fivefold increase. Funding for drug-law enforcement
increased as well during this period, but at only half the rate of the increases for treatment and prevention. As a result, by 1972, federal funding for treatment and prevention efforts was twice as much as that for
law enforcement efforts.[25]

Why did the Nixon administration come to support such a dramatic
reversal in drug policy? One interpretation is that the turn toward the
treatment approach and its distinctive methadone maintenance form
was a political ploy devised by Nixon advisors as a method for appearing
to show results with respect to drugs and crime in time for the reelection
campaign. Nixon had, after all, come to office with crime and disorder as
one of his main campaign themes. Once in office, Nixon must quickly
have discovered the difficulty of delivering on his law-and-order
promises. "It was a local issue, and the federal government, short of giving money and aid, was severely limited in what it could accomplish.
This led Nixon to rely on dramatic gestures and symbolic leadership in
the crime area."[26] By 1970, according to Michael Genovese, Nixon was
ordering his chief of staff, H. R. Haldeman, to "do something on crime
now":

> But the president didn't know *what* to do. In a June 9,1971 meeting with his
> chief of staff, Haldeman's notes reveal the president saying:
> look in terms of how create issues
> need an enemy, controversy
> drugs and law enforcement
> esp. since so weak in polls[27]

In his influential interpretation, Jay Epstein describes how Jeffrey
Donfeld, a low-level staffer on the president's Domestic Policy Council,
learned in 1970 of emerging research and clinical practice involving
methadone and saw the potential for "a magical solution to both the nar-

cotics and law-and-order problems."[28] Despite initial reservations among some, the concept of a major drug initiative centered on methadone treatment was eventually accepted by key members of Nixon's top staff, and they apparently "sold" it to him on the grounds that it was the only action that could yield results in time for the 1972 election:

> Substantive measures, such as court reform or reorganizing police departments, could not possibly have an effect on crime statistics in time for the 1972 election.... One of the largest categories of arrests in urban centers was ... the revolving door arrests of junkies.... Donfeld pointed out that if large numbers of addicts received legal methadone rather than illegal heroin ... narcotics violations could be expected to decrease dramatically in major cities, and this alone might bring about diminished crime reporting by local police departments.[29]

In addition, Dole and Nyswander's research on methadone maintenance had suggested that this therapy would deter predatory crime by heroin addicts by removing their need to steal and rob. According to the political logic described by Epstein, however, methadone maintenance was highly attractive to Nixon's closest staff because even if the crime deterrent effect suggested by Dole and Nyswander was *not* forthcoming, simply reducing arrests for drug possession and use would yield diminished crime statistics for which the Nixon reelection campaign could claim credit.

The End of the Nixon War on Drugs

The rapid mobilization toward a treatment-oriented war on drugs was followed by an equally dramatic demobilization. The demobilization was signaled in what is commonly referred to as Nixon's "turning the corner" speech. In that statement at a White House conference on drug treatment issues, Nixon claimed that the nation had "turned the corner on drug addiction." "In addition to being a statement of 'victory,' the president's message also implied disengagement from the war" on drugs.[30]

And, in fact, there was a notable disengagement, though reductions in the newly established funding took longer to be realized than the more precipitate decline in presidential rhetoric, legislative initiatives, and administrative reorganizing that had propelled the drug issue into the limelight in the 1970–1972 period. The federal budget for drug treatment and rehabilitation began to decline after 1973, in absolute as well as inflation-adjusted dollars, while the budget for drug-law enforcement continued to increase.

There are a number of likely reasons for this rapid demobilization. One possibility is that the drug war had actually yielded dramatic results in terms of decreased drug addiction and attendant crime. The Nixon administration had certainly begun to claim credit for results even before the 1973 "turning the corner" speech. Those who interpret the entire war on drugs as a reelection ploy point out the claims of success made during the 1972 campaign months. On August 15, 1972, for example, Nixon administration officials marshaled a variety of statistics to show that there had been substantial progress in preventing importation of drugs, in domestic enforcement of drug laws, and in treating the victims of drug abuse.[31] Meanwhile, decreases in crime rates in general and in Washington, D.C., in particular were being touted as evidence that the Nixon administration's strategy had yielded results.[32]

But there are substantial grounds for doubting the validity of these statistical claims of success. As noted earlier, the law enforcement side of this war on drugs involved massive numbers of arrests of street-level dealers. A suspension of this policy after a year or so of heavy arrest activity would, in itself, yield a showing of decreasing drug-related crime, perhaps especially in a single focal city such as Washington, D.C. But such a reduction would clearly be artificial. Jay Epstein provides an even more intriguing description of the Nixon administration's manipulation of figures on the number of heroin addicts. According to this description, the Nixon administration first created an artificial "increase" in the number of known heroin addicts by changing its method for estimating this number, which had for years been based upon figures compiled by the Bureau of Narcotics and Dangerous Drugs (BNDD) from local police reports. In 1969, the figure stood at 68,088. But in 1970 and 1971, the BNDD applied a statistical adjustment formula to the raw data, an adjustment keyed to the number of arrests of addicts. Particularly since the latter was escalating rapidly due to law enforcement policies calling for more arrests, the statistical adjustment led to an estimate of 315,000 addicts in 1970 and 559,000 in 1972—a whopping increase that was heavily publicized as evidence that there was a heroin epidemic. However, in the reelection year of 1972, Nixon's chief domestic policy counselor, Egil Krogh, demanded that the BNDD executive cease this:

> Krogh ordered Ingersoll not to release "any more numbers" and to clear all his public statements with a special White House press officer, Richard Harkness. The epidemic thus peaked at 559,000 addicts—and then was arbitrarily reduced to 150,000 addicts. The elimination of 409,000 addicts (who might never have existed) was subsequently cited as evidence of success in the Nixon crusade.[33]

This sort of evidence of manipulation of data for political ends undermines any argument that the rapid demobilization of Nixon's drug war was the result of a victory over the drug problem. What other explanations for demobilization are there? The most obvious is tied to the reelection rationale that has been offered as an explanation for the initiation of the drug war. Presumably, once reelected, Nixon no longer needed to keep pressure on the drug issue. Furthermore, the war on drugs was yielding some embarrassing bloopers, as when ODALE agents, using no-knock powers, barged into the homes of innocent and terrorized citizens in Collinsville, Illinois, in 1973, leading to outrage and a formal review of the special agency. And finally, the new tactics of Nixon's drug war "had in their combined effect failed to measure up to original expectations, and it seemed unlikely that any further improvement would result from an expanded or intensified effort in these areas."[34]

CONCLUSIONS

What lessons can be learned about drug politics and drug policy from this Nixon-era episode? First, the episode is an example of the mobilization model of agenda setting. It reveals the special susceptibility of the drug issue to symbolic politics—specifically, politicians manipulate symbols to arouse fears and anxieties in the mass public, then introduce highly visible and dramatic policy efforts that assuage the anxieties. As this episode shows, political entrepreneurs can seize upon opportunities presented by prevailing conditions of turmoil to forge anxiety-provoking symbolic links between drugs, crime, and social dislocation. Drug policy-making under these circumstances is not simply a straightforward response to public demands for drug control; it creates the demand for drug control.

Second, the episode is suggestive about the type of drug policy that is likely to emerge as the product of mobilization-style agenda setting. The mobilization of public fears is presumably not orchestrated unless there are likely means for quickly allaying those fears. In this case, there were two. One, the synthetic drug methadone, offered the pharmacological version of a surefire answer. Heroin addicts who were on methadone would not need to engage in predatory crime. The other, involving the manipulation of statistical evidence on crime and addiction, offered a guaranteed avenue for claiming success and assuring the public that the drug problem was being effectively addressed. Note that this was made possible in part by the relatively primitive state of social indicators on the drug issue in the early 1970s. The regular household and high school surveys of drug use that are described in Chapter 1, for example, were not instituted until right after the Nixon drug war. Today, the existence of these surveys, along with the alternative data sources outlined in Chapter 1, would presumably make a policy "solution" based upon statistical manipulation less plausible.

And third, this episode suggests that although public concern about the drug issue can be quickly galvanized, it can disappear just as quickly. As Figure 1.4 shows, public attention to the drug problem dropped precipitously after 1973. President Nixon's demobilization of the war on drugs, as signaled in the 1973 "turning the corner" speech, was presumably instrumental in this dramatic decline in public concern. But the receptivity of the American public to such claims, and the resulting roller coaster pattern of public concern about drugs, is of more general interest. It illustrates that the "issue attention cycle"[35] for the drug problem can be quite short, not so much because of "saturation" effects[36] (i.e., loss of interest due to the repetitiveness of messages over time) but because of receptivity to symbolic reassurances.[37] This, unfortunately, is not a pattern that lends itself to rational public discourse and comprehensive problem-solving efforts.

NOTES

1. David F. Musto, *The American Disease: Origins of Narcotic Control* (New Haven: Yale University Press, 1973), pp. 40–41.
2. Arnold Trebach, *The Heroin Solution* (New Haven: Yale University Press, 1982), p. 120.
3. Trebach, 1982, p. 125.
4. Trebach, 1982, p. 125
5. Trebach, 1982, p. 128.
6. Musto, 1973, pp. 5–8.
7. Trebach, 1982, p. 160.
8. John C. McWilliams, *The Protectors: Harry J. Anslinger and the Federal Bureau of Narcotics, 1930–1962* (Newark: University of Delaware Press, 1990), p. 70.
9. McWilliams, 1990, pp. 66, 90.
10. McWilliams, 1990, p. 108.
11. McWilliams, 1990, pp. 109–110.
12. McWilliams, 1990, p. 112.
13. McWilliams, 1990, p. 116.
14. Examples in this section are from the *New York Times Index* for 1971.
15. U.S. House of Representatives, Committee on Armed Services, Special Subcommittee on Alleged Drug Abuse in the Armed Services, *Alleged Drug Abuse in the Armed Services* (Washington, DC: U.S. Government Printing Office, 1971).
16. "Comprehensive Drug Control Bill Cleared by Congress," *CQ Almanac,* vol. 26 (Washington, DC: Congressional Quarterly, 1970), p. 531.
17. "Congress Clears Comprehensive Drug Control Bill," *CQ Weekly Report,* October 16, 1970, pp. 2539–2542.
18. Michael Lyman, *Practical Drug Enforcement* (New York: Elsevier, 1989), p. 363.
19. Steven Wisotsky, *Beyond the War on Drugs* (Buffalo: Prometheus Books, 1990), p. 68.
20. Peter Goldberg, "The Federal Government's Response to Illicit Drugs, 1969–1978," in Drug Abuse Council, *The Facts About "Drug Abuse"* (New York: Free Press, 1980), p. 39.

21. "Excerpts from President's Message on Drug Abuse Control," *New York Times*, June 18, 1971, p. 22.
22. Goldberg, 1980, pp. 33–34.
23. David J. Bellis, *Heroin and Politicians: The Failure of Public Policy to Control Addiction in America* (Westport, CT: Greenwood Press, 1981), pp. 61–62.
24. Richard P. Nathan, *The Plot That Failed: Nixon and the Administrative Presidency* (New York: Wiley, 1975).
25. Goldberg, 1980, p. 57.
26. Michael A. Genovese, *The Nixon Presidency: Power and Politics in Turbulent Times* (New York: Greenwood Press, 1990), p. 90.
27. Genovese, 1990, p. 88.
28. Jay Epstein, *Agency of Fear* (New York: Putnam, 1977), p. 123.
29. Epstein, 1977, p. 137.
30. Goldberg, 1980, p. 42.
31. Dana Adams Schmidt, "U.S. Officials Report Progress in Stopping Drugs," *New York Times*, August 17, 1972, p. 16.
32. Bellis, 1981, p. 72.
33. Epstein, 1977, p. 177.
34. Goldberg, 1980, p. 43.
35. Anthony Downs, "Up and Down with Ecology—the 'Issue-Attention Cycle,'" *The Public Interest* 32 (1973), pp. 38–50.
36. Stephen Hilgartner and Charles L. Bosk, "The Rise and Fall of Social Problems: A Public Arenas Model," *American Journal of Sociology* 94 (July 1988), pp. 53–78.
37. Murray Edelman, *The Symbolic Uses of Politics* (Urbana: University of Illinois Press, 1974).

Chapter 3

Drug Policy in the Carter Administration

INTRODUCTION

Another notable episode of national attention to drug policy, different in many ways from Nixon's war on drugs, occurred during the Carter administration. This episode did *not* galvanize public attention to the drug issue. Figure 1.4 shows that although it did increase somewhat, popular attention to the drug issue was remarkably low in the 1977–1979 period, as measured by Gallup poll mentions of the drug issue as "the most important problem facing the country" and by the number of magazine articles about drugs. On the basis of the evidence in Figure 1.4, one might be tempted to conclude that there was no drug policy episode in this period.

However, even though drugs were not on the popular agenda in any major way, they were definitely on the government's agenda. As Figure 3.1 shows, the number of congressional hearings involving drug topics in the late 1970s approached the number devoted to the issue during Nixon's war on drugs. The character of this attention to drugs was considerably different in the two administrations, however. To a considerable extent, drugs were on the congressional agenda not because new initiatives were being proposed or dramatic new developments were being investigated, but because drug programs and organizations were coming up for reauthorization or being subjected to oversight review. For example, drug-related hearings held in 1977 included one on reauthorization of the Drug Enforcement Administration (DEA), a review of narcotics funding channeled through the Law Enforcement Assistance Administration, one devoted to amendments to the existing veterans health care law, several on a presidential reorganization plan that would affect the organizational arrangements for drug policy formulation and coordination, and two devoted to confirmation proceedings for new

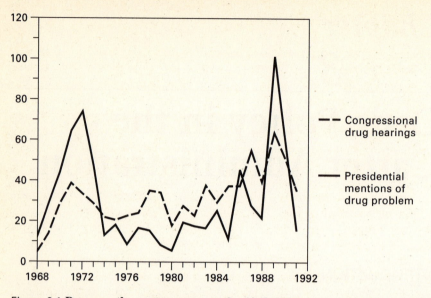

Figure 3.1 **Drugs on the government agenda, 1968–1991.** (*Source:* Author's original coding of hearings using Congressional Information Service on compact disc and the *New York Times Index* for the years represented.)

presidential appointees in the drug control area. In short, the drug issue was largely being handled as a matter of routine procedure and technical correction of existing programs. With one notable exception—a hearing on decriminalization of marijuana—drug policy was not in the high-visibility, controversial mode of the Nixon years.

Figure 3.1 also shows that presidential attention to the drug issue during the Carter administration differed from that in the Nixon administration. Throughout his presidency, Jimmy Carter spoke publicly about the drug issue much less frequently than did either Nixon before him or Reagan after him. This difference in the extent of presidential rhetoric about the drug issue does not mean that drugs were not on Carter's agenda. Rather, it reveals a difference in the style of agenda setting that was being used. As we have seen, Nixon used a *mobilization* form of agenda setting, which relies upon the evocation of high levels of concern about the problem among the general public. By contrast, Carter used the *inside-access* approach to agenda setting for the drug issue. This approach emphasizes control of the issue by interests and experts within government, with less publicly visible attention to the problem. As this chapter will show, the approach may have been effective in resolving many small-scale technical problems with existing drug programs and policies, but it was not an effective approach for the one dramatic policy change that Carter recommended—the decriminalization of marijuana.

CARTER'S DRUG AGENDA

In contrast with Nixon, whose drug policy initiative was linked to core symbolic themes that he brought to office (law and order, crime control) and was strongly motivated by reelection entrepreneurship, Carter's drug policy was unrelated to any campaign themes or reelection imperatives. Rather, the drug issue was pursued as one among many policy problems that deserved immediate attention, yet needed to be approached from a standpoint of making comprehensive and detailed reform. In this respect, Carter's handling of the drug issue was typical of his approach to problems generally. As governor of Georgia, his administration had been characterized by "a comprehensive approach, based on close study and a long view, resulting in more than incremental gains, over a wide variety of policy fields."[1] Carter was, in short, a rational-technocratic president, oriented toward technical expertise and problem solving rather than political skills and issue leadership. The drug policy initiatives of this period, and their ultimate fate, were shaped by this orientation.

They were also strongly influenced by the president's drug policy advisor, Peter Bourne. In stark contrast with the political operatives who shaped Nixon's drug policy responses, Bourne was a technically trained specialist in the field of mental health and substance abuse. He was a psychiatrist and had served in Georgia's narcotics treatment program when Carter was governor of that state. His published writings on drug policy were reformist in character, with a clear emphasis on the need for a rethinking of the "war on drugs" mentality and a turn toward serious innovation on the treatment side.[2] Perhaps most important, Bourne provided Carter with a link to a substantial network of reform-minded drug policy experts. This network centered around the Drug Abuse Council, a foundation-funded organization of drug abuse experts that had begun to function as an important lobby for drug policy change during the Nixon administration.[3] This institutionalized network of experts was important given the inside-access model of agenda setting that characterized Carter's approach to drug policy-making.

The Carter administration's drug policy agenda included a variety of ideas and initiatives that at first seem to have no coherent focus or thematic emphasis. On closer inspection, however, we see that Carter's drug policy agenda had several important themes, including (1) the need for a more comprehensive and balanced approach to the drug issue, (2) the need for rational discourse and research to overcome undue hysteria and false premises about the drug problem, and (3) the need to rationalize federal drug policy-making through reorganization.

The most notable drug policy initiative of the Carter era was a proposal to decriminalize marijuana, detailed later in this chapter. Although this initiative seemed to de-emphasize the seriousness of one illicit substance, the Carter administration simultaneously pressed for more federal attention to substances that were legal in prescription form but were nonetheless abused. In particular, the administration highlighted the abuse of barbiturates and other sedatives, which, according to Peter Bourne,

> are too often overprescribed and over-utilized. There is no doubt that for certain indications there are safer and more effective drugs available. Yet out of lack of knowledge, or in some cases desire for financial gain, physicians continue to inappropriately prescribe them . . . we will determine whether those sedative/hypnotic drugs particularly subject to abuse should be removed from the market.[4]

The president had signaled his personal emphasis on this version of the drug problem in response to a questioner in a televised question-and-answer show in Los Angeles in May 1977:

> There's also a need for us to recognize that you don't have to have scarce and exotic drugs like heroin before somebody can be damaged, because barbiturates, for instance, are by far the major cause of death among all drugs, and they are prescribed sometimes. . . . So a comprehensive analysis of the entire drug field, including both alcohol and the addictive and nonaddictive drugs, plus a treatment of those who are damaged by the drugs, will be a part of our . . . program.[5]

And in his major statement on drug abuse, a message to Congress on August 2, 1977, Carter emphasized, "Federal programs have given disproportionate attention to the heroin addict while neglecting those who are dependent on other drugs"; he therefore directed the secretary of Health, Education, and Welfare "to expand resources devoted to care for abusers of barbiturates, amphetamines, and multiple drugs used in combination, including alcohol."[6]

These comments reveal the first theme of drug policy in this era: movement toward a comprehensive and balanced approach to the drug issue. Drug policy was to be more comprehensive in the sense that a fuller spectrum of abused substances would be subject to government attention; it was to be more balanced in that the emphasis given to particular substances would be based on objective consideration of the severity of health problems posed and the pervasiveness of abuse. In this respect, drug policy in the Carter era was substantially different from that in the Nixon era, which focused heavily on heroin despite the fact that the drug was used by very small numbers of Americans.

An emphasis on research and orderly improvements to the drug policy system replaced the more dramatic rhetoric of Nixon's war on drugs. This was most evident in the Carter administration's call for research on the potential therapeutic uses of drugs. Peter Bourne summarized the administration's approach to drugs:

Cannabis may help patients having glaucoma where it apparently reduced intraocular pressure and those having cancer where it may serve as an antiemetic in chemotherapy. Likewise, heroin (diacetylmorphine) may be useful for the treatment of pain in terminal cancer and for other carefully circumscribed medical conditions. I feel strongly that, to the fullest extent possible, research into the potential therapeutic usefulness of marihuana and heroin should be dealt with exclusively as a medical issue, with a completely objective assessment of the available scientific data, without being biased by historical precedent, legal status of the drug or public prejudice.[7]

This may seem a modest and unsurprising thing to ask. Yet it represented an important change in tone and policy direction. As Chapter 2 shows, when drugs are on the government agenda, the discussion often verges on the hysterical. The demonization of drugs and those who use them is not conducive to a rational discussion of possible legitimate medical uses of some of those same drugs. Thus, the call for an assessment of legitimate medical uses was a genuine policy innovation. Carter was "the first president in our history, as far as the public record shows, who openly entertained the possibility of relaxing prohibition on the use of these substances in ordinary medicine, that is, for treating the organically ill."[8]

More generally, the drug issue was being handled with a much lower-key tone and with an approach designed for troubleshooting and remediation of problems with existing programs rather than dramatic exhortations about the need for major new initiatives. As a result, much of the Carter drug policy agenda involved relatively narrow technical matters. For example, with respect to drug-law enforcement, the first year of policy activity in the Carter administration included efforts to enhance coordination between U.S. Customs and the DEA, efforts to improve liaison with state and local law enforcement agencies, and a review of border control activities.[9]

The Carter administration's drug policy agenda also included reorganization efforts. These were actually part of a more comprehensive reorganization plan, designed to abolish a number of the special units that had accumulated within the Executive Office of the President and to elevate the cabinet to a more prominent role in policy development. This new "policy management system" was to exemplify "lean but efficient Government organization,"[10] according to Harrison Wellford, the president's executive associate director for reorganization and management:

Replacing the [Domestic Policy] Council will be ad hoc task forces of Cabinet and agency officials convened for specific issues. The domestic policy staff will function as conveners, coordinators, and neutral brokers, wherever and whenever appropriate. . . . This flexible assembly and disassembly of ad hoc working groups will allow maximum use of the expertise in the Cabinet departments and other agencies.[11]

The most dramatic element of Carter's drug policy agenda, however, was his call for the decriminalization of marijuana. This initiative ultimately failed. But the attempt itself was an important episode in American drug policy history, and the story of the attempt reveals much about drug policy-making generally and about the Carter administration in particular.

The Marijuana Decriminalization Debate of 1977–1978

In several respects, it could be argued that by 1977 the time was ripe for change in the federal government's policy toward marijuana. Indeed, there had already been a modest change during the Nixon administration. Prior to 1970, federal penalties for marijuana possession were as severe as those for "hard" drugs such as heroin or cocaine. They could involve 5 to 20 years of imprisonment for conviction of a first offense and 10 to 40 years for a second.[12] The Comprehensive Drug Abuse and Control Act of 1970 did keep marijuana in the same control category as heroin, LSD, and cocaine. But it reduced federal penalties for possession *and distribution* to a maximum of 5 years in prison and $15,000 in fines for a first offense, and double this for a second. First offenders could also be placed on probation and exempted from having a guilty verdict on their record.

There were other indications that the time for change had come. A number of states had already begun to change their laws involving marijuana. In 1968, Alaska, California, and Vermont reduced penalties for marijuana possession, and by 1970, 33 states had decreased marijuana possession to a misdemeanor offense with a penalty of typically no more than seven days in jail. In 1973, Oregon fully decriminalized marijuana possession, establishing only a fine of $100 for possession of less than 1 ounce of marijuana.[13] By 1977, eight states (Oregon, Alaska, Maine, Colorado, California, Ohio, Minnesota, and Mississippi) had only civil penalties of $100 to $200 for possession of small amounts of marijuana.[14]

The climate for marijuana decriminalization also seemed ripe because of apparent change in public attitudes on the issue. By 1977, commentators could claim, "In the past few years, public attitudes toward marijuana have shifted sufficiently so that favoring its decriminalization has become a politically safe position."[15] Gallup poll results for 1976 and 1977 provide some support for the claim. When asked whether they thought the possession of small amounts of marijuana should or should not be treated as a criminal offense, the majority of respondents (53 percent) said it should not; 41 percent said it should and 6 percent had no opinion.[16]

In an important analysis of this period, Jerome Himmelstein[17] argues that change in the social composition of the marijuana user group was the key to this changed climate of public opinion about marijuana. Until the later 1960s, marijuana use was not particularly widespread, and the American public largely accepted the characterization of the Bureau of Narcotics and Dangerous Drugs (BNDD), which called marijuana a very dangerous drug—a characterization that fit nicely with public images of its use by ethnic minorities and fringe elements such as jazz musicians and other bohemians. But the late 1960s and 1970s witnessed the "embourgeoisement" of marijuana, as large numbers of middle-class youth and adults began using marijuana. As Figure 1.2 shows, by the later 1970s nearly half of all 18- to 25-year-olds reported on surveys that they had used marijuana within the past year and about one-third of this age group reported use within the past month.

This spread of marijuana use led to changes in the American public's perceptions of marijuana users. Americans learned through the media or through personal experience that their own children and other apparently normal middle-class individuals—rather than deviants, criminals, or members of the "dangerous classes"—represented the marijuana user group. The embourgeoisement of marijuana also created new political forces because youthful middle-class users were in a position to mobilize groups to engage in political lobbying over the issue—groups such as the National Student Association and the National Organization for the Reform of Marihuana Laws (NORML). The combination of these new perceptions of who marijuana users were and these new political forces helped to convince many Americans that marijuana was not as bad as had once been thought and to make the general public more receptive to reduced penalties for marijuana possession.[18]

However, despite these changes, it may have been premature to characterize marijuana decriminalization as a politically safe issue. Gallup poll results showed that only a bare majority supported decriminalization; the country was still deeply divided on the issue. Furthermore, public attitudes toward marijuana were not particularly favorable, despite the extent of support for decriminalization. Two-thirds of Americans surveyed in the Gallup poll said that marijuana should not be made completely legal, and a majority (55%) agreed that for most people, the use of marijuana is physically harmful. Characterizations of marijuana as a "killer weed" were fading away, but the public was beginning to accept authoritative statements about marijuana as the cause of "amotivational syndrome"—that is, people believed marijuana tended to "destroy ambition and initiative, to interfere with the effort to cope with the world, and to facilitate withdrawal from reality."[19] In short, while attitudes had shifted enough to make the time ripe for policy change, the marijuana issue still was a divisive one and marijuana was still broadly viewed as a very problematic substance.

Marijuana decriminalization was being propelled onto the government agenda through the efforts of a number of lobby groups, the most important of which was NORML. NORML was founded in 1971 by Keith Stroup, a graduate of the Georgetown University Law School and a former employee of the National Commission on Product Safety. Inspired by the consumerist approach of that Ralph Nader–oriented organization, galvanized by the marijuana arrest of a friend, supportively advised by former attorney general Ramsey Clark, and initially financed by a grant from Hugh Hefner's Playboy Foundation, Stroup set out to build a lobbying organization that could succeed in getting the federal government to end criminal penalties for the use of marijuana.[20]

Stroup was able to build NORML into a highly visible lobbying organization. In its early years, he attracted prominent individuals to join its board of directors. These included the national director of the American Civil Liberties Union, two members of the faculty of the Harvard Medical School, a noted professor of pediatrics from Georgetown University, and a recently retired senior official from the BNDD.[21]

The issue of marijuana decriminalization had also been propelled onto the government agenda by the National Commission on Marihuana, created during the Nixon administration as a compromise feature of the comprehensive 1970 drug legislation. The Marihuana Commission had reported its findings in 1972. Much to the dismay of then-President Nixon, who promptly disavowed the commission, these findings supported decriminalization of marijuana. The commission found that unless use was heavy and long-term, there was no evidence that marijuana caused physical or psychological harm or that it led to physical dependency. As a result, the commission concluded that possession of small amounts of marijuana did not warrant a criminal penalty and urged corresponding changes in state laws as well.[22] Despite Nixon's rejection of these findings, the report was influential in changing public thinking about marijuana, in large part because of the commission's composition. Its members, appointed by Nixon, included mainstream politicians (i.e., several U.S. senators and representatives) as well as scientists, and it was chaired by Republican governor Raymond Shafer of Pennsylvania. Groups such as NORML were therefore able to make use of the commission's findings in their battle to get legitimacy for the idea of marijuana decriminalization.

By 1977 the issue of marijuana decriminalization had been rumbling through the public consciousness and threatening to burst onto the government agenda for at least five years. Viewed from this perspective, the issue was far from innovative. However, Carter's decision to put the weight of the presidency behind the decriminalization movement was the most visible and the only truly controversial feature of his drug policy agenda. It was "a historic step—however modest it may seem to some observers—because it was the first presidential recommendation for a relaxation of criminal penalties on the *nonmedical* use of any of the drugs that carry such negative emotional freight among many members of the electorate."[23]

The arguments of administration spokespersons at the 1977 marijuana decriminalization hearings suggested three reasons for administration efforts in this direction: (1) the counterproductive and inappropriately damaging aspects of then-current marijuana penalties; (2) the inconsistency between the law on the books and actual enforcement practice; and (3) the limited importance of marijuana from a health effects perspective, especially compared to other substances being abused. With respect to the first rationale, Peter Bourne, then the director-designate of the Office of Drug Abuse Policy, indicated the administration's reasoning: "We have seen in the past where criminal penalties have resulted in otherwise law-abiding young people spending time in prison and incurring permanent damage to their careers and their ability to enter professions. This causes far greater harm to their lives than any effect the drug would have had and the penalties are counter-productive."[24]

Second, the administration implicitly acknowledged that the federal government did not have the resources to actually enforce existing laws against simple possession of marijuana. Benjamin Civiletti, an assistant attorney general in the Department of Justice, explained his position on the subject:

I think that it erodes the law and respect for the law to have laws . . . on the books, that make certain actions criminal and yet people aren't prosecuted for it, or they are only prosecuted in certain areas. . . . Yet that is the circumstance that exists today with regard to marihuana.[25]

At other points in the hearing, Bourne made it clear that part of the impetus for reforming marijuana law had to do with its priority as an abuse issue on medical grounds:

There was a state of panic in the country 10 years ago because people were misinformed. There was a feeling that marihuana was a very, very dangerous drug, comparable to heroin or even more dangerous in some people's minds. We have done an extensive amount of research and, contrary to much of the prejudice that existed, we have yet to find a serious medical consequence related to marihuana.[26]

By the same token, this hearing suggested how narrowly drawn this decriminalization reform proposal really was, despite the apparent radicalness of the idea. Although the penalty for simple possession of marijuana was to be reduced to a small civil fine, marijuana would still remain a prohibited substance. Peter Bourne indicated, "We are not talking about people getting legal marijuana. This is still a prohibited substance. It is just that the deterrents are different. . . . We are not changing our attitude that we should deter the use of marihuana. And I think the findings that use has not gone up significantly in those States which have decriminalized tends to support this."[27]

THE FAILURE OF
CARTER'S DRUG POLICY INITIATIVES

To a large extent, the Carter administration's drug policy agenda failed to be realized. In particular, the call for marijuana decriminalization and the promise of a more rational, medically grounded approach to drug abuse policy were derailed when Peter Bourne, who had spearheaded the administration's efforts at drug policy redirection, was forced to resign under a cloud because of a drug incident. The precipitating incident involved a prescription for a tranquilizer (Quaalude) that Bourne wrote for one of his assistants, Ellen Metsky, who had been complaining of having trouble sleeping. Bourne, a medical doctor, was qualified and licensed to prescribe such medications. The problem, however, was that the prescription was written for a fictitious name rather than under Ellen Metsky's name, evidently to protect her privacy. This is not a legal practice. Consequently, when state authorities arrested the individual who was attempting to get the prescription filled for Metsky, word of Bourne's involvement immediately transformed the incident into a media event.[28]

Bourne's legitimacy was completely destroyed, however, when in the wake of the prescription incident, the journalist Jack Anderson reported that Bourne had taken cocaine at a party the previous winter in Washington, D.C. Bourne admitted to having been at the party and being among others using cocaine, but he denied actually having used it himself. Others who were at the party claimed that Bourne did take cocaine:

> As the bullet [container of cocaine] slowly made its way around the circle toward Peter Bourne, one young woman, a friend of his from the campaign, whispered to him that he should not be doing this, but he only laughed self-confidently. Bourne had a fatal desire to be one of the boys. When the bullet reached him, he too took a one-and-one [a hit in each nostril]. All around the room people were stunned. And well they might have been, for they were witnessing one of the turning points in the war over drug policy that had been so bitterly contested in America in the 1970s.[29]

In any case, Bourne's resignation was inevitable under the circumstances, and the credibility of Carter's drug policy initiatives was completely destroyed. As one commentator noted, "The drug-law reform movement vanished up Peter Bourne's nose."[30]

CONCLUSIONS

It may be overly simplistic to attribute the failure of Carter's drug policy agenda solely to the Bourne incident. It is possible to identify other factors that limited the possibilities for policy change in this period. One is the diffuse character of the president's policy agenda. As Barber notes,

Carter, by his own admission, attempted too many different things at once in his initial year or two in office.[31] The result of this was an inevitable retreat on many of the policy fronts, especially given Carter's limitations as a wheeler-dealer among entrenched power bases in Washington.

Another limitation may be the character of agenda setting for drug policy in particular. As noted at the beginning of this chapter, Carter used an inside-access model rather than a mobilization model of agenda setting. Unlike Nixon, who made the drug issue highly visible by heightening public concerns and media attention to it, Carter approached drug issues as technical problems that could be ameliorated through quiet, rational reassessment by experts in the drug policy field. Such a low-visibility approach might have been ideal if the agenda were restricted to narrow technical issues, such as research on therapeutic uses of controlled substances and attention to abuse of amphetamines and barbiturates relative to other drugs such as heroin. But the call for decriminalization of marijuana was not a narrow, routine, or technical matter. Despite the many factors that brought this matter onto the government agenda and made the issue seem ripe for discussion, it was still a volatile, explosive topic. Change could not simply be a matter of obtaining technical consensus on the relatively innocuous medical consequences of marijuana smoking, then altering policy accordingly. In this instance, efforts at policy change inevitably involved confrontations between expert judgments and public fears about a substance that had for many years been portrayed in highly negative terms. Successful policy change would have required the forging of a new public consensus. But unlike the mobilization model, the inside-access approach to policy formulation ignores the need for manipulation of the attitudes of the mass public. In short, much as the inside-access approach to policy change may have fit Carter's own technocratic style, it was a poor fit with the political imperatives of the marijuana decriminalization issue.

NOTES

1. James David Barber, *The Presidential Character*, 3rd ed. (Englewood Cliffs, NJ: Prentice-Hall, 1985), p. 432.
2. Arnold Trebach, *The Heroin Solution* (New Haven: Yale University Press, 1982), pp. 237–238.
3. Trebach, 1982, p. 236.
4. U.S. House of Representatives, Select Committee on Narcotics Abuse and Control, *Oversight Hearings on Federal Drug Strategy* (Washington, DC: U.S. Government Printing Office, 1978), p. 10.
5. *Public Papers of the Presidents of the United States. Jimmy Carter, Book I, 1977* (Washington, DC: U.S. Government Printing Office, 1977), p. 904.
6. *Public Papers of the Presidents*, 1977, p. 1404.
7. Select Committee on Narcotics Abuse and Control, 1978, p. 10.

8. Trebach, 1982, p. 239.
9. Select Committee on Narcotics Abuse and Control, 1978, p. 10.
10. Select Committee on Narcotics Abuse and Control, 1978, p. 20.
11. Select Committee on Narcotics Abuse and Control, 1978, p. 21.
12. U.S. House of Representatives, Select Committee on Narcotics Abuse and Control, *Decriminalization of Marihuana* (Washington, DC: U.S. Government Printing Office, 1977), p. 2.
13. Select Committee on Narcotics Abuse and Control, 1977, pp. 2–3.
14. Robert Reinhold, "Smoking of Marijuana Wins Wider Acceptance," *New York Times*, May 23, 1977, p. 46.
15. Tom Goldstein, "Backing Grows for Easing Marijuana Laws," *New York Times*, February 3, 1977, p. 14.
16. George Gallup, *The Gallup Poll: Public Opinion 1972–1977*, vol. 2, 1976–1977 (Wilmington, DE: Scholarly Resources, 1977), p. 1081.
17. Jerome Himmelstein, *The Strange Career of Marihuana* (Westport, CT: Greenwood Press, 1983), pp. 98–120.
18. Himmelstein, 1983, p. 107.
19. Himmelstein, 1983, p. 125.
20. Patrick Anderson, *High in America: The True Story Behind NORML and the Politics of Marijuana* (New York: Viking Press, 1981), pp. 25–45.
21. Anderson, 1981, pp. 58–62.
22. Anderson, 1981, pp. 91–92.
23. Trebach, 1982, p. 239.
24. Select Committee on Narcotics Abuse and Control, 1977, p. 5.
25. Select Committee on Narcotics Abuse and Control, 1977, p. 72.
26. Select Committee on Narcotics Abuse and Control, 1977, p. 56.
27. Select Committee on Narcotics Abuse and Control, 1977, p. 12.
28. Trebach, 1982, p. 240.
29. Anderson, 1981, p. 21.
30. Anderson, 1981, p. 22.
31. Barber, 1985, p. 440.

The Contemporary War on Drugs

INTRODUCTION

It would seem that by 1980, the American public would have reached the point of exhaustion over the drug issue. Having experienced an explosion of attention to drug issues eight years earlier, then rapid demobilization from Nixon's war on drugs, followed by a drug policy reform effort in the Carter administration that disintegrated in a cloud of controversy over the behavior of the president's drug policy spokesman, the American public might reasonably be expected to be jaded over the drug issue. As Figure 1.4 shows, popular concern with the drug issue was, in fact, at a low level in 1980. In contrast with frequent mentions of the drug issue as "the most important problem facing the country" on Gallup polls in the early 1970s, negligible numbers of Americans identified drugs as the most important national problem in 1980. The popular media had begun to focus somewhat more heavily on drug-related articles during the Carter administration—a pattern that continued into the 1980 presidential election year. But the avalanche of popular articles on drugs that would be evident by mid-decade was not yet in sight in 1980.

Furthermore, in the early years of the decade, drug-related news events, and consequently the character of popular articles on drugs, were vastly different from those that had alarmed people in the early 1970s. In particular, there were many stories and articles on drug use, and especially cocaine use, by athletes, entertainers, and other celebrities. In 1982 alone, *Time* magazine ran an article on drug use by football players ("Coke and No Smile") and another on drug use in professional basketball ("Highs and Lows Under the Basket"); *Macleans* ("Playing Football Under a Snowdrift" and "Drawing the Line on Cocaine") and *Sports Illustrated* ("I'm Not Worth a Damn" and "A Test with Nothing But Tough Questions") also ran articles on drug use in professional football. In the same year, popular magazines were also filled with articles on the drug overdose death of entertainer John Belushi and allegations of sexual activity and drug abuse involving congressional pages. The popular image of drugs, it would seem, no longer evoked the impoverished heroin addict nodding off in a slum doorway but envisioned the rich and famous living the high life and occasionally falling victim to its pleasures. We noted in Chapter 1 that Americans have typically been galvanized toward antidrug activity when drugs can be linked to underclass elements and alien outsiders. Because the images of drug use in the early 1980s were quite different, the relatively low levels of public concern with the drug issue are not surprising.

As Figure 3.1 shows, the drug issue was also at a low level of salience on the government agenda. President Carter rarely made mention of the drug issue in 1980, and presidential candidate Ronald Reagan made no public statements about the drug issue, choosing instead to focus on economic issues and the theme of "big government." The volume of congressional hearings on drug-related topics was relatively low; most involved routine appropriations hearings for agencies with drug treatment or drug-law enforcement missions.

But, as Figure 3.1 shows, drugs were not to remain off the government agenda for long. Beginning in 1981, both congressional and presidential attention to the drug issue began to ratchet upward, and the escalation continued throughout the decade. By 1989, presidential attention to the topic, as measured by *New York Times* indexing of articles in which President Bush dealt with the drug issue, was at an all-time peak, far exceeding the magnitude of attention to drugs even at the height of Nixon's war on drugs.

In contrast with the Nixon era, however, popular attention to the drug issue was *not* quickly galvanized in the 1980s (see Figure 1.4). There were small increases in the numbers of drug-related articles in popular magazines in the early 1980s, but not until 1985 did Gallup poll results suggest a reawakening of public concern about drug problems, and not until 1986 did the media lock into the nearly frenzied attention to the drug issue that would characterize the remainder of the decade.

In short, there appear to be two stages to the 1980s drug policy episode—an early stage in which there was government attention to the issue without public attention, followed by a stage in which ever-increasing government attention to the issue was matched and perhaps ultimately driven by very high levels of public concern about the problem. This pattern could be interpreted in two ways. On the one hand, perhaps the 1980s illustrate agenda setting of the mobilization type, but with a lag time between politicians' focus on the issue and public response; on the other hand, the same pattern would be observed if politicians were pursuing the drug issue via the inside-access model in the early 1980s *but lost control* of the issue as dramatic events caused the unintended mobilization of public attention to the drug problem. This chapter argues that although unexpected precipitating incidents galvanized public concern about drug problems in the mid-1980s, the Reagan administration had been attempting to direct public attention toward the issue even in the early years of the 1980s when public concern was low. In short, the decade of the 1980s is best understood as an example of mobilization-style agenda setting. What makes the decade so interesting is the sustained character of the mobilization.

STAGE 1: MOBILIZING THE PUBLIC

In the initial years of President Ronald Reagan's first term in office, the drug policy agenda consisted of two distinctive initiatives: (1) largely symbolic efforts directed toward reduction of demand for drugs and (2) an effort to target law enforcement efforts to a specific geographic location where drug trafficking was especially problematic and where focused effort could presumably yield dramatic results. As this section shows, however, these limited initiatives quickly expanded into more substantial ones; the war on drugs spread to 13 different geographical focal points, and Congress enacted crime legislation in 1984 providing substantial new weapons for drug-law enforcement.

Demand Reduction and Symbolic Policy

The emphasis on demand reduction was evident within three months of the new president's inauguration. At a news conference on March 7, 1981, President Reagan was asked what his priorities would be with respect to the drug problem. In stark contrast with actual policy developments that would shortly unfold, his response criticized supply reduction policies:

> I've had people talk to me about increased efforts to head off the export into the United States of drugs from neighboring nations. With borders like ours, that as the main method of halting the drug problem in America is virtually impossible: It's like carrying water in a sieve. It is my belief—firm belief— that the answer to the drug problem comes through winning over the users to the point that we take the customers away from the drugs.[1]

More than a year later, as the midterm congressional elections loomed in the fall of 1982, the theme of demand reduction was still being developed. In October 1982, Dr. Carlton Turner, then the White House advisor on drug abuse policy, announced a new campaign against drug abuse that would emphasize the short-circuiting of demand for drugs and that would rely upon help from the private sector. Officials throughout the Reagan administration were reported as acknowledging the limitations of law enforcement approaches to drugs and supporting a revamped, demand-oriented approach. Although the new policy approach included some specific goals, such as a 30 percent reduction in daily drug use by high school seniors, there was little detail about actual programs or resource commitments that would lead to these desired reductions in demand.[2]

The government did not establish and fund new programs for treatment and prevention of drug abuse. The emphasis was largely on rhetorical efforts and symbolic gestures, including a high-visibility series of public appearances and statements by First Lady Nancy Reagan. In February 1982, Mrs. Reagan vowed just such a campaign, saying that she would make "an increasing number of appearances devoted to social issues, particularly the problem of drug abuse among young children."[3] The ensuing months saw a flurry of appearances and statements: Mrs. Reagan claiming on April 24 that television and movies glamorized drug use, visiting drug treatment facilities such as Gateway House and Phoenix House in May and June, visiting Little Rock High School in September to discuss concerns about alcohol and drug abuse, and serving as the star speaker at the organizational conference of the National Federation of Parents for Drug-FreeYouth in Arlington, Virginia, in October.[4]

Geographically Targeted Law Enforcement Initiatives

The Reagan administration had acknowledged the limitations and difficulties of solving the drug problem through supply reduction efforts such as border interdiction and enforcement activities aimed at traffickers. Nevertheless, one year after first taking office, President Reagan instituted a new initiative aimed at reducing the drug supply. This was the creation of the South Florida Task Force on Crime, which was meant to focus the government's efforts against drug trafficking by (1) targeting a single geographic area where drug trafficking was especially problematic and (2) engaging the joint efforts of different government agencies that had too often pursued drug-law enforcement in uncoordinated ways. Vice President George Bush was placed in command of the South Florida Task Force.

The choice of South Florida as a geographic focal point needs little explanation. The Miami–Dade County area had become a major center for the importation of drugs from Central and South America, leading to enormous strains on its law enforcement system and a national image as a place for drug-related activity, as captured in the television series *Miami Vice.*

The emphasis on joint efforts by many different government agencies is, in many ways, a more interesting aspect of the South Florida Task Force. It meant that interorganizational cooperation was being demanded from federal agencies such as the Drug Enforcement Administration (DEA) and the Customs Bureau, which had previously exhibited rivalries; and it meant that these federal agencies also had to work more closely with state and local law enforcement agencies, which had not always been well coordinated in the past.

More important, the South Florida Task Force drew upon the resources of a number of agencies that had not previously played important roles in drug enforcement activity. The Coast Guard joined the task force effort by stepping up patrol activity in areas of the Caribbean that were known for smuggling. In order to support this initiative, the Coast Guard was provided with "285 additional seamen and other personnel and new equipment—initially, two high-speed surface-effect ships and two new cutters and later, helicopters and new Falcon jet long-distance search aircraft."[5]

Still more significant was the introduction of the military into the drug-fighting effort. Prior to 1981, the U.S. military was prohibited from engaging in civilian law enforcement activity by the Posse Comitatus Act. That act, passed in the wake of the Civil War, reflected concerns about civilian-military relations during the period of military occupation of the South. In the late 1950s, as the era of civil rights activity in the South opened, branches of the military that had not been covered by the original Posse Comitatus Act were brought under its restrictions. As a result of this long-standing policy, the U.S. military had been limited to only indirect, supportive relationships with civilian law enforcement agencies, such as the loan of equipment, training of personnel, or use of facilities. In 1981, however, Congress amended the Posse Comitatus Act to broaden the interpretation of allowable military support activity for civilian enforcement.[6] The South Florida Task Force was therefore able to make considerable use of the military in its efforts to step up interdiction of drugs. Army helicopters were used by the Customs Bureau, sophisticated Navy radar tracking planes and Air Force radar balloons were enlisted in the drug interdiction effort, and the Navy began to participate much more directly in actual drug interdiction operations.[7]

Not surprisingly, the task force approach, which attained great visibility in South Florida, was immediately adopted as a model to be replicated elsewhere. After all, the administration's arguments for the South Florida Task Force were equally compelling for other regions; interagency and intergovernmental coordination of drug enforcement efforts would be more useful than turf battles and disconnected activities, and focused effort on high-level traffickers would be more successful than scattered efforts netting only lower-level traffickers. Furthermore, if the South Florida Task Force were successful, it would presumably displace drug-trafficking activity to alternative locations. Logically, a national effort would have to involve a network of regional task forces. And this is precisely what the Reagan administration implemented in 1983.

By 1984, drug enforcement task forces were in operation in 13 cities: Detroit, Houston, Los Angeles, Baltimore, Denver, Boston, New York, Chicago, San Francisco, St. Louis, Atlanta, San Diego, and Miami. These constituted the Organized Crime Drug Enforcement Task Force Program, under the direction of the attorney general of the United States. Each task force was headed by the United States attorney for that city, who supervised "agents from the DEA, FBI, Customs, Bureau of Alcohol, Tobacco and Firearms (BATF), IRS, Coast Guard, and U.S. Marshals Service" in addition to a number of assistant U.S. attorneys.[8]

Drug-Related Anticrime Legislation in 1984

In 1984, under strong pressure from the Reagan administration, Congress enacted anticrime legislation (PL 98-473) that had a number of major provisions of substantial importance to the developing war on drugs. For one thing, the legislation expanded the government's ability to use *forfeiture* as a weapon against drug traffickers. Forfeiture involves a process by which the government can seize and keep property or other assets allegedly obtained through criminal activity. Before 1984, a civil court hearing was required for forfeiture of properties worth more than $10,000; assets worth less than that could be taken by default, without a regular court proceeding. PL 98-473 increased the threshold value for required court proceedings to $100,000. In addition, special funds were set up in the Justice and Treasury departments to process, maintain, and facilitate the use of forfeited properties.[9]

In an interesting application of this tool, Justice Department officials in the Reagan administration began using forfeiture to seize the fees paid to defense attorneys by drug traffickers. The logic of this tactic is that if drug traffickers should not be allowed to enjoy the "ill-gotten gains" of their criminal activity, they should not be allowed to use such gains to purchase the best defense that drug money can buy. "The fees of criminal defense attorneys are attractive to government prosecutors not only because of the funds' roots in criminality, but because they represent a flaunting of the suspected criminal's illicit wealth in a legal arena where government prosecutors are significantly less remunerated."[10] But, as Steven Wisotsky argues, this extension of the forfeiture tool is a clear example of creeping erosion of civil liberties:

> Forfeiture of fees seriously cranks the balance wheel of justice in the Government's favor. It hurts defendants by discouraging experienced attorneys from wanting to work on such cases, and by diverting energy of counsel from defense of the charge to defense of the fee.[11]

Wisotsky quotes one notable drug defense lawyer, "Diamond" Joel Hirschhorn, who withdrew from handling drug cases in the wake of these developments. According to Hirschhorn, "It's just not worth the aggravation to represent major drug dealers. The government comes after your fees. It's not worth it. . . . I'm doing tax fraud. And I like to do one murder case a year. It's OK to represent a murderer. Everyone approves of that."[12]

The 1984 legislation also increased penalties for drug-law offenders and gave the attorney general emergency powers to more easily categorize a new drug under Schedule I—the most restrictive category of the existing drug law—if the new drug were deemed to be an immediate threat to public safety. Finally, the legislation established strict new bail and preventive detention requirements, particularly for those accused of drug offenses. The law entitled judges to deny a defendant pretrial release "if there was enough evidence to charge him with a major drug offense or specified other serious crimes."[13] This substantial change resulted from arguments that drug traffickers were such a danger to the community, and so likely to flee before trial, that bail should be denied to those being tried as such, even though their guilt had not yet been established at trial. In testimony leading to the enactment of PL 98-473, Associate Attorney General Rudolph Giuliani made this position clear:

> In Miami, for example, although the average money bond for drug defendants is $75,000, 17 percent of these defendants never appear for trial. For them, money bonds are nothing more than a cost of doing business, and a means of escaping prosecution. . . . In short, Federal bail laws do not adequately protect the public from violent criminals and dope traffickers.[14]

STAGE 2: FURTHER DRUG POLICY IN RESPONSE TO A MOBILIZED PUBLIC

Not surprisingly, popular attention to the drug issue, which was very low from 1980 to 1984, was influenced by the high-profile government drug policy activity from 1981 to 1984. By 1985, popular concern about drugs was noticeably on the upswing (see Figure 1.4). But just as popular concern was beginning to come into line with the pace of government action, a series of events escalated the drug issue to still higher levels of attention, prompting an even more frenetic cycle of drug policy activity.

In particular, three developments caused the mutation of the drug issue into newer and more frightening forms: the spread of "crack," a smokable, highly addictive, and relatively inexpensive form of cocaine; reports that drug use was a key activity in the spread of the AIDS virus; and reports that a new and highly visible category of victims of drug abuse—crack babies—was emerging.

The emergence of crack cocaine in the mid-1980s was especially frightening. First, crack was reported to be more highly addictive than regular cocaine. Second, because it was less expensive, crack was much more readily accessible to the poor than regular cocaine. Consequently, as news reports of an epidemic of crack use proliferated, they were accompanied by images of impoverished black and Hispanic individuals.

The glamorous image of celebrity cocaine use had been replaced by the type of association that has historically escalated fears about drugs—that is, drug use by the "dangerous classes," and especially racial minorities.

Drug use was also implicated in the ongoing spread of AIDS, particularly among minorities. Public health professionals knew that AIDS could be spread through use of contaminated needles or through heterosexual activity with an infected partner who had been exposed through drug abuse. The American public still saw AIDS as primarily a disease of homosexual men, but the role of drug abuse in the spread of the disease began to sink into public consciousness as the realities of the ongoing AIDS epidemic became known. By 1987, officials from the Centers for Disease Control were reporting that 40 percent of black and Hispanic men with AIDS and 12 percent of white men with AIDS were intravenous drug abusers. Among children with AIDS, 31 percent of whites, 61 percent of blacks, and 76 percent of Hispanics had a parent with a history of intravenous drug abuse.[15]

Recognition that drug use by pregnant women was leading to the birth of crack babies added a new and even more dramatic definition to the drug problem. Testifying before Congress in 1987, the director of a newborn intensive care unit at Broward General Medical Center in Florida explained that as recently as 1985 he hardly ever saw babies with cocaine-related problems, but less than three years later one in five babies in the unit had cocaine in their systems. Crack babies cost at least $100,000 each in neonatal hospital intensive care.[16] Apart from this enormous financial burden, the suffering of crack babies, who are born medically distressed and may face long-term health problems, added an important and extremely dramatic twist to thinking about the drug problem. In the words of Congressman Clay Shaw, "We have heard, all of us, that drug abuse is referred to as a victimless crime. We have just seen the ultimate victim of this crime, the unborn, whose lives are destroyed before they even leave their mother's womb. Many of these, if not all of these, youngsters are destroyed by the absolute reckless ignorance of their mother in the use of drugs."[17]

In addition to these developments, dramatic news items triggered the spiraling of the drug issue to new heights of public and government attention in 1986 and 1987. In particular, the cocaine-caused death of star basketball player Len Bias in June 1986 galvanized public attention to cocaine use.

Three months after the death of Len Bias, President and Mrs. Reagan gave a nationally televised address to the nation, devoted solely to the drug issue. This address included Nancy Reagan's famous appeal to the nation's youth to "just say no" to drugs. The address mentioned no particular programmatic initiatives, nor did the Reagans promise any new resource commitments. This fact and the "just say no" theme were quickly seized upon by partisan and other critics of the administration's drug policy. To critics, Reagan's drug policy was mere symbolism, without resources and prevention programs that would have an effect on the demand for drugs.

If it was symbolism, it was powerful symbolism nonetheless. The context and setting of the televised address served to underscore the importance of the drug issue. On that September evening in 1986, Americans were treated to a prime-time televised visit from their president *and* first lady, with the sole purpose of highlighting the drug issue. The content of the address was equally dramatic. President Reagan called upon the American public to join a "national crusade" against drugs—a crusade that he claimed "must include a combination of government and private efforts which complement one another."[18] But the most dramatic rhetoric came from Nancy Reagan, who argued, "There's no moral middle ground. Indifference is not an option. We want you to help us create an outspoken intolerance of drug use. For the sake of our children, I implore each of you to be unyielding and inflexible in your opposition to drugs."[19]

In September 1986, then, the drug issue was highly salient and highly politicized. The American public had been mobilized about the issue, and as congressional elections approached, the president elevated the issue to a prominent place on the government agenda. In this context, Congress passed the *Anti–Drug Abuse Act of 1986*. That legislation increased penalties for drug-trafficking offenses, including provisions that doubled the penalty for adults who used juveniles in drug trafficking and tripled the penalty for those convicted of trafficking near a school. The legislation also authorized $230 million per year for three years in federal grants to the states for drug-law enforcement and a total of $700 million over three years in federal grants to state governments, local schools, colleges, and universities for drug education programs. In addition, the legislation made "designer drugs" illegal. These drugs had eluded law enforcement control; although functionally they had the same effects as various controlled substances, trivial differences in chemical makeup had made them technically legal substances.[20]

Two features of the 1986 legislation were equally notable: the provisions that were eventually dropped from it, and the political posturing that surrounded its passage. The House version of the legislation had originally included a provision to "ease restrictions on prosecutors' use of illegally seized evidence" as well as a death penalty provision for major drug traffickers.[21] The former was dropped from the final bill because of Senate opposition. The handling of the death penalty provision, however, is suggestive of the election-year posturing that characterized this legislation. Although the Senate had made clear that it would not accept the death penalty measure, House members refused to compromise; they did not want to be seen as backing down from what was believed to be a popular symbol of getting tough in the war on drugs. Consequently, two versions of the Anti–Drug Abuse Act of 1986 were sent on from the House to the Senate—one with the death penalty provision and one without—thus forcing the Senate to fully take any blame for the absence of a death penalty provision.[22]

Drug Legislation in 1988

The development of drug legislation in 1986 underscored the extent to which the drug issue had become politicized, with the White House and members of Congress from both parties jockeying to have a leadership role on policy development, or at least to avoid embarrassment on the issue as elections loomed. But if the politicization of the drug issue in the off-year elections of 1986 was notable, it is not surprising that in the superheated politics of a presidential election year, the drug issue would be even more salient. In 1988, this led to passage of the most comprehensive drug legislation to date.

In particular, the Reverend Jesse Jackson, then a contender for the Democratic nomination for the presidency, seized upon the drug issue. In his campaign, Jackson "repeatedly criticized the Reagan administration for failing to mount an all-out, well-coordinated attack on the drug problem."[23]

From the White House, it was clear in early 1988 that the drug issue would continue to be pushed. In February 1988, the Reagan administration held a White House Conference for a Drug-Free America, a high-visibility gathering that provided a platform for the administration to showcase its drug-fighting efforts and philosophy. At that conference, Nancy Reagan made clear what the newest theme of the continuing drug war would be—a harsh crackdown on "casual" drug users:

> The casual user may think when he takes a line of cocaine or smokes a joint in the privacy of his nice condo, listening to his expensive stereo, that he's somehow not bothering anyone. But there is a trail of death and destruction that leads directly to his door. The casual user cannot morally escape responsibility for the action of drug traffickers and dealings. I'm saying that if you're a casual drug user you're an accomplice to murder.[24]

President Reagan's frequent statements about the drug issue in 1988 also typically involved attacks on drug users. In remarks to media executives at a White House briefing on drug abuse in March 1988, for example, Reagan argued, "Drug use is not a victimless crime; it is not a private matter. . . . we must demonstrate our great concern for the millions of innocent citizens who pay the high price for the illegal drug use of some."[25]

As the following section shows, these White House comments directing righteous anger against casual drug users were not empty rhetoric. They were soon to be institutionalized in legislation that provided for special penalties (above and beyond the usual criminal law penalties) for those convicted of trafficking in drugs, using drugs, or even tolerating family members' or friends' use of drugs in public housing. More immediately, they were institutionalized in the administration's "zero-tolerance" policy—a policy of aggressive enforcement by the Coast Guard and U.S. Customs of laws against possession of illegal drugs, even in small amounts. Paul Yost, commandant of the Coast Guard, explained the policy as follows:

> Zero tolerance means that the Coast Guard, in the course of its regular patrols, boarding and inspections, will now, within the limits of the law, seize vessels and arrest individuals when "personal use" quantities of illegal drugs are discovered.... Customs has developed an administrative procedure by which the owner can present evidence to establish that he was an innocent party and took reasonable steps to prevent the vessel from being used in violation of the law.... If the owner is successful in meeting this burden, it is Custom's policy to return the vessel. If he is unable to sustain his burden of proof, an appropriate penalty, up to forfeiture of the vessel, will be applied.[26]

It is important to note that under this zero-tolerance policy, the burden of proof is upon the accused rather than the accuser. People so accused had to prove not only that they were not themselves in possession of drugs but that they had no knowledge of or ability to control drug possession and use by other individuals present on the seized vessel.

In the autumn of 1988, with the drug issue ranked by pollsters as Americans' number one concern and with antidrug themes playing a role in the presidential campaign, PL 100-690 was passed by Congress and signed into law. This omnibus antidrug bill included a host of provisions designed to coordinate drug-fighting efforts, enhance treatment and education programs, and beef up law enforcement approaches to the drug problem. Perhaps the most widely noted aspect of this legislation was its creation of a cabinet-level official to coordinate federal drug-control policy. This official, informally dubbed a "drug czar," was to head a new office of National Drug Control Policy charged with advising the president on organizational and budget matters involving drug enforcement agencies. The czar had the task of presenting national drug-control policy statements, the first due within 180 days of appointment and others mandated for presentation to Congress by February 1 each year.[27] Not since Peter Bourne had advised President Carter was the drug issue elevated to such prominence; and never before had the drug issue warranted cabinet-level rank. The nation's first drug policy czar, William Bennett, was confirmed by the Senate in March 1989.

PL 100-690 also provided expanded authorizations for several treatment and prevention programs and attempted to target their use. Financial assistance to states and local governments for these purposes had been consolidated with alcoholism treatment and general mental health programming assistance in a single block grant administered by the Alcohol, Drug Abuse, and Mental Health Administration. The 1988 legislation authorized spending of $1.5 billion in fiscal year 1989 under this block grant, but the amount a state could receive in such grants was restricted unless the state earmarked the funds exclusively for drug abuse programming. Priority was to be given to treatment for people infected with the AIDS virus, but funds could not be used for programs distributing sterile needles to addicts.[28] The Office of Substance Abuse Prevention, a small federal agency located within the Alcohol, Drug Abuse, and Mental Health Administration, was given an authorization of $95 million for fiscal 1989 and a mandate to expand its data collection efforts; another $100 million was authorized to assist public and nonprofit treatment centers that had long waiting lists for treatment. Additional authorizations were included for special treatment programs and facilities for Indian youth and for veterans.[29]

With respect to education programs, PL 100-690 increased the authorized funding for the Drug-Free Schools and Communities Act. This act, originally passed as part of the Anti–Drug Abuse Act of 1986, was slated for $100 million; PL 100-690 increased this to $350 million, including $16 million for grants to schools and colleges for "teacher-training programs concerning alcohol and drug abuse prevention," $15 million for "grants to non-profit private and public organizations to prevent and reduce the youth participation in gangs that engaged in drug-related activities," and $40 million for grants to state "community-youth-activity programs."[30]

These treatment and prevention aspects of PL 100-690 were overshadowed, however, by the enforcement and interdiction aspects of the legislation. Among the more innovative provisions in this regard were several "user accountability" components. The law provided authority for public housing managers to evict tenants who engaged in drug-related or other criminal activity or whose household members or guests engaged in such activities in or near the public housing unit. Federal benefits in the form of grants, contracts, and loans (but not retirement, welfare, Social Security, and similar entitlements) could be denied to an individual for up to five years for a first conviction of drug trafficking, and permanently for a third. A similar benefit exclusion could be imposed for one year on anyone convicted of simple possession of illegal drugs.[31]

The government's powers to seize and gain control of criminal assets through forfeiture proceedings had been strengthened in 1984 legislation. The 1988 law further enhanced the government's ability to use forfeiture as a law enforcement tool, while simultaneously adding provisions responsive to concerns that innocent individuals not be ensnared in legal nightmares resulting from forfeiture efforts. With respect to the latter, the legislation stipulated that forfeiture proceedings involving automobiles and other vehicles, aircraft, or boats had to be completed within 21 days when only "personal use" quantities of drugs were at issue and that the vehicle, aircraft, or boat had to be returned to the owner if the owner could show that he or she had no knowledge of and did not consent to the drug possession or use that had occurred on the conveyance.

These provisions institutionalized some of the procedures that the Coast Guard and Customs had been using under the administration's zero-tolerance policy and responded to some concerns over the use of that policy. In particular, the confiscation of fishing boats and other commercial vessels had created some stir in Congress. Congressman Earl Hutto explained the problem as he opened hearings on the zero-tolerance policy in 1988:

> We must support those who fight at the front in this war on drugs, but we must not forget what it is we are fighting for. When innocent persons are precluded from making a living due to overzealous enforcement of the law— when shrimpers lose a week's work or more because of trace amounts of marijuana dropped by a crewman, when a charter boat captain has his vessel seized because of a joint left by a passenger, when a father has his car confiscated because of some residue left by his children's friends—it is time to take a hard look at all of these things, to reevaluate and to adjust.[32]

To enhance use of the forfeiture tool in drug enforcement, the legislation created a special fund that the attorney general could use to cover "expenses necessary to seize, detain, inventory, safeguard, maintain, advertise or sell property under seizure or detention."[33] This fund was necessary because a huge amount of property had accumulated in the possession of the federal government from use of forfeiture over the years. Property acquired prior to the 1984 legislation had to be forfeited through a time-consuming court proceeding if it was valued at more than $10,000, and a backlog of seized properties awaited court disposition. For example, as of 1985, the Miami district of the Customs Service had 415 boats, 42 planes, and 119 motor vehicles in its possession.[34] Meanwhile, federal drug enforcement agencies had vastly increased the number of properties seized for forfeit after the 1984 legislation. By 1988, the value of the inventory of assets seized by the Justice Department and the U.S. Customs Service was $800 million.[35]

The 1988 legislation provided the financial resources that federal agencies needed in order to manage all of this property as it worked its way through administrative or judicial forfeiture proceedings and to expedite the sale of successfully forfeited properties. The Asset Forfeiture Fund had the potential to enhance the prospects for drug enforcement to become a "self-financing, or even money-making, operation"—sustaining the achievement noted by the attorney general in 1985, who reported that the value of forfeitures and fines for the year was greater than the cost of operating the drug enforcement task force program.[36]

CONTINUING SALIENCE OF THE DRUG ISSUE: POST-1988 DEVELOPMENTS

One might have thought that after the elections and the passage of comprehensive drug legislation in 1988, drugs would have quickly faded from attention. After all, drugs had been on the government agenda almost continuously since 1982, and the issue had been highly salient among the American public for almost four years. Constant attention to the drug problem would be expected to lead to "saturation" on this issue, with public attention fading because of sheer repetitiveness.[37]

But once again, dramatic triggering events extended the life of the issue attention cycle for drugs. In particular, ominous news reports of drug-related violence fed public concern. In 1989 the Crime Control Institute reported that a record number of police officers had been killed the previous year.[38] In addition, the nation was experiencing record homicide rates in some cities, which were attributed to the violence among drug dealers.[39] By the end of the 1980s, a new term—*drive-by shooting*—had been added to the common language of the American public.

In response to this continuing concern over drugs, President George Bush announced a comprehensive and expensive drug-control strategy in September 1989. Like his predecessor, Bush chose the spotlight of a televised evening speech devoted exclusively to the drug issue. In that speech, President Bush made clear that although attention would be given to all aspects of the drug problem, the major emphasis would be on drug-law enforcement. The president proposed that the federal government more than double its financial assistance to state and local law enforcement agencies, and he recommended other increases in resource commitments devoted to drug enforcement: "I am also proposing that we enlarge our criminal justice system across the board—at the local, state and Federal levels alike. We need more prisons, more jails, more courts, more prosecutors. So tonight, I'm requesting—altogether—an almost billion-and-a-half dollar increase in drug-related Federal spending on law enforcement."[40] The president also called for more attention to treatment and prevention. Specifically, he proposed an increase of $322 million in spending for drug treatment, along with an increase of $250 million in funds for school and community drug prevention programs.[41]

The difficulty with this proposed expansion in the nation's war on drugs was financing. The president's proposal came at a time of enormous budget difficulty, exacerbated by partisan wrangling over how to minimize budget deficits. What is more, Bush had campaigned in 1988 with the strong stand of "Read my lips—no new taxes." Under these circumstances, the president's proposal for an expanded war on drugs would inevitably face difficulty in Congress. This was acknowledged by the president in a news conference the day after his dramatic televised presentation:

We have sent specific suggestions as to how to pay for this program to the Hill, and it does not require additional taxes. And I've been in this town long enough to know that there are always going to be people out there who are saying, "More taxes." If it's not for this subject, it will be for something else. And that isn't necessary to fully fund the national strategy that we came up with, that I unveiled last night.[42]

The Bush administration suggested that nearly half of the resources for the proposed drug program could come from cuts in federal aid to states for assistance with immigration impacts and that the remainder could come from abolishing the Economic Development Administration, cuts in the juvenile justice programs of the Justice Department, a delay in the purchase of a new communications system for the Defense Department, and use of monies originally intended for operating public housing projects.[43]

The president's drug policy proposal quickly became the focus of a number of other conflicts in addition to the financing quandary: (1) conflicts over the adequacy of the resource commitments promised in the president's proposal, (2) conflicts over the balance of attention to law enforcement relative to treatment and prevention, and (3) conflicts over state versus city control of the grant funds.

The proposed expansion was criticized when it became clear that despite the huge-sounding numbers in the president's televised speech, what was actually being proposed was an increase of "only" $716 million in antidrug spending for 1990. In the context of a total federal budget of $1.1 trillion, this is not a large amount.[44] More important, it was a relatively small amount compared to what state and local governments spent from their own resources and compared to the additional costs that would be borne by those governments as they actually implemented the war on drugs at the street level. Within two days of the president's televised speech, William Bennett, the president's drug policy director, was forced to admit, "State and local governments would have to spend billions of dollars to meet the goals of Mr. Bush's national drug strategy, perhaps $5 billion to $10 billion next year for new prisons alone."[45] The limited federal antidrug funds for state and local governments became particularly controversial in light of the fact that these subnational governments would be required to establish expensive new programs, such as "drug-testing programs for all arrestees, convicts, parolees and prison guards" in order to get the new drug-law enforcement funds.[46] Highlighting the partisan nature of this conflict as well, Democratic Senator Joseph Biden, chair of the Senate Judiciary Committee, argued that the administration was "trying to require the states to carry the overwhelming bulk of the load" in the war on drugs; as he waved a copy of the president's national drug-strategy plan, Biden said, "The real question I'm waiting for Bennett to answer is 'How much does this little red book cost?'"[47]

Not surprisingly, there was also criticism of the fact that more than two-thirds of the resource commitments in the president's drug strategy would go to law enforcement while less than one-third would go to treatment and prevention. For example, at a congressional hearing devoted to presentation of the new drug strategy by Secretary Bennett, Congressman James H. Scheuer argued that the priorities were wrong: "It seems to me that when we're spending two-thirds of all of these dollars in punitive law enforcement efforts that don't have a history of accomplishing a great deal, I think we all can agree on that, and we're not providing any extra funds for drug education, that on a cost benefit basis we are missing a boat, we are missing a major window of opportunity."[48]

Finally, there were conflicts over the intergovernmental system for channeling federal aid for the war on drugs. Within one month of the president's drug policy proposal, the United States Conference of Mayors was agitating to have federal grant funds for drug prevention and treatment sent directly to them rather than being channeled through state governments, because, as Mayor Norquist of Milwaukee indicated, "the cities are where this fight is being waged and where the resources should be directed."[49] The National Governor's Association, meanwhile, insisted that the monies should continue to be funneled through state government, which could exercise oversight concerning their distribution to localities within the state. Like so many of the other aspects of drug policy by this time, this debate was in part rooted in partisan differences. Big-city mayors are largely oriented toward the Democratic party and believe that their cities will be disadvantaged when funds are distributed by state administrations which, if not Republican, must at least show some responsiveness to predominantly Republican rural and suburban areas.

Despite these conflicts and despite successful efforts by congressional Democrats to increase the amount of spending authorized for the drug war by $1.1 billion, the scope and character of drug policy in George Bush's presidency was largely that suggested by the administration. William Bennett, then drug czar, claimed, "Our strategy set the terms of the debate. If some people are adding hood ornaments and chrome and other accouterments, so be it. Our strategy is the vehicle."[50] That strategy was one of continuing emphasis on law enforcement and interdiction relative to treatment and prevention, but with ever-increasing budgetary commitments to both and continuous partisan wrangling over the scope, character, and success of the drug policy effort.

CONCLUSIONS

In contrast with earlier episodes during the Nixon and Carter administrations, the Reagan-Bush drug policy episode was most notable for its duration. Defying the logic of issue saturation, drugs occupied a prominent place on the government agenda for a decade and on the popular agenda for more than five years. How might we account for the surprising durability of this issue? And what are the implications of the continuous drug policy-making that marked this episode?

Perhaps the best answer to these questions is that the drug issue has clearly become an important vehicle for a variety of other agenda items. The capacity of the drug issue to galvanize popular concern has not been lost upon politicians. Not surprisingly, politicians have taken advantage of the power of the drug issue to direct attention to other interests and problems that can, in some fashion, be characterized as a part of the drug issue. In the process, the drug issue is transformed; but it also endures. Thus, for example, the drug problem has become the springboard for arguments about the need for greater federal support for law enforcement at the state and local level, about the need for more money for America's schools, about the growing urban health crisis in America, and about the need for policies to deal more effectively with poverty and hopelessness in urban America.

Years of federal drug policy-making have also helped to institutionalize a variety of organized interests with stakes in the character of the nation's drug policy strategy and the magnitude of the nation's drug policy budget. Federal agencies—the Coast Guard; the DEA; the Justice Department; the Customs Bureau; NIDA; the Alcohol, Drug Abuse, and Mental Health Administration; and the Department of Education, to name but a few—are substantially invested players in the ongoing game of drug policy development, as are state and local law enforcement agencies, local schools, private and nonprofit treatment centers, state and local health bureaucracies, and many more. As Chapter 8 shows, the interplay of these organized interests is of considerable importance in understanding the continuity of drug policy in the United States.

At the outset of this chapter, drug policy-making in the 1980s was characterized as fitting a mobilization model of agenda setting: public officials took the lead in directing attention to the problem, and public concern followed on the heels of government initiatives. As this chapter has shown, however, once the public is mobilized, organized interests are institutionalized, and partisan lines are drawn, it is difficult to bump that issue off the government agenda, especially if the topic has the dramatic potential of the drug issue.

NOTES

1. "Transcripts of the President's News Conference on Foreign and Domestic Matters," *New York Times*, March 7, 1981, p. 10.
2. "U.S. Shifts Emphasis in New Drive on Drug Abuse," *New York Times*, October 6, 1982, p. 14.
3. Enid Nemy, "First Lady Finds a Cause," *New York Times*, February 19, 1982, p. B5.

4. *New York Times Index, 1982* (New York: New York Times Company, 1983).

5. Steven Wisotsky, *Beyond the War on Drugs* (Buffalo: Prometheus Books, 1990), p. 92.

6. Wisotsky, 1990, p. 92.

7. Wisotsky, 1990, pp. 93–94.

8. Wisotsky, 1990, p. 100.

9. "Major Crime Package Cleared by Congress," *CQ Almanac* (Washington, DC: Congressional Quarterly, 1984), p. 216.

10. John Dombrink, James Meeker, and Julie Paik, "Fighting for Fees—Drug Trafficking and the Forfeiture of Attorney's Fees," *Journal of Drug Issues* 18 (1988), p. 429.

11. Wisotsky, 1990, p. 122.

12. Wisotsky, 1990, p. 122

13. "Major Crime Package," 1984, pp. 215–216.

14. U.S. Senate, Committee on the Judiciary, Subcommittee on Criminal Law, *Comprehensive Crime Control Act of 1983* (Washington, DC: U.S. Government Printing Office, 1984), p. 13.

15. U.S. House of Representatives, Select Committee on Narcotics Abuse and Control, *Intravenous Drug Use and AIDS: The Impact on the Black Community* (Washington, DC: U.S. Government Printing Office, 1988a), p. 9.

16. U.S. House of Representatives, Select Committee on Narcotics Abuse and Control, *Cocaine Babies* (Washington, DC: U.S. Government Printing Office, 1988b), p. 6.

17. Select Committee on Narcotics Abuse and Control, 1988b, p. 2.

18. "Excerpts from Speech on Halting Drug Abuse," *New York Times,* September 15, 1986, p. B10.

19. "Excerpts from Speech," 1986, p. B10.

20. Linda Greenhouse, "Congress Approves Anti-Drug Bill as Senate Bars a Death Provision," *New York Times,* October 18, 1986, p. 33.

21. Greenhouse, 1986, p. 33.

22. Greenhouse, 1986, p. 33.

23. "Election-Year Anti-Drug Bill Enacted," *CQ Almanac* (Washington, DC: Congressional Quarterly, 1988), pp. 85–86.

24. *Public Papers of the Presidents of the United States. Ronald Reagan, Book I, 1988* (Washington, DC: U.S. Government Printing Office, 1990), p. 269.

25. *Public Papers of the Presidents,* 1990, p. 300.

26. U.S. House of Representatives, Committee on Merchant Marine and Fisheries, Subcommittee on Coast Guard and Navigation, *"Zero Tolerance" Drug Policy and Confiscation of Property* (Washington, DC: U.S. Government Printing Office, 1988), p. 12.

27. "Election-Year Anti-Drug Bill Enacted," 1988, p. 86.

28. "Election-Year Anti-Drug Bill Enacted," 1988, pp. 86–87.

29. "Election-Year Anti-Drug Bill Enacted," 1988, p. 87.

30. "Election-Year Anti-Drug Bill Enacted," 1988, p. 87.

31. "Election-Year Anti-Drug Bill Enacted," 1988, p. 87.

32. Subcommittee on Coast Guard and Navigation, 1988, p. 3.

33. "Election-Year Anti-Drug Bill Enacted," 1988, p. 89.

34. U.S. House of Representatives, Committee on the Judiciary, Subcommittee on Crime, *Forfeiture Issues* (Washington, DC: U.S. Government Printing Office, 1986), p. 144.

35. Gene L. Dodaro, *Asset Forfeiture Programs: Corrective Actions Underway But Additional Improvements Needed* (Washington, DC: U.S. General Accounting Office, 1988), p. 1.
36. Wisotsky, 1990, p. 175.
37. Stephen Hilgartner and Charles L. Bosk, "The Rise and Fall of Social Problems: A Public Arenas Model," *American Journal of Sociology* 94 (July 1988), pp. 53–78.
38. Richard Berke, "A Record 14 Officers Killed in '88 in Drug Incidents, a Study Shows," *New York Times*, September 3, 1989, p. 11.
39. Richard Berke, "Public Enemy No. 1," *New York Times*, September 3, 1989, sec. 4, p. 1.
40. "Text of President's Speech on National Drug Control Strategy," *New York Times*, September 6, 1989, p. 10.
41. "Text of President's Speech," 1989, p. 10.
42. *Public Papers of the Presidents of the United States. George Bush, Book II, 1989* (Washington, DC: U.S. Government Printing Office, 1990), p. 1144.
43. David Rosenbaum, "Cost Is Estimated on Bush Drug War," *New York Times*, September 6, 1989, p. 11.
44. Rosenbaum, 1989, p. 11.
45. Bernard Weinraub, "States Would Pay Much of the Bill for the Drug War," *New York Times*, September 8, 1989, p. 1.
46. Todd Sloane, "States: Read Our Lips, Send More Money," *City & State*, September 11–24, 1989, p. 30.
47. Weinraub, 1989, p. 10.
48. U.S. House of Representatives, Select Committee on Narcotics Abuse and Control, *National Drug Control Strategy* (Washington, DC: U.S. Government Printing Office, 1990b), p. 44.
49. William E. Schmidt, "Drug War Funds Arouse Conflict," *New York Times*, November 12, 1989, p. 1.
50. David Johnston, "Democrats Claim Success in Drug Policy," *New York Times*, October 8, 1989, p. 14.

Chapter
5

Drug Treatment: Programs and Results

INTRODUCTION

The various policy-making episodes documented in Chapters 2 through 4 have left us with a legacy of many different programs for drug treatment, prevention, and enforcement, many of them funded with federal dollars but implemented at the state and local levels. Chapters 5 through 7 describe these programs in some detail, to provide a clear picture of the policy outputs that have been generated.

More important, each chapter documents what is known about the effectiveness of drug treatment, prevention, and enforcement programs. In some areas, evaluation research has provided substantial evidence about program effectiveness, or the lack of it. But drug programs also epitomize the many difficulties and limitations of program evaluation that have been acknowledged by scholars of public policy. The existence of multiple and conflicting goals, for example, creates substantial difficulties for the assessment of goal attainment.[1] This problem is very much in evidence with respect to evaluation of drug-law enforcement (see Chapter 7). Even where there is agreement on goals, measurement of goal attainment is often problematic. For one thing, there is difficulty in obtaining reliable and valid indicators, as is the case with respect to drug use, abuse, and trafficking.

There is also the problem of attributing observed change to particular programs. Virtually every jurisdiction in America is the site of a variety of drug-related "programs," including prevention programs in the schools, law enforcement efforts of one or more agencies, national media campaigns against drugs, publicly funded drug treatment, and private drug rehabiliation programs. Attributing aggregate changes in the incidence of drug use or trafficking to any one of these is impossible because the relative impact of each cannot be determined. And even sophisticated evaluation studies of drug treatment programs, like those discussed in this chapter, rely upon relatively crude comparison groups, not random assignment of subjects to experimental and control groups. This compounds the problem of attributing observed changes to particular public programs.[2]

Timing issues are a challenge in the drug program area, as they are for program evaluation generally.[3] The ultimate success of drug abuse prevention programs, for example, is observable only years after school-children have been exposed to the programs; yet policymakers must decide immediately whether to continue to invest tax dollars in such programs. Some of the enforcement programs described in Chapter 7 and many of the treatment programs described in this chapter yield impressive immediate results that decay over time. For example, drug traffickers may move back into areas that they temporarily vacated in response to an enforcement crackdown; and clients of drug treatment facilities may relapse into drug use after some months of abstinence. The existence of these "letdown" effects[4] suggests that longer-term evaluation is in order. But long-term evaluation is problematic, not only because of the shorter time horizon of political leaders but also because of technical problems in long-term evaluation. After release from a treatment program, for example, some clients become increasingly more difficult to keep in a study.

The field of program evaluation has adapted in a number of ways to difficulties and challenges. New types of evaluations have been devised. For example, formative (or process) evaluation, which focuses on how a program is implemented, avoids many of the problems of impact evaluation, which looks at results. Process evaluation helps managers to determine *what* is going wrong with a program—not simply whether or not the program has failed.[5] There have also been efforts to support large-scale impact evaluations that can generate relatively definitive findings. Two of these are described in this chapter.

But evaluation of drug programs, like program evaluation generally, has not had the central role in policy change that its proponents initially envisioned for it. In particular, formal program evaluations do not, and perhaps cannot, serve as the primary basis for sweeping decisions about program discontinuance.[6] Apart from technical challenges that limit the conclusiveness of evaluations, a host of political and organizational dynamics stand in the way of objective, straightforward use of program evaluation results for decision making about needed policy change. These obstacles are considered at length in Chapter 8. Here, it is important to note only that drug program evaluations, like program evaluations generally, are utilized in a variety of ways, such as to "reinforce official commitment to a program, reduce uncertainty, neutralize critics, bolster supporters, shift responsibility for failure to researchers, and legitimize decisions made on other grounds."[7]

In addition to these roles, evaluation research plays an important enlightenment function.[8] That is, it provides decision makers with information and evidence that shapes their ideas. Thus, while it may not have an immediate and dramatic effect at a single, identifiable decision point, the results of evaluation research can gradually create a climate for policy change.

As this chapter will show, however, evaluation research on drug treatment programs may be limited even in its capacity to serve the enlightenment function. This is because research results have been so mixed. Compared with drug prevention and drug enforcement programs, drug treatment programs have been heavily evaluated. But the sheer volume and complexity of research results may have virtually guaranteed that a definitive and persuasive "bottom line" about drug treatment will remain elusive. The resulting lack of confidence about which, if any, programs are effective may be contributing to the underfunding of drug treatment relative to drug-law enforcement. This is certainly the viewpoint of the National Association of State Alcohol and Drug Abuse Directors, which argues that skepticism about the effectiveness of drug treatment is very much responsible for what the group perceives as underfunding of treatment.[9]

THE SCOPE OF DRUG TREATMENT EFFORTS

Although it has generally received less federal funding than law enforcement approaches, treatment of drug abuse and addiction is an important part of the nation's response to the drug problem. Official estimates are that in 1989, nearly $2.7 million in resources were allocated in the United States for drug treatment—nearly half (48 percent) from private sources, 31 percent from state and local government, and 21 percent from the federal government. This national "system" is estimated to have the capacity to treat about 2 million individuals.[10]

These resources fund literally thousands of drug treatment units across the United States. According to surveys conducted by the National Institute on Drug Abuse (NIDA) and the National Institute on Alcohol Abuse and Alcoholism, there were over 6,200 treatment units in 1989—1,266 drug treatment units and 5,021 units that treat both alcoholism and drug abuse.[11] As Figure 5.1 shows, the vast majority of these are private-sector units, especially private nonprofit facilities that treat both drug abuse and alcoholism. Fewer than one-fifth of the treatment units in the United States are government facilities; most of these are state or local government units that treat both drug abuse and alcoholism.

Another way to view the scope of drug treatment in the United States is to consider the number of drug treatment clients. NIDA reports that over 603,000 individuals were in drug treatment or drug and alcoholism treatment programs as of September 1989.[12] As Table 5.1 shows, clients are handled in facilities ranging from prisons to hospitals to community mental health centers to specialized residential treatment cen-

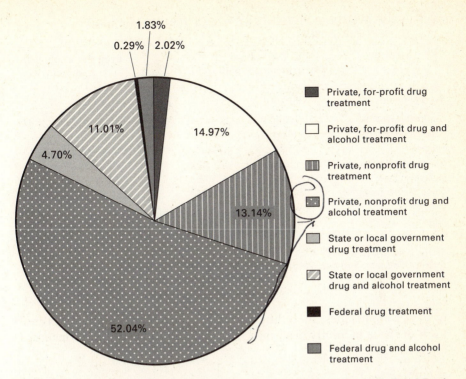

1.83%

0.29%   2.02%

11.01%

14.97%

4.70%

13.14%

52.04%

- Private, for-profit drug treatment
- Private, for-profit drug and alcohol treatment
- Private, nonprofit drug treatment
- Private, nonprofit drug and alcohol treatment
- State or local government drug treatment
- State or local government drug and alcohol treatment
- Federal drug treatment
- Federal drug and alcohol treatment

Figure 5.1 **Availability of treatment facilities by type, 1989.** (*Source:* **National Institute on Drug Abuse and National Institute on Alcohol Abuse and Alcoholism, 1990,** *National Drug and Alcoholism Treatment Unit Survey (NDATUS) 1989 Main Findings Report,* **p. 17.**)

ters. However, the most common type of facility for treatment is the outpatient clinic. The reason for the prevalence of outpatient treatment is primarily economic—outpatient treatment is considerably less expensive than inpatient hospital stays or treatment in residential facilities. Private insurers may not have questioned the need for expensive, month-long residential treatments in the past, but in many cases they now limit coverage for such treatment or demand that outpatient services be used first. A number of large health maintenance organizations are placing virtually all of their policyholders with drug or alcoholism problems in outpatient programs.[13]

TYPES OF DRUG ABUSE TREATMENT

There are only a few distinctive treatment strategies (often referred to as "modalities") in use for handling drug addicts. In fact, treatment practice and research has long been dominated by four types: chemically based treatment, especially methadone maintenance; simple detoxification; nonresidential self-help groups; and therapeutic communities. A handful

Table 5.1   DISTRIBUTION OF CLIENTS BY TYPE OF TREATMENT FACILITY,
SEPTEMBER 1989

Type of facility	Drug abuse treatment only		Drug and alcoholism treatment	
	Number	%	Number	%
Community mental health center	6,929	4.0	93,838	22.1
Hospital	15,363	8.8	58,578	13.8
Correctional facility	5,517	3.2	8,302	2.0
Halfway house	860	0.5	10,827	2.5
Other residential facility	16,595	9.6	26,898	6.3
Outpatient	98,656	53.9	197,374	46.5
Other	34,731	20.0	28,932	6.8

Source: National Institute on Drug Abuse and National Institute on Alcohol Abuse and Alcoholism, *National Drug and Alcoholism Treatment Unit Survey (NDATUS) 1989 Main Findings Report,* 1990, p. 18.

of newer approaches, including family therapy, round out the picture.[14] Each of these is briefly described here, followed by evidence concerning effectiveness.

Detoxification Programs

Detoxification programs are short-term programs, often hospital- or clinic-based, designed to get addicts through the withdrawal period after they stop drug use. Withdrawal involves physical discomforts, so various drugs, such as methadone, barbiturates, and sedatives, are used to relieve the patient's physical symptoms. Some detoxification programs include longer-term drug treatment goals and therapies, most involve only the immediate process of physically detoxifying the patient.[15] Detoxification per se is not really a rehabilitative program; rather, it is more properly viewed as an entry point or gateway to other drug abuse therapies. For this reason, detoxification is omitted from most of the following discussion.

The Pharmacological Approach: Methadone Maintenance

Methadone maintenance is undoubtedly the most controversial of the treatment strategies, in large part because it involves stabilization of the addict through regular administration of a synthetic drug, methadone, which is itself a potent narcotic. As discovered in pioneering research by Professors Dole and Nyswander at the Rockefeller Institute in the 1960s, a properly administered dose of methadone can block the addict's craving for heroin without providing a euphoric high. Furthermore, the necessary dosage of methadone need only be administered once every 24 hours; in contrast, maintenance on heroin itself would require administration every few hours.[16] Maintenance doses of methadone therefore allow the addict to lead a relatively normal and productive life, interrupting the desperate cycle of craving for a fix and the criminal activity that has been alleged to result from addiction. The majority of methadone clinics function on an outpatient basis, with maintenance doses of methadone being dispensed on-site; under some circumstances, a client may be entrusted with a multiday prescription of methadone doses, though the potential for the development of a black market in methadone necessarily means that this must be strictly limited and monitored.

Many methadone clinics offer a variety of forms of problem-solving assistance, such as vocational counseling, but the intensive counseling therapy that is part of other treatment approaches is not a feature of all methadone maintenance. Furthermore, while some clients are eventually weaned completely from methadone, total abstinence from all chemical dependency is not necessarily the major goal of methadone maintenance programs. There are, in fact, two contrasting forms of methadone treatment. One, which might be called the *adaptive form*, is based on the assumption that drug abuse is a chronic disease in which peculiarities of the individual's metabolism lead to the physical need for drugs. In its adaptive form, methadone treatment means long-term methadone maintenance, without the presumption that treatment will lead to eventual abstinence. The second type of methadone treatment might be called the *change-oriented form*. This form is based on the assumption that drug abuse is based in emotional disorder, which can eventually be cured with proper psychotherapeutic treatment. In this form of treatment, methadone is only a supportive device while psychotherapy is the centerpiece of treatment. As psychotherapy begins to yield results, the individual is expected to move off of methadone treatment and to be able to function in abstinence from drugs.[17]

The adaptive form reflects the earliest view of methadone treatment and is therefore most prevalent in those programs institutionalized in the late 1960s and early 1970s. The change-oriented approach began to emerge in the 1980s. A survey of 17 methadone clinics in the most recent large-scale study of drug treatment suggests, however, that the newer, change-oriented form has by no means supplanted the adaptive form. In all but 1 of the 17 clinics studied, the majority of clients were on long-term methadone maintenance.[18]

Meanwhile, the emergence of cocaine and its derivative crack as focal drugs of concern has led to efforts to develop a drug to deal with cocaine addiction, the way methadone is used for heroin addiction. Recently, researchers have found that drugs such as desipramine and carbamazepine, both antidepressants, can reduce patients' craving for co-caine, and the Addiction Research Center has used drugs called calcium-channel blockers to limit the euphoria that crack can produce in a user.[19] Although the pharmacological approach to cocaine treatment is still in its early stages, these developments have led some observers to hope that such drugs can be used to stave off cocaine use long enough for the individual to be receptive to other forms of therapy.

Residential Programs

Therapeutic communities, exemplified by such well-known programs as Daytop Village and Phoenix House, treat drug abusers in residential settings for an extended period, typically from 15 months to 2 years. This treatment approach is based upon the assumption that drug abuse is a symptom of broader problems in the character and social adjustment of the individual, such that a restructuring of the whole person is needed.[20] Treatment is characterized by the following features: (1) a high degree of structure, with virtually all of the client's time scheduled; (2) heavy reliance upon graduates of the residential program itself, rather than credentialed professionals, as leaders and counselors in the program; (3) the use of confrontational group counseling; and (4) staged movement through a series of roles of greater responsibility and privilege. Many residential treatment programs, especially those based upon the principles of Synanon and Alcoholics Anonymous, presume that drug addiction is never cured. Rather, one must learn how to maintain a life of abstinence while in "remission" from this lifelong disease.[21]

Drug-Free Outpatient Programs

Another important approach to drug abuse rehabilitation is drug-free nonresidential or outpatient treatment. Some of these clinics make some use of either methadone or other drugs to assist with rehabilitation, but many do not; the focal point of the treatment strategy is never pharmacological, as it is in methadone maintenance.[22] One of the most important subtypes of drug-free nonresidential treatment is the self-help group. Based on the Alcoholics Anonymous model, this approach relies upon voluntary groups of members who have the same addiction problem and who help each other through group counseling and support.[23]

Not all drug-free outpatient programs are based on the Alcoholics Anonymous model. In fact, these programs are exceptionally diverse and are therefore less easily characterized than the other treatment approaches. The most recent large-scale national study of drug treatment programs included ten drug-free outpatient programs in its sample. The vast majority (80%) of clients of these programs indicated that the treatment they received consisted primarily of individual counseling, although most of the programs included weekly group counseling sessions. Almost half the clients of these programs reported receiving family counseling as well; a variety of other services, such as educational, job, or financial counseling, were provided to some clients.[24]

Family Therapy

The drug treatment field has recently turned to the use of family therapy as a strategic approach. Rooted in the assumption that drug abuse, perhaps especially among youth, derives from flawed relationships within the family, this strategy targets the family as a whole for counseling and draws upon the family for therapeutic resources.[25] Unlike nonresidential self-help groups, family therapy is typically handled by mental health professionals. There is considerable variation in the treatment techniques used and the length of time that therapy is expected to take.[26]

As the preceding sections point out, the major types of drug treatment programs in America differ substantially in terms of philosophy and activities. The following section outlines what is currently known about the effectiveness of these various forms of treatment. Before turning to effectiveness, however, we should look at the vastly different costs of these various forms of treatment. As Table 5.2 shows, residential programs are considerably more expensive than outpatient programs, and drug-free outpatient programs are by far the least expensive type of treatment *on an annual basis.* However, many methadone maintenance programs are very long-term in character. Those with a strictly adaptive approach would presumably have clients permanently on methadone maintenance treatment. Viewed from this perspective, the *lifetime* cost per client is a more comparable figure than the annual cost. These and other difficulties make simple cost comparisons difficult, if not impossible. However, the annual costs presented in Table 5.2 at least provide

Table 5.2   COMPARATIVE ANNUAL COSTS OF VARIOUS FORMS
OF DRUG TREATMENT, 1989

Type of treatment	Dollars per client	Number of clients
Methadone maintenance outpatient program	$2,040	46,900
Drug-free outpatient program	845	251,593
Multimodality outpatient program	1,136	110,877
Residential program	3,247	100,961

Source: National Institute on Drug Abuse and National Institute on Alcohol Abuse and Alcoholism, *National Drug and Alcoholism Treatment Unit Survey (NDATUS) 1989 Main Findings Report,* 1990, p. 72.

some perspective that may be useful in the comparative assessment of the various treatment programs.

THE EFFECTIVENESS OF DRUG TREATMENT

It is not difficult to find suggestions that drug treatment and rehabilitation programs are ineffective. For example, in response to a request from the House Select Committee on Narcotics Abuse and Control, the General Accounting Office (GAO) studied the effectiveness of methadone maintenance clinics. Preliminary results focused on 15 clinics studied in 1989 in five states with large numbers of intravenous drug users. Most of the clinics failed to get many of their patients off of heroin and other opiates. Even among patients in treatment for more than six months, from 2 to 47 percent still used drugs.[27] Indeed, only 10 of the 15 clinics had cessation of all drug use, or cessation of all drugs except methadone, as a goal; the other 5 attempted to stop only use of heroin and other opiates. Yet the GAO study found that the use of cocaine and other drugs constitutes a serious problem among patients of these methadone clinics.[28] Stated another way, the effectiveness of methadone maintenance depends upon the time frame for evaluation and the presumed goals of treatment. Over the longer term, and with the presumption that total abstinence from heroin and methadone might be a realistic goal, the results are disappointing. Fewer than 10 percent of the cases reported on by Dr. Dole in his long-term follow-up were considered successful a decade after treatment.[29]

Methadone maintenance can also be criticized for certain unintended consequences, as reported in 1989 by Gene Haislip, an official of the Drug Enforcement Administration (DEA). Haislip notes that 857 programs are registered with the DEA for use of methadone in treatment, and argues that the methadone dispensed from these clinics is subject to abuse. Deaths and injuries from methadone use are reported through the Drug Abuse Warning Network, and a DEA probe showed that "methadone was frequently, in some cases commonly being sold in the neighborhood of these [methadone maintenance] programs for about $35.00 a dose."[30]

Some officials believe that many drug treatment programs are not only ineffective but are designed for making money off federal largesse rather than a sincere effort to yield effective treatment results. The director of NIDA, for example, states, "But I just get a little pain thinking about the lack of success rates for many of these drug treatment programs and the fact that there are a lot of people, quite frankly, who are in that business to make money and they make their money and they make it off of us."[31]

One of the harshest critics of drug treatment is Stanton Peele. In his book *Diseasing of America*,[32] Peele argues that the treatment of addiction has become a major industry and that America has been ill served by this industry. In particular, Peele argues that "addictionologists" and others in the drug treatment field have self-serving interests in defining drug use, as well as many other activities ranging from overeating to gambling, as diseases. The definition of such behaviors as diseases sets the stage for an overemphasis on treatment by professionals and a trivialization of the alternative—people's ability to cure themselves of addictions. Drawing upon research on heroin addicts from the early 1960s, Peele argues that natural "maturing out" of drug addiction is the means by which a substantial number of individuals withdraw from drug addiction, without the intervention of any treatment professionals.

How valid are these criticisms of the drug treatment industry and these concerns about the effectiveness of drug treatment programs? In recent years, there has been a veritable flood of research on the nature of drug addiction and on the outcomes of various treatment programs and strategies. A substantial portion of the research has been financed and coordinated by the federal government, through agencies such as the National Institute of Mental Health and NIDA. When viewed in the aggregate, this research on the effectiveness of drug treatment offers mixed results. Virtually all types of drug treatment programs have been shown to yield some positive outcomes, especially for those who remain in treatment long enough. However, the results offer less promising signs as well. The absolute magnitude of reported treatment effects is sometimes disappointingly small, and retention rates in treatment programs border on the abysmal. This section elaborates on these frustratingly mixed results.

On the positive side, John Gustafson, the deputy director of New York State's Division of Substance Abuse Services, has testified that "virtually all studies conducted over the last 15 years show that drug abuse treatment is effective in reducing drug abuse, increasing employment, improving psychological adjustment, and decreasing crime along with other negative behaviors."[33] Similarly, Dr. Charles Schuster, then director of NIDA, testified in 1989 that among those who stay in drug treatment long enough, success rates are very high:

> For those individuals who stay in therapeutic communities for 6 months or longer, and most therapeutic communities recommend 12 to 18 months, the success rate is very high. Studies by George DeLeon and others from Phoenix House have indicated that as many as 85 to 90 percent of these people are drug-free 3 to 5 years after graduating from a program.[34]

And Edward Senary argues that the overall picture is one of positive results:

The number and quality of studies carried out demonstrate, as well as can be realistically expected from any set of studies, that positive changes in client functioning occur during and after treatment. While there have been programs that have been poorly run and have encountered serious credibility problems, there can be little question that, from a public health point of view, many people have been helped by drug treatment.[35]

On the other hand, some of what is claimed to be success seems rather modest. Dr. Joseph Chambers, a psychiatrist and addictionologist, testified in 1989 that a 30 percent "cure" rate is to be expected for patients who complete a course of treatment costing $8,000 to $10,000, providing they have families who can help them with recovery afterward. Chambers argues that this is a "wonderful" recovery rate, one that compares favorably with the cure rate for cancer, but the highly favorable circumstances upon which the cure rate depends should be kept in mind.[36]

Furthermore, there is clearly a lot of variability across programs. In congressional hearings on the matter in 1990, the Select Committee on Narcotics Abuse and Control was informed that in some programs all but 8 percent of clients are off of illicit drugs within three years while in other programs 57 percent of clients continue to use illicit drugs.[37]

A closer look at the major research studies on the effectiveness of drug treatment offers us a clearer understanding. One of the largest systematic studies of the outcomes of drug treatment programs is the Drug Abuse Reporting Program (DARP), which collected data from 43,943 clients of 52 different treatment programs in the United States in the mid-1970s and conducted follow-up research on those clients for as long as seven years after admission. The study also had a comparison group who had completed intake procedures for one of the programs but did not come back to receive treatment.[38]

The results of this data collection project suggest that treatment may yield improvements but that posttreatment improvements are not clearly attributable to the treatment itself. Table 5.3, for example, shows some of the one-year posttreatment results from the study. Note that each of the treatment groups shows improvement in employment status, but the comparison group does as well. Patients in the treatment groups are also markedly less likely to have been arrested or incarcerated in the year after treatment than in the year before, though once again the comparison group also shows these improved outcomes. Finally, the DARP data show that there are substantial declines in use of opiates for each of the treatment groups. Here again, however, the same improvement is to be found in the comparison group. Furthermore, the absolute level of drug abstinence achieved is not that impressive. Over one-third of the clients of each of the treatment approaches used an opiate daily at some period in the year following treatment, and over half used such drugs at least occasionally after treatment.

Table 5.3   DRUG ABUSE REPORTING PROGRAM (DARP) FIRST-YEAR OUTCOMES, BY TREATMENT TYPE

| | Percentage reporting outcomes | | | | |
| | Any Drug Use[a] | Daily drug use | Criminality | | Employed 6 mos or more |
			Arrested	Incarcerated	
Methadone maintenance					
Pretreatment[b]	100	100	88	75	33
Posttreatment	56	36	27	28	57
Therapeutic community					
Pretreatment	100	100	95	83	20
Posttreatment	58	39	33	33	61
Drug-free outpatient program					
Pretreatment	100	100	87	66	24
Posttreatment	64	44	34	34	52
Intake only (comparison group)					
Pretreatment	100	100	86	68	21
Posttreatment	70	53	39	41	44

[a]Daily drug use posttreatment means daily use in one or more months during the year.

[b]Pretreatment indicators of drug use are based on the two months prior to admission to the treatment program, criminality is based on lifetime before admission, and employment is based on the year before admission.

Source: Simpson and Sells, 1983, p. 14.

More recently, NIDA funded a large-scale study of drug abuse treatment, the Treatment Outcome Prospective Study (TOPS). The study included 11,750 individuals who were admitted to various treatment programs in the period from 1979 to 1981. Follow-up study of these individuals is providing information about both short- and longer-term effects of treatment.[39] Figures 5.2 through 5.4 display some of the results of the TOPS study.

Figure 5.2 shows that two of the three types of treatment—methadone maintenance and therapeutic community programs—seem to lead to a notable and durable decline in heroin use. Clients of drug-free outpatient programs are relatively unlikely to have been regular heroin users prior to treatment, and the impact of treatment is less dramatic. As with the DARP study results, however, the comparison groups in the TOPS study put these treatment effects into perspective. In the TOPS study, those who were initially assigned to a drug treatment program, but who had relatively little treatment (i.e., less than three months) or none because they dropped out, served as the comparison groups. Figure 5.2 shows that the decline in heroin use can be about as dramatic for a comparison group as for a group that completes a treatment program. For example, among clients of outpatient methadone programs, the prevalence of heroin use declined from nearly 65 percent in the year before

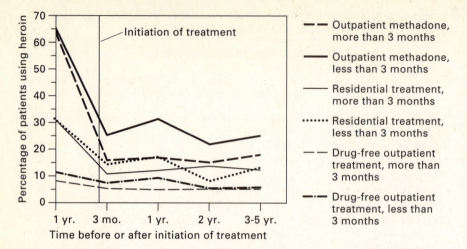

Figure 5.2 **Impact of treatment on heroin use, by type of treatment.** (*Source:* **Hubbard, Marsden, Rachal, Harwood, Cavanaugh, and Ginzburg, 1989, p. 180.**)

treatment was initiated to less than 20 percent three to five years after treatment, but the prevalence of heroin use among those who were in outpatient methadone treatment for less than three months was down to 25 percent by the three- to five-year follow-up period. Results such as these suggest that either a much more limited exposure to treatment is as effective as longer-term treatment, or factors other than treatment itself (such as maturation or changes in social climate) are responsible for much of the observed decline in heroin use.

Figure 5.3 shows somewhat similar results concerning the impact of treatment on cocaine use. Treatment programs apparently diminish the prevalence of cocaine use among long-term clients. However, parallel improvements occur for those with minimal exposure to the treatment programs, though the effects are not quite as dramatic. In the case of outpatient methadone treatment, cocaine use outcomes at the three- to five-year follow-up point are actually better for those who had less than three months of treatment than for those who had more than three months. While this result may be a fluke, it illustrates the way in which the data from the comparison group weaken the generally favorable results from the treatment group.

Drug treatment is also expected to have an impact on criminal activity. Methadone maintenance, for example, initially gained the attention of federal decision makers because its pioneers reported that in clinical trials, methadone patients showed dramatic declines in the predatory illegal acts that they had relied upon to sustain their drug habit. While not as simplistically keyed to the crime issue, other forms of drug treatment also are expected to yield these socially desirable results. Figure 5.4 shows the impact on illegal acts for the three major forms of treatment. The illegal activity indicated here is self-reported and includes only

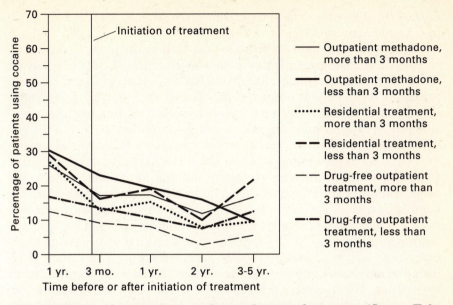

Figure 5.3 **Impact of treatment on cocaine use, by type of treatment. (*Source:* Hubbard, Marsden, Rachal, Harwood, Cananaugh, and Ginzburg, 1989, p. 180.)**

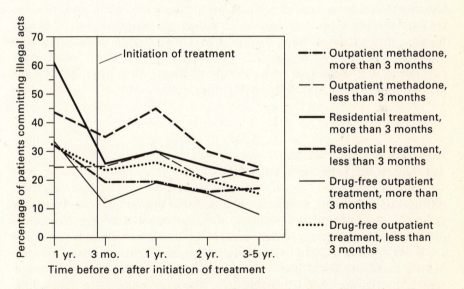

Figure 5.4 **Impact of drug treatment on illegal acts, by type of treatment. (*Source:* Hubbard, Marsden, Rachal, Harwood, Cavanaugh, and Ginzburg, 1989, p. 181.)**

predatory crimes, such as burglary, robbery, and assault; illegal drug possession, for example, is not included. As with drug use outcomes, the impact of treatment on illegal activity appears to be substantial, but those with little or no exposure to treatment often showed parallel reductions in criminal activity.

Both the TOPS and DARP studies, as well as the professional literature on drug abuse treatment outcomes more generally, focus mostly on heroin abuse and treatment. Relatively little scholarly research has been published on treatment outcomes for cocaine abuse.[40] This is undoubtedly because the movement for scientific studies of drug treatment outcomes largely dates from a period in which heroin was viewed as the primary drug abuse problem. However, the emergence of cocaine as a major drug of abuse in the United States in the 1980s led to the development of some treatment approaches especially tailored to cocaine abusers, and some studies of the effectiveness of these treatment approaches are becoming available. For example, one program for treating cocaine abuse involves what is called *contingency contracting.* Clients provide the treatment professional with information, such as letters admitting to cocaine use, that would be personally very damaging to the client if released to employers, professional licensing agencies, or law enforcement authorities. The treatment professional agrees to hold the damaging documentation while the client goes through the program of psychotherapy, but to mail it if the client tests positive for cocaine use or fails to take the mandatory urinalysis test. While abstinence from cocaine use is quite high (90 percent) during the course of this contingency contracting treatment, there is considerable relapse afterward. Over half resume cocaine use after the contingency contracting period is over.[41] Siegel reports on a program using a more conventional mix of therapies for cocaine abusers, such as hospitalization for detoxification and psychotherapy, combined with exercise therapy. After nine months, 80 percent of the clients were still abstaining from cocaine.[42]

MAJOR CHALLENGES
TO IMPROVED EFFECTIVENESS

As this chapter shows, a substantial amount of public funds, and an even greater volume of private resources, are being devoted to drug treatment programs in this country. Many critics argue that not enough resources are being committed and that we should expand treatment until anyone having problems with drug abuse has access to treatment on demand rather than going onto a waiting list. Major expansions in the public funding of drug treatment are constrained, however, both by the budget limits that face all programs in contemporary America and, perhaps more importantly, by skepticism over the effectiveness of drug treatment and confusion over which treatment programs should be funded. William Bennett, then the nation's drug policy director, argued in 1989, "Despite our interest and our sense of urgency about helping people who are genuinely interested in seeking treatment, the state of the art isn't up to it. I think that suggests the importance of research and models."[43] The following sections outline a number of obstacles that stand in the way of enhanced drug treatment effectiveness.

The Retention Problem

One of the biggest barriers to effectiveness for treatment programs—especially those such as therapeutic communities, which involve a longer time commitment—is the dropout problem. Many clients leave before completing the treatment program, sometimes at the very beginning. For example, one of the test programs being funded by NIDA is the Argus Community in New York City, and in particular its Harbor House program for the addicted mentally ill. However, out of the 168 individuals who have been in the program, 123 dropped out.[44] The most recent national-sample study of treatment programs shows that over 80 percent of the clients of drug-free outpatient and residential programs remained in treatment for less than six months, although completion of these sorts of programs takes considerably longer. Many of these individuals, and especially the drug-free outpatient clients, dropped out virtually immediately. More than 22 percent of the clients of drug-free outpatient programs left within the first week of treatment.[45] Research from other types of treatment programs also documents high dropout rates. A recent study of treatment programs for cocaine abusers found that 42% of the subjects dropped out after only one or two evaluation interviews and received no therapy.[46]

Treatment of Criminal Offenders

A substantial number of individuals with drug problems are to be found among the ranks of America's prison population. The widespread drug involvement of those caught up in the criminal justice system is suggested by the large proportion of those arrested for serious nondrug crimes who test positive for drug use. In the last quarter of 1990, a large proportion of male arrestees yielded positive urinalyses for drugs: 23 percent in Omaha; 42 percent in Kansas City, Missouri; 55 percent in Houston and in Washington, D.C.; 72 percent in Chicago; 74 percent in San Diego; and 75 percent in New York City.[47]

The challenges that face drug treatment programs in general are in many ways compounded in programs for drug-abusing felons. In contrast with well-off citizens who have substance abuse problems, who can use high-priced private clinics, incarcerated addicts are likely to find little in the way of treatment programming. At a time when Americans are unwilling to pay for prison construction despite their approval of increased prison terms for drug offenses, elaborate and expensive drug treatment programs for offenders will not be easy to finance.

Nevertheless, treatment of the drug problems of criminal offenders is important, from the viewpoint of society as well as the individual offender. While America's prison system has not been a notable success at rehabilitating criminals generally, its ability to perform any rehabilitative function is surely compromised still further by the drug problems of many offenders.

Several innovative programs to deal with substance-abusing criminal offenders were instituted in the 1960s, both at the state level and through the federal Narcotic Addict Rehabilitation Act of 1966. These "civil commitment" programs provided access to drug treatment facilities for addicts convicted of certain crimes. The results of these programs were disappointing, largely because of implementation problems. An evaluation of California's civil commitment program, for example, suggests that although the concept was a positive one, the program's enormous costs and presumptions of favorable circumstances were unrealistic.[48] The federal civil commitment program was abandoned after a relatively short existence. Because only two federal facilities were equipped to handle addicted offenders, the system quickly became overwhelmed; and program administrators became so preoccupied with weeding out unsuitable candidates for rehabilitation that within four years, nearly two-thirds of all applicants for the program were being rejected.[49] Under these circumstances, the demise of the program is not surprising.

Despite the problems of civil commitment programs in this earlier period, the concept of some form of prison-based treatment for criminal addicts has reemerged. However, many of the challenges that confronted earlier drug programs for criminal offenders have yet to be resolved. For example, there is controversy over the efficacy of compulsory drug abuse treatment for criminal offenders. On this matter, a judge with expertise in the matter warned Congress that the effective programs that he has seen are ones in which offenders had volunteered rather than been coerced into treatment.[50] Many in the criminal justice system agree with the judge; others cite evidence that "correctional drug-treatment programs can have a substantial effect on the behavior of chronic drug-abusing offenders."[51] Even if compulsory drug treatment has the potential for effectiveness, its wisdom is questionable when the resources available for treatment are limited. In 1992, the federal Bureau of Prisons devoted $22 million to drug treatment within prisons, and the U.S. government provided another $105 million to state and local governments for such treatment.[52] These amounts are quite limited relative to the number of drug-abusing individuals in prisons. Since there are inadequate resources to treat all drug-abusing offenders, systems must be devised to identify those whose drug use constitutes the most serious threat to themselves and society.[53] But these may not be the individuals who would voluntarily undertake treatment.

Drug Testing: A Diagnostic Tool for Treatment Referral?

One of the most controversial topics relating to drug abuse treatment is drug testing. Drug testing can and has been used purely as an enforcement device, for example, to monitor whether athletes should be disqualified from competition because they have used performance-enhancing drugs. A more interesting and controversial application of drug-testing technology is in the workplace. In both the public and private sectors, testing of certain categories of employees or job applicants has been used as a method of screening for individuals with substance abuse problems. To the extent that such screening is a vehicle for referring individuals to an employee assistance program (EAP) for rehabilitation, it constitutes yet another tool for drug treatment. As we will see, however, one of the many reasons for controversy over workplace drug testing is the fact that such screening can be used simply to weed out undesirables rather than as a helping hand. Questions can also be raised about the appropriateness of drug testing as a basis for determining the most effective use of scarce treatment slots.

In the public sector, testing of employees for drug use dates from the military's decision in 1971 to test returning Vietnam veterans. The U.S. armed forces continue to test military personnel, based on random selection, generating a large volume of drug-testing activity. The navy alone tests nearly 2 million urine specimens annually, and the army has been increasing testing from the 1.2 million drug tests conducted in 1986.[54]

In addition to the military, a number of U.S. government agencies, such as the Departments of Transportation and Energy, had drug-testing programs in effect prior to 1986. But in that year, the magnitude and visibility of public-sector drug testing increased dramatically with President Reagan's issuance of Executive Order 12564. That executive order mandated that federal agencies take a leadership role in establishing drug-free workplaces by using drug testing to detect and deal with illegal drug users. Congress responded by enacting requirements that drug-testing programs in federal agencies would have to meet. In particular, agencies had to develop drug-testing plans and submit them to the Department of Health and Human Services for approval, and the laboratories used for drug testing had to be certified for high levels of accuracy.[55] By 1990, over 100 federal agencies that had engaged in no drug testing prior to Executive Order 12564 had certified plans for such testing.[56]

The amount of drug testing of civilians by federal agencies is substantial. In a single half-year period from late 1989 to early 1990, federal agencies conducted over 12,000 random drug tests of employees and another 12,000 tests of job applicants. The overwhelming majority of random tests of employees (93%) were conducted by the Treasury Department, the DEA, and the Department of Transportation; drug testing of job applicants, however, was much more widespread.[57]

According to Executive Order 12564, employees found to be using illegal drugs are to be referred to an EAP for "assessment, counseling, and referral for treatment or rehabilitation as appropriate"; disciplinary action is to be taken against employees found to be using illegal drugs unless they voluntarily admit to drug use or volunteer for drug testing *and* receive counseling or rehabilitation through an EAP *and* refrain from further use of illegal drugs. In particular, any employee who tests positive as an illegal drug user but refuses the services of an EAP or refuses to discontinue illegal drug use is to be removed from government service.[58]

However, only a tiny fraction of federal drug tests on civilians have turned out positive. About 0.5 percent of tested employees and about the same minuscule percentage of job applicants tested positive for illegal drug use between October 1989 and April 1990.[59] Either despite or because of the stern warnings of Executive Order 12564 concerning recalcitrants, drug testing has rarely led to employees losing their jobs. Out of the very small number who test positive, only about one in five are severed from federal government service.[60]

In the private sector, drug testing of applicants and employees has also become relatively common, especially in larger companies and in certain sectors of the economy. A survey of private employers by the U.S. Bureau of Labor Statistics found that in 1988, about one out of five private-sector employees in the United States worked in an establishment with a drug-testing program. Among establishments having between 500 and 999 employees, 31 percent had such programs in 1988, as did 45 percent of establishments with 1,000 or more employees. Drug testing is particularly prevalent in the mining industry (where 22% of establishments have such programs), in the communication and public utilities sector (17.6%), and in the transportation industry (14.9%).[61]

Not surprisingly, workplace drug testing has spawned concerns about individual rights, along with legal challenges and court cases. In the five-year period ending in September 1990, there were 136 court decisions involving drug testing—67 involving private-sector programs and 69 involving public-sector drug testing. Nine of the decisions came from the Supreme Court.[62]

Perhaps the most significant of these were the two U.S. Supreme Court decisions rendered in March 1989. In *National Treasury Employees' Union v. von Raab*, 86-1879, the Court found in favor of the government's urine-testing program for applicants for work in drug enforcement areas of the Customs Bureau; in *Skinner v. Railway Labor Executives' Association*, 87-1555, the Court sustained the government's policy of forcing railroad workers involved in accidents to submit to blood and urine tests. The Supreme Court has also let stand rulings by lower courts that allow random drug testing of law enforcement officers (*Guiney v. Roache* and *Policeman's Benevolent Association v. Washington Township*). All these decisions are seen as signaling the Supreme Court's willingness "to allow widespread testing of employees in jobs that affect public safety."[63] In contrast, many lower court decisions are conflicting; unless the Supreme Court rules again to clarify matters, the legal issues involved in drug testing will remain unsettled. As a result, "employees who challenge universal or random drug testing in the courts stand a fighting chance of success."[64]

Widespread drug testing has evoked a strong reaction from many individuals who find it an offensive assault on individual privacy and, if conducted by government, an infringement of constitutional protections against unreasonable search. In addition, there have been concerns about the accuracy of drug testing (urine tests are far from error-free) and about the potentially damaging consequences to individuals who are falsely identified as drug users. These concerns have been exacerbated by publicity over incidents such as the firing of Juanita Jones, a 51-year-old grandmother and school bus attendant in Washington, D.C., who was fired after an erroneous drug test result. Her story, as told to a congressional oversight hearing, has many of the features that epitomize the concerns of opponents of drug testing. Although her employer had no cause to suspect drug use, she was "herded into a bus" with other employees and taken to a clinic to leave a sample of urine. Her sample generated a positive result for marijuana on preliminary screening, and she was immediately fired. The employer did not conduct a follow-up test to corroborate the result or give her a chance to defend herself. Although the results were negative on a second urine test that she volunteered to take right away, the employer refused to give her a hearing to appeal her dismissal. Eventually, the U.S. District Court ruled that she should be reinstated with full back pay. But in the intervening 15 months, she underwent a substantial ordeal:

> As a result of my termination, I was branded before my co-workers, family, and community as a drug user. My best friend, wrongfully believing that I was a drug user, refused to speak to me. For over a year, I was unable to find another job, especially one which would involve caring for children.[65]

In response to concerns about the accuracy of drug-testing programs, the federal government has issued standards that government programs must meet, and they serve as benchmarks for the private sector as well. According to J. Michael Walsh and Jeanne Trumble, "the rigor of the federal standards has virtually dispensed with concerns regarding accuracy and reliability."[66] This may prove to be an overstatement, but the standards do appear to obviate the sorts of problems that caused nightmares for Juanita Jones. In particular, all urine tests that are positive on the initial screening using immunoassay methods must be confirmed in a second test using gas chromatography or mass spectrometry. In addition, a specialized medical officer must draw the final conclusions, based not only on the lab results but also upon "conversations with the employee and other evidence" that could yield "alternative medical explanations for the results."[67]

Much of the debate over drug testing in the workplace has focused on how the testing is carried out (i.e., randomly or only when there is cause for suspicion, with expensive standards for laboratory accuracy or with less expensive but less accurate methods). But perhaps the most important question about workplace drug testing is its purpose. On one hand, drug testing can be used primarily to detect and get rid of any applicants or employees who use drugs; on the other hand, testing can be used to detect employees who should be referred to rehabilitation programs that will enable them to overcome substance abuse problems and return to their jobs as more productive workers. Just as drug policy responses in general can involve sharp differences between those holding to a medical model of the problem and those holding to a criminal model, so also does drug testing have the potential to be handled with either emphasis. As the scope of workplace drug testing expands, this matter of purpose or orientation may, for example, shape the courts' ongoing interpretation of the acceptability of drug testing. As Franklin Zimring and Gordon Hawkins argue, "the courts are traditionally more vigilant in providing right-to-privacy and search-and-seizure limits in criminal law than in government intrusions that are justified for reasons of public health."[68] Consequently, drug-testing programs that are an integrated part of a rehabilitative strategy for troubled employees might be more likely to be sustained by the court.

Others argue that the orientation to workplace drug testing has in fact moved toward precisely this "helping-hand" approach.[69] Corporate experience with alcoholism problems has paved the way. Many companies established EAPs in the 1970s to provide counseling and assistance to employees with alcoholism and other personal problems. Responses to a Conference Board survey of businesses in 1988 suggest that private companies with drug-testing programs are also likely to have them nested within a more elaborate system that includes an EAP and drug education.[70]

Although this helpful rehabilitative orientation gives a positive face to workplace drug testing, there are some reasons to question whether such testing should be in widespread use. Workplace drug testing is often justified on the grounds that drug use constitutes a serious safety problem and creates substantial productivity losses for American business and industry. But as many critics have pointed out, alcoholism is a much more widespread form of substance abuse, yet drug-testing programs are irrelevant to it. Many managers believe that an individual whose alcohol use jeopardizes workplace safety or productivity manifests directly observable behaviors such as excessive absenteeism, lateness, and unsatisfactory job performance. But surely the same can be said of drug use.

Given the costs of large-scale random drug testing and the legal issues that it evokes, its use is questionable. The value of widespread drug testing is further cast into doubt because only extremely small numbers of drug abusers are detected. But perhaps most important, the appropriateness of viewing drug testing as a helping hand is questionable as long as our ability to successfully rehabilitate drug users is limited. Drug testing may have the virtue of motivating individuals to seek drug abuse treatment when they would not otherwise do so. Concern about loss of one's job constitutes the kind of crisis that forces an addict out of a state of denial and into therapy.[71] But as the research reviewed in this chapter shows, drug treatment is an extended, expensive proposition, with a modest rate of full success in the sense of total abstinence. Because businesses are unlikely to have the patience to be supportive of troubled employees through such a process, it is difficult to view workplace drug testing as primarily a tool to help rehabilitate employees.

CONCLUSIONS

Treatment of drug abusers is an important component of the nation's efforts to deal with the problem of drugs in the United States. Although the share of governmental resources devoted to drug treatment is smaller than that devoted to drug-law enforcement, the combined total of government and private resources devoted to drug treatment is substantial, and large numbers of individuals are being treated at methadone clinics, in residential therapy programs, in outpatient programs, and in family therapy sessions. There have also been major efforts to evaluate the effectiveness of these programs, and this evaluation research leaves us with many troubling questions. Exposure to drug treatment seems to be linked with decreased drug use, less arrests, and more employment; but similar improvements are shown for comparison groups of drug abusers who have not completed treatment programs. Hence, there are lingering questions about the necessity for professional treatment programs for all drug abusers and about the extent to which solutions to the drug abuse problem can be attributed to treatment programs.

The drug abuse treatment field is plagued by other troubles as well. The dismal retention rates in many treatment programs raise serious questions, especially for those programs that are premised on relatively long-term treatment. Methadone maintenance still operates under a cloud of controversy because it substitutes one narcotic for another. Prison officials are grappling with the challenge of providing drug treatment within their limited budgets for a population with an extraordinary proportion of drug users, many of whom may not be motivated to make good use of drug treatment programming. And efforts to detect drug users in the workplace through expanded use of drug testing raise the issue of privacy, as well as questions about the availability of suitable and effective treatment programs for drug-abusing workers.

In short, drug abuse treatment is an intriguing part of the ongoing war on drugs in the United States. Underfunded in the eyes of many proponents, struggling to improve its credibility with government officials, grappling with problems of effectiveness, and touching upon a variety of explosive issues involving rights, drug abuse treatment is an enterprise under pressure on many fronts. It is also an enterprise that many addicts, drug abusers, and their families have come to rely on in a time of crisis.

NOTES

1. B. Guy Peters, *American Public Policy: Promise and Performance*, 3rd ed. (Chatham, NJ: Chatham House, 1993), pp. 150–151.
2. Thomas R. Dye, *Understanding Public Policy*, 7th ed. (Englewood Cliffs, NJ: Prentice-Hall, 1992), pp. 360–362.
3. Peters, 1993, pp. 153–154.
4. Lester M. Salamon, "The Time Dimension in Policy Evaluation: The Case of New Deal Land Relief Programs," *Public Policy* (Spring 1979), pp. 129–183.
5. Dennis Palumbo, *Public Policy in America* (New York: Harcourt Brace Jovanovich, 1988), p. 131.
6. Palumbo, 1988, pp. 148–149.
7. Palumbo, 1988, p. 154.
8. Carol H. Weiss, "Research for Policy's Sake: The Enlightenment Function of Social Research," *Policy Analysis* 3 (1977), pp. 531–545.
9. Barbara Shelly, "Experts Debate Value of Therapy," *Kansas City Star*, Wednesday, April 18, 1990, pp. A1, A16.
10. White House, *National Drug Control Strategy* (Washington, DC: U.S. Government Printing Office, 1991), pp. 46–47.
11. National Institute on Drug Abuse (NIDA) and National Institute on Alcohol Abuse and Alcoholism, *National Drug and Alcoholism Treatment Unit Survey (NDATUS) 1989 Main Findings Report* (Rockville, MD: U.S. Department of Health and Human Services, 1990), p. 12.
12. NIDA, 1990, p. 18.
13. Barbara Shelly, "Insurers Tighten Controls," *Kansas City Star*, Tuesday, April 17, 1990, p. A6.
14. Richard C. Stephens, *Mind-Altering Drugs: Use, Abuse, and Treatment* (Newbury Park, CA: Sage, 1987), pp. 87–101.
15. Stephens, 1987, pp. 87–88.
16. Stephens, 1987, p. 89.
17. Robert Hubbard, J. Valley Rachal, S. Gail Craddock, and Elizabeth R. Cavanaugh, "Treatment Outcome Prospective Study (TOPS): Client Characteristics and Behaviors Before, During, and After Treatment," in Frank Tims and Jacqueline Ludford, eds., *Drug Abuse Treatment Evaluation: Strategies, Progress, and Prospects* (Rockville, MD: National Institute on Drug Abuse, 1984), p. 45.
18. Hubbard et al., 1984, p. 48.
19. Mary Cooper, *The Business of Drugs* (Washington, DC: Congressional Quarterly, 1990), p. 134.
20. George De Leon, "Treatment Strategies," in James Inciardi, ed., *Handbook of Drug Control in the United States* (New York: Greenwood Press, 1990), pp. 119–120.
21. Robert Hubbard, Mary Ellen Marsden, J. Valley Rachal, Henrick Harwood, Elizabeth Cavanaugh, and Harold Ginzburg, *Drug Abuse Treatment: A National Study of Effectiveness* (Chapel Hill: University of North Carolina Press, 1989), p. 56.
22. De Leon, 1990, p. 118.
23. Stephens, 1987, p. 96.
24. Hubbard et al., 1989, p. 67.
25. Stephens, 1987, p. 101.

26. De Leon, 1990, p. 123.
27. U.S. House of Representatives, Select Committee on Narcotics Abuse and Control, *Efficacy of Drug Abuse Treatment Programs, Part II* (Washington, DC: U.S. Government Printing Office, 1990a), pp. 36–37.
28. Select Committee on Narcotics Abuse and Control, 1990a, p. 37.
29. De Leon, 1990, p. 117.
30. Select Committee on Narcotics Abuse and Control, 1990a, pp. 40–41.
31. Select Committee on Narcotics Abuse and Control, 1990a, p. 34.
32. Stanton Peele, *Diseasing of America: Addiction Treatment Out of Control* (Lexington, MA: Heath, 1989).
33. U.S. House of Representatives, Select Committee on Narcotics Abuse and Control, *Efficacy of Drug Abuse Treatment Programs, Part I* (Washington, DC: U.S. Government Printing Office, 1989a), p. 34.
34. Select Committee on Narcotics Abuse and Control, 1990a, p. 19.
35. Edward C. Senary, "Clinical Implications of Drug Abuse Treatment Outcome Research," in Frank Tims and Jacqueline Ludford, eds., *Drug Abuse Treatment Evaluation: Strategies, Progress, and Prospects* (Rockville, MD: National Institute on Drug Abuse, 1984), p. 139.
36. Select Committee on Narcotics Abuse and Control, 1989a, p. 12.
37. Select Committee on Narcotics Abuse and Control, 1990a, p. 24.
38. D. Dwayne Simpson and S. B. Sells, "Effectiveness of Treatment for Drug Abuse: An Overview of the DARP Research Program," in Barry Stimmel, ed., *Evaluation of Drug Treatment Programs* (New York: Haworth Press, 1983).
39. Hubbard et al., 1989.
40. Herbert Kleber and Frank H. Gawin, "Cocaine Abuse: A Review of Current and Experimental Treatments," in John Grabowski, ed., *Cocaine: Pharmacology, Effects, and Treatment of Abuse*, NIDA Research Monograph 50 (Washington, DC: U.S. Government Printing Office, 1984), p. 111; and Jerome Jaffe, "Evaluating Drug Abuse Treatment: A Comment on the State of the Art," in Frank Tims and Jacqueline Ludford, eds., *Drug Abuse Treatment Evaluation: Strategies, Progress, and Prospects* (Rockville, MD: National Institute on Drug Abuse, 1984), p. 24.
41. Kleber and Gawin, 1984, p. 115.
42. R. K. Siegel, "Cocaine Smoking," *Journal of Psychoactive Drugs* 14 (1982), pp. 271–359.
43. U.S. House of Representatives, Select Committee on Narcotics Abuse and Control, *National Drug Control Strategy* (Washington, DC: U.S. Government Printing Office, 1990b), p. 14.
44. Douglas Martin, "'Tough Love' for Those Most in Need," *New York Times*, Wednesday, June 5, 1991, p. A16.
45. Hubbard et al., 1989, p. 95.
46. Paula Kleinman, George Woody, Thomas Todd, Robert Millman, Sung-Yeon Kang, Jack Kemp, and Douglas Lipton, "Crack and Cocaine Abusers in Outpatient Psychotherapy," *Psychotherapy and Counselling in the Treatment of Drug Abuse*, NIDA Research Monograph 104 (Washington, DC: U.S. Government Printing Office, 1990) p. 28.
47. U.S. Bureau of the Census, *Statistical Abstract of the United States 1992*, 112th ed. (Washington, DC: U.S. Government Printing Office, 1991), p. 183.
48. M. Douglas Anglin, "The Efficacy of Civil Commitment in Treating Narcotics Addictions," *Journal of Drug Issues* 18 (Fall 1988), pp. 527–545.

49. Richard Lindblad, "Civil Commitment Under the Federal Narcotic Act," *Journal of Drug Issues* 18 (Fall 1988), p. 599.

50. U.S. House of Representatives, Select Committee on Narcotics Abuse and Control, *National Drug Control Strategy* (Washington, DC: U.S. Government Printing Office, 1991), p. 17.

51. M. Douglas Anglin and Yih-Ing Hser, "Treatment of Drug Abuse," in Michael Tonry and James Q. Wilson, eds., *Drugs and Crime* (Chicago: University of Chicago Press, 1990), p. 427.

52. Select Committee on Narcotics Abuse and Control, 1991, p. 16.

53. Carl Leukefeld and Frank Tims, "Compulsory Treatment: A Review of Findings," in Leukefeld and Tims, eds., *Compulsory Treatment of Drug Abuse: Research and Clinical Practice* (Washington, DC: National Institute on Drug Abuse, 1988), p. 246.

54. Craig M. Cornish, *Drugs and Alcohol in the Workplace: Testing and Privacy* (Wilmette, IL: Callaghan, 1988), p. 52.

55. Frank J. Thompson, Norma M. Riccucci, and Carolyn Ban, "Drug Testing in the Federal Workplace: An Instrumental and Symbolic Assessment," *Public Administration Review* 51 (November/December 1991), pp. 515–516.

56. Thompson et al., 1991, p. 517.

57. Thompson et al., 1991, pp. 517–518.

58. Cornish, 1988, p. 263.

59. Thompson et al., 1991, p. 520.

60. Thompson et al., 1991, p. 521.

61. U.S. Bureau of the Census, 1991, p. 535.

62. Thompson et al., 1991, p. 516.

63. Deborah L. Ackerman, "A History of Drug Testing," in Robert H. Coombs and Louis J. West, eds., *Drug Testing: Issues and Options* (New York: Oxford University Press, 1991), pp. 16–17.

64. Thompson et al., 1991, p. 517.

65. U.S. House of Representatives, Committee on Education and Labor, Subcommittee on Employment Opportunities, *Oversight Hearing on Drug Testing in the Work Force* (Washington, DC: U.S. Government Printing Office, 1988), p. 28.

66. J. Michael Walsh and Jeanne G. Trumble, "The Politics of Drug Testing," in Robert H. Coombs and Louis J. West, eds., *Drug Testing: Issues and Options* (New York: Oxford University Press, 1991), p. 25.

67. Thompson et al., 1991, pp. 518–519.

68. Franklin Zimring and Gordon Hawkins, *The Search for Rational Drug Control* (New York: Cambridge University Press, 1992), p. 18.

69. Walsh and Trumble, 1991, p. 27.

70. Helen Axel, "Drug Testing in Private Industry," in Robert H. Coombs and Louis J. West, eds., *Drug Testing: Issues and Options* (New York: Oxford University Press, 1991), pp. 144–145.

71. Ronald M. Paolino, "Identifying, Treating, and Counseling Drug Abusers," in Robert H. Coombs and Louis J. West, eds., *Drug Testing: Issues and Options* (New York: Oxford University Press, 1991), p. 229.

Chapter
6
Drug Abuse Prevention

INTRODUCTION

This chapter focuses on a second major approach to the drug problem—
prevention of drug use and abuse. At the most abstract level, it might be
argued that prevention incorporates both drug-law enforcement and drug
treatment and rehabilitation. To the extent that aggressive drug-law enforcement deters would-be drug users and drug treatment takes former
users out of the market for drugs, such programs contribute to drug
abuse prevention. However, in public policy discussions surrounding the
drug issue, prevention is typically characterized more narrowly and dis-
tinguished from both drug-law enforcement and drug treatment and rehabilitation. Specifically, the traditional approach to drug prevention involves *educational* campaigns designed to influence citizens as they
make choices about whether or not to use drugs. As this chapter shows,
such educational campaigns are often targeted toward youth, but the machinery of the mass media has also been mobilized to direct advertising
campaigns about drug dangers to the American public more generally.

Two types of constraints have been important in shaping drug prevention programs. One is the essential ambivalence in American political thinking about the role of the state in changing people's preferences.
The American political economy is built upon liberal principles, one of
the most potent of which is the assumption of consumer sovereignty.[1]
According to this principle, citizens have various tastes and preferences,
most of which are met by a private sector that supplies goods and services in response to those tastes and preferences. The role of government
in such a political economy is to ensure that the market operates fairly
and that market failures—such as negative effects on third parties, lack
of competition, and market exchanges based on fraudulent information—are corrected. There is scant role in such a framework for inquiry
into the legitimacy or propriety of people's preferences. Such preferences
are taken as given, and both private markets and government, as it
patches over private-market failures, are assumed to be responsive to
those preferences.

In actuality, this pure model of liberal political economy does not exist. Through various public policies, ranging from the subsidizing of fine arts programming on television and radio to requirements for health warnings on cigarette packages, government has taken on the role of attempting to shape people's consumer behavior. But this does not mean that the liberal principle of consumer sovereignty is irrelevant. The power of this conception constrains the vigor of government initiatives involving the modification of citizens' preferences. As a result, government is typically relatively unsophisticated in its methods for modifying consumer preferences. For example, consider the difference between the sophistication and pervasiveness of private sector advertising for automobiles, soft drinks, and the like as compared to the typical government brochure or public service announcement designed to discourage smoking, drug use, or behaviors that can lead to the transmission of AIDS. Furthermore, consider what public reaction would likely be if the federal government mounted an antidrug advertising campaign of a magnitude, sophistication, and expense comparable to contemporary advertising campaigns by car manufacturers, beer makers, soft drink companies, or any number of other corporations. The evident lack of legitimacy for such preference manipulation on the part of government can be traced to the liberal principle of consumer sovereignty.

The second type of constraint in the development of drug prevention programs is the dilemma of unintended consequences of information dissemination. Although many educational campaigns about drugs are designed to discourage drug use by making individuals, and especially youth, more aware of the potential harmful effects of drugs, many people fear that heightened awareness of drugs may actually lead to drug use. In part, this is because antidrug campaigns that use celebrities who have overcome drug problems can unintentionally glamorize drug use and subtly suggest that drug abuse is an easily surmountable problem. In addition, drug use may seem more acceptable if it appears to be a widespread activity in society, and saturating the schools and the airwaves with messages about drug use can give just such an impression. Finally, prevention programs that offer an accurate portrayal of the pharmacological effects of drugs may encourage drug use because some of those effects seem enticingly pleasurable to youth and because accurate information underscores the fact that not all users die or become permanently addicted. In contrast, antidrug campaigns that sacrifice some accuracy for the sake of scaring youth away from drugs run the risk of delegitimizing the entire antidrug effort as individuals discover from other sources that the information is inaccurate.

Because of the constraints just discussed, drug abuse prevention programming is far from fully developed and lacks much in sophistication. As this chapter will show, existing research suggests that most of what has been done in the name of drug abuse prevention has been of very limited effectiveness. However, some newer approaches to drug prevention are being attempted. These approaches, and the available effectiveness data on them, are considered as well.

THE SCOPE OF DRUG ABUSE PREVENTION

Just as law enforcement and treatment responses to the drug problem have a relatively long policy history in the United States, drug prevention policies extend back many years before the contemporary war on drugs. As early as 1970, the federal government had a small drug education program within the Office of Education, designed as a formula grant program to provide monies for teacher training in school systems nationally and to set up demonstration programs in a number of colleges and communities. By 1972, $13 million was budgeted for these Office of Education programs.[2] In 1973, however, an interesting hiatus developed. In response to recommendations by the National Commission on Marihuana and Drug Abuse, the White House agency responsible for coordinating drug policy at the time called a temporary halt to the dissemination of drug information.[3] Presumably, criticism regarding the ineffectiveness of drug education messages and even concerns that drug education might be counterproductive prompted this unusual policy reversal.

In the years between 1973 and 1979, drug prevention programs languished within the bureaucracy of the federal government, with relatively low levels of funding. There was considerable discussion, planning, and research about suitable approaches. In 1979, prevention was given added visibility and funding when Congress stipulated that a certain portion of the budget of the National Institute on Drug Abuse (NIDA) be earmarked for prevention programming. As a result, spending on drug abuse prevention increased from $6.2 million in 1979 to $12.8 million in 1980 and $16.1 million in 1981.[4]

Yet another large jump in funding for drug prevention occurred as a result of the Anti–Drug Abuse Act of 1986 (enacted, as noted in Chapter 4, when crack cocaine catapulted to high levels of public and government concern). The Drug-Free Schools and Communities Act, incorporated within that omnibus drug legislation, strongly emphasized prevention efforts and created yet another new bureaucratic organization—the Office of Substance Abuse Prevention (OSAP). OSAP was to devise demonstration programs in the drug prevention area, provide technical assistance to state and local government, and serve as a central clearinghouse for dissemination of drug prevention information. With this new legislation, federal funding for drug abuse prevention jumped from $24 million in 1986 to $249 million in 1987. Most of this funding went to the federal Department of Education, which provides grants to states and local schools for drug abuse prevention programming; $43 million went to

OSAP.[5] As of March 1989, over $125 million had been expended through the Drug-Free Schools and Communities Act, largely in grants to states and localities.[6] Actual expenditures for drug abuse prevention programs run out of the Department of Education amounted to $608.9 million in 1991 and are estimated to total $626.8 million in 1992.[7]

Spending on prevention programs has clearly increased, especially since passage of the Drug-Free Schools and Communities Act, but it is still a tiny portion of the total federal drug budget. And, as Edward Zubrow, a school official in Philadelphia, noted before Congress in 1989, the amount of federal funding devoted to drug prevention is very small compared to the magnitude of the problem:

> Congress currently appropriates about $345.5 million nationally for the drug abuse education efforts under the Drug-Free Schools and Communities Act, of which inner-city schools receive about $13.7 million or 4 percent—in contrast to the 12 percent of the Nation's students they enroll, most of whom are those highly at risk for drug use. Not only is the $9—on average—spent per child by the Federal Government inadequate to address the Nation's drug problems, but the $3.50 spent for each urban child borders on the scandalous.[8]

TYPES OF DRUG ABUSE PREVENTION PROGRAMS

Whether enough resources are being devoted to drug prevention, especially relative to drug-law enforcement and treatment, is a debatable and highly charged issue. At the moment, however, millions of public dollars are being devoted to drug abuse prevention. What sorts of efforts are being supported with these funds? Are there competing approaches, as there are competing approaches to drug treatment? The following sections describe various drug prevention programs that have been used.

Prevention: Educational Approaches

A recent study suggests that drug education programs can be divided into three different types that "(1) focus on providing factual information about drugs; (2) emphasize attitudes, feelings, and values; or (3) try to influence behavior" through the introduction of alternatives to drug use.[9] A fourth type focusing on "social resistance skills" has recently emerged, with the intent to provide the young with skills necessary to resist social pressures for substance use.

The first, the informational approach, is based upon the assumption that full, factual information about the dangers of drug use will deter individuals, and especially young people, from using drugs. The importance of using accurate, factual information rather than hyperbole and scare tactics can be illustrated by the reaction to the film *Reefer Madness*, developed in the 1930s as part of the campaign against marijuana use in that period. That film, which shows people instantly degenerating into fiendishly antisocial characters after a single puff of marijuana smoke, was never an effective deterrent. Instead, it became a cult classic among youth who found its exaggerated approach to be hilarious. More contemporary antidrug campaigns may run the same danger in their effort to deliver high-impact messages, according to Jean Rhodes and Leonard Jason. They argue that a particular television ad comparing the effects of drugs on the brain with two eggs frying in a pan "may run contrary to the experience of many adolescents, and ultimately this unrealistic message may reduce the believability of entire drug related campaigns."[10]

As indicated in the introduction to this chapter, the informational approach labors under the problem of unintended consequences—the possibility that full and accurate information may actually encourage drug use among some individuals. There is, in fact, some evidence that drug information programs have had this effect.[11] Furthermore, the informational approach is based upon the assumption that the use of drugs is a purely rational decision based upon an assessment of the costs and benefits of drug use. By implication, information campaigns that more fully lay out the dangers of drug use are expected to deter drug use through changing the individual's cost-benefit calculus.[12] However, most studies of drug use by youth suggest that this rational model is not accurate. Rather than an individual, rational decision-making process, the choice of drugs is evidently a social, emotive process. It is, in other words, based more upon peer pressure, exerted in social settings and playing upon the individual's need for acceptance, fear of embarrassment, and desire to be part of the group.[13]

Drug prevention programs that are purely informational can also be criticized because they do nothing to directly affect the *motivation* of the individual or the person's ability to respond appropriately to the information that is presented. In response to this limitation, a second, affective type of prevention program attempts to reinforce self-esteem, clarify values, and improve interpersonal skills, presumably strengthening resources the individual can use to resist the temptations of drugs. This approach is based on recognition that people's behavior is strongly influenced by their peers and that the desire to be accepted by others can prompt young people to experiment with drugs despite warnings from the adult world. Consequently, effective prevention programs have to equip young people with specific skills and psychological support so that they are less likely to be overwhelmed by peer pressure.

The third type of program, offering alternatives, emphasizes the provision of wholesome social and recreational activities that are alternatives to drug use. "The underlying assumption is that if adolescents have satisfying real-life experiences, involvement in these activities will take the place of involvement with substance abuse."[14] For example, in some communities, local organizations run late-night youth basketball leagues to provide an activity that is an explicit alternative to involvement with gangs and drugs. The more primitive of the alternatives programs simply involve the creation of youth centers where an array of activities presumed to be appealing to youth could be organized. A more complex form of the alternatives approach attempts to tailor specific activities to specific individuals whose unmet needs are presumed to leave them vulnerable to substance abuse. Gilbert Botvin describes the approach:

> For example, the desire for physical relaxation or more energy might be satisfied by alternative activities such as athletics, exercise, or hiking. The desire for sensory stimulation might be satisfied through alternatives that enhance sensory awareness, such as learning to appreciate the sensory aspects of music, art, and nature. Interpersonal needs, such as gaining peer acceptance for individuals who are rebelling against authority, might be satisfied through participation in sensitivity training or encounter groups.[15]

Like informational approaches, the alternatives approach carries some potential for unintended, counterproductive results. Studies have suggested that drug use is more, rather than less, likely among youth who are more involved in social and entertainment activities. For this reason, researchers caution that the choice of alternative activities must be made carefully, not only to fit with the unmet needs of youth but also with an awareness of the potential for facilitating occasions for substance use.[16]

The fourth and newest type of substance abuse prevention program draws elements from both the informational and the affective types but primarily emphasizes the teaching of skills needed to resist social pressures toward tobacco, alcohol, and drug use. This type of program is based upon the innovative efforts of a group of University of Houston researchers in the late 1970s. They drew upon a theory called psychological inoculation to develop their program for substance abuse prevention. According to this theory, people are as regularly exposed to social pressures for alcohol, tobacco, and drug use as they are to disease-causing germs. Hence, just as they must be inoculated in order to develop antibodies to resist disease, so also must they be exposed to artificially induced versions of social pressures for drug or alcohol use so that they can develop resistance to substance abuse pressures. Initial programs, directed at prevention of smoking by adolescents, yielded very promising results.[17]

Resistance skills training has also been applied to the drug prevention area. One of the most widely used and best-known of these drug resistance programs is Project DARE (Drug Abuse Resistance Education), initiated by the Los Angeles Police Department and the Los Angeles schools. It is aimed at students in the fifth through seventh grades and is designed to give them "the skills and motivation needed to resist peer pressure to use drugs, alcohol, and tobacco."[18] The program uses uni-

formed police officers, who teach a 17-session curriculum at each participating school. A similar program called Project SPECDA (School Program to Educate and Control Drug Abuse) was implemented in the New
York City schools in 1987,[19] and Project DARE itself has been implemented in a host of communities across the country. Kentucky Fried
Chicken, Inc., which has become a corporate sponsor of the program,
states that there are more than 500 DARE programs across the country,
reaching 1.5 million children.[20]

Because of widespread recognition of the power of peer influence,
other programs utilizing the resistance skills training approach make use
of peer leaders and trainers in addition to teachers, police officers, and
other adult authority figures. One example, called STAR (Student-
Taught Awareness and Resistance), consists of ten sessions of about an
hour each, handled by a teacher, a program assistant, and peer leaders se-
lected by their classmates and given special training. Through role playing, peer leaders illustrate the use of skills for resisting pressures toward
substance abuse in a variety of social situations. The other students are
then taught to identify the social situations in which they are likely to
be placed at risk, and they practice the use of those skills for resisting social pressures.[21]

In their most elaborate form, social resistance programs incorporate
training in a broad array of personal and social skills, some directly related to potential substance abuse and some much more indirectly.
These broad programs, focusing on "life skills," are designed to prevent
problem behavior of many kinds. Life skills programs typically involve
at least two of the following emphases: (1) problem-solving skills, (2) cognitive skills for resisting persuasive appeals, (3) training to build self-
esteem, (4) stress-reduction techniques, (5) general interpersonal skills,
and (6) assertiveness training.[22]

A combination of these approaches can be used. Consider, for example, the Philadelphia schools. That district spent nearly $1.5 million on
drug prevention programming in 1988–1989. A standardized curriculum
on drugs, provided by the Department of Health and Physical Education,
is taught in kindergarten through grade 12. In addition, kindergarten and
grade school students are taught a state-approved alcohol and drug abuse
curriculum emphasizing social skills, bonding, refusal skills, and information about the effects of chemical dependence. Middle school students are exposed to a program offered by the Jewish Family and Children's Service Agency, which stresses peer support groups to help young
people resist drugs. The schools also cooperate with Project DARE, the
police department–based drug prevention program. In the high schools,
some 48,000 students are in peer-group counseling programs. Other programs train teachers to identify substance abuse problems and make re-
ferrals to appropriate intervention and treatment agencies. Meanwhile,
the city board of education has banned the use of beepers, expelled students found to be involved with drugs and weapons, and initiated its own

drug activity investigative unit. Edward Zubrow, special assistant to the superintendent of the Philadelphia public schools, notes that each school in the Philadelphia system has been asked to establish a 1,000-foot drug-free zone around the school and to work with law enforcement authorities and community leaders to find ways to determine how a zero tolerance for drugs within the zone can be implemented.[23]

Prevention: Deterrence Methods

The various types of drug prevention programming are largely targeted to youth and based upon educational models of prevention. Recently, a different form of drug prevention program has been developed—targeted to adults as well as youth and based upon a deterrence model of prevention. At the federal level, this approach to drug prevention was spearheaded by initiatives in the Reagan administration. The philosophy behind this approach was clearly articulated by William Bennett, then secretary of the federal Department of Education, in congressional testimony in 1986:

> We are strongly in favor of drug education programs, but I have to point out, Mr. Chairman, whether mandated or not, almost every school district in this country has drug education programs, and we are still awash in drugs. Education programs can be helpful. They can be a useful auxiliary. But what we need, and what the evidence shows works, is a firm, clear and consistent policy on the part of the adult's and the child's community—principals, teachers, parents, police. . . . We need to get tough, and we need to get tough as hell, and we need to do it right now.[24]

Support for this philosophy of drug prevention is also evident in the comments of Congressman E. Clay Shaw, Jr., of Florida:

> The problem cannot be solved just simply by teaching kids that drugs will hurt them, that drugs are wrong. The kids already know that. . . . The answer to this problem, if there is an answer . . . is discipline within the school itself. . . . The schools themselves are putting up with the rotten apples that are poisoning the whole barrel. They ought to make the kids either straighten up or throw their bottoms out of school.[25]

"Zero tolerance" became the label for this philosophy of prevention. Zero tolerance meant "clear and firm enforcement of the laws and rules against drug use and drug dealing in schools, and expulsion of violators."[26] Although it may have been largely symbolic policy, the zero-tolerance or deterrence approach was evident in 1989 amendments to the Drug-Free Schools and Communities Act. These amendments mandate that schools and colleges document for the federal Department of Education that they have implemented a plan to prevent use of illegal drugs and abuse of alcohol by both students and staff. The prevention strategy has to include yearly dissemination to all students and employees of a code of conduct that clearly prohibits possession, use, or distribution of illicit drugs, along with a list of penalties (such as expulsion, firing, and turning in for prosecution) for violating the code. Educational institutions that fail to meet the requirements of the Drug-Free Schools and Communities Act are threatened with loss of eligibility for federal funds.[27]

This deterrence or zero-tolerance approach has also been reflected in a number of state-level initiatives. For example, Secretary of Education Bennett praised the state of Oregon, which "says that if you use drugs, you forfeit the right to get your driver's license for six months or a year. . . . This is tough. That's a tough law, but it sure gets young people's attention because people want to drive."[28]

The demand reduction program implemented in 1989 in Maricopa County, Arizona, also illustrates this approach. Its goal is to deter demand for drugs from casual or occasional drug users through the use of high-visibility crackdowns on those buying drugs. People arrested in such crackdowns are formally booked so that they get a taste of some time in the jail intake facility. If they meet specified criteria (such as no prior felony drug arrests), they are then offered an alternative to prosecution. Prosecution on the drug charge is temporarily suspended if the individual agrees to a specified set of activities, typically including a written admission to the drug charge, completion of a drug abuse treatment program, and mandatory drug testing for the duration of the treatment program. The individual is also expected to pay a fee to cover the cost of participation in the treatment and monitoring program. Those who do not successfully complete the requirements of their alternative agreement are prosecuted on the original drug charge.[29]

The Maricopa County program is obviously based in law enforcement institutions. But several features make it a prevention program, not a drug-law enforcement program. First, it is intended to reduce demand rather than to interrupt the supply of drugs. Second, the law is used more as a threat to deter drug use than as a penalty. This is evident in the design of the program, which diverts arrestees from the criminal justice process once they have had a preliminary exposure to instill a fear of jail time. It is also evident in the use of the media to convey deterrence messages. The program relies upon the local broadcast and print media to convey the message that anyone caught using drugs will face felony drug charges and a prison sentence or else have to pay for a year-long treatment program.[30]

The deterrence methods introduced in the Reagan administration under Secretary of Education William Bennett and manifested in state and local programs continued to receive emphasis in the Bush administration, under the label "user accountability." As explained in the national drug policy statement for 1992, user accountability is viewed as a key to prevention:

Holding casual users accountable for their actions through meaningful criminal, civil, and social sanctions is integral to the National Drug Control Strategy . . . . the casual user . . . imparts the message that you can use drugs and still do well in school or maintain a career and family. On the presumption that law enforcement not only punishes but also instructs, laws and policies directed toward holding users accountable deter drug use by providing clear consequences for possessing or using illegal drugs.[31]

Prevention: Mass Media Approaches

Much of the attention in the drug abuse prevention field is focused on school-based programs directed at youth. However, no assessment of the nation's efforts at drug abuse prevention would be complete without acknowledgement of the use of the mass media for antidrug publicity. While not nearly as pervasive or as sophisticated as the advertising for many products, advertising directed against drug use had become noticeably more prevalent by the late 1980s. In 1986, for example, NIDA developed an advertising campaign called "Cocaine, the Big Lie," targeted at the young adult audience and designed to provide information about the social, medical, and psychiatric problems caused by cocaine use. The campaign, which featured ex-users of cocaine, baseball stars, and First Lady Nancy Reagan, was developed with the help of the Advertising Council, a group of advertising agencies and media organizations that help to develop and disseminate public service announcements. The 13 ads developed as part of this campaign were aired between 1,500 and 2,500 times per month in the 75 local television markets monitored by NIDA.[32]

A considerable amount of antidrug advertising is the handiwork of the Media Partnership for a Drug-Free America, whose ads can be found everywhere from billboards to newspapers to television ads to the yellow pages of telephone books. The Media Partnership is a voluntary organization rather than a government agency, and it relies upon donated air time and advertising space. Its spokespersons indicate that the group has been making use of $1 billion worth of such donated time and space per year.[33] Many media-based antidrug spots have featured well-known personalities (athletes or actors) insisting in somber tones that drug use has serious consequences, including death.

EFFECTIVENESS OF PREVENTION PROGRAMS

The conventional wisdom about drug prevention programs generally, and the traditional informational types in particular, is that they are simply ineffective. This conventional wisdom is to be found not only in the conversations of average Americans but in the statements of some of the most important drug policy decision makers in the United States. For example, in testimony in 1987 before the House Select Committee on Narcotics Abuse and Control, William J. Bennett, then secretary of education, articulated this conclusion:

> You know, there's an awful lot of drug education going on in the United States. Before these Acts were passed into law, we estimated some 80 or 85 percent of American schools had drug education programs and drug use was still increasing. I know there is a modest kind of sweet faith on the part of some that if you have a drug education course, young people will change their minds. In fact, there's no evidence that that's the case at all.[34]

Unfortunately, evaluation research tends to confirm that educational programs have disappointing results. In general, the research suggests that educational and prevention programs can transfer information to target populations and can even enhance negative attitudes about drug abuse; yet there is no evidence that they can affect behavior itself in the form of lessened use of drugs.[35] This is especially true of straightforward information approaches; effectiveness studies "indicate quite clearly that increased knowledge has virtually no impact on substance use or on intentions to engage in tobacco, alcohol, or drug use in the future."[36] Despite this unencouraging evidence, substance abuse prevention programs of the informational type are the most widespread. Jean Rhodes and Leonard Jason speculate that school officials may not be aware of the professional research showing the ineffectiveness of this approach and that this approach remains popular because straightforward informational programs are "inexpensive and easily delivered."[37]

Drug prevention programs of the affective type appear to be equally ineffective. "Although affective-education approaches have, in some instances, been able to demonstrate an impact on one or more of the correlates of substances abuse, they have not been able to affect substance-use behavior."[38] Improving self-esteem and developing negative attitudes about substance abuse, it seems, do not necessarily translate into changes in individuals' actual decisions about the use of alcohol, tobacco, and drugs.

To round out the disappointing news, antidrug campaigns in the mass media have yielded mixed results at best. Many public service ad campaigns are not evaluated at all. One exception is an evaluation of the Media Partnership for a Drug-Free America, which suggests that in areas targeted for more intense exposure to the antidrug campaign, the drug attitudes of people surveyed afterward were more strongly influenced than were the attitudes of people in areas less intensively exposed to the campaign.[39] But generally, media antidrug campaigns have no effects on behavior, and some have even been linked to an increase in substance abuse.[40]

These disappointing results should hardly be surprising. Research on public service advertising in general suggests that in order to have any chance of impact, such advertising must meet a number of obvious but difficult standards. For one thing, public service ads must reach their intended audience, and do so with a reasonable amount of repetition. Since public service announcements rely upon donated air time and publishing space, however, they have often been relegated to non–prime time television spots and print-copy fill-in spots. There have been improvements in this regard. For example, almost half of the substance abuse spots aired on ABC in 1985 were, according to the network, aired in prime time. Nevertheless, one-fifth of ABC's public service announcements were aired late at night.[41]

In addition, media campaigns need to "de-emphasize the use of information-dissemination and fear-arousal strategies and place greater emphasis on strategies designed to combat the powerful social influences to smoke, drink, or use drugs."[42] Unfortunately, it is not necessarily self-evident what strategies other than simple information dissemination and fear arousal could be used in mass media campaigns. The American advertising industry uses highly sophisticated strategies and techniques to sell a variety of products; ads appear to rely largely upon associating the product with pleasurable images (e.g., driving through gorgeous scenery with an attractive companion in the next seat, or being immersed in the sun, fun, and excitement of a youthful romp at the beach while enjoying one's beer). However, it is not clear how one might "sell" the refusal of a product rather than the product itself. And there has been virtually no research on "the styles and content formats that may most attract audience attention"[43] to public service announcements.

In contrast with the discouraging evidence reported so far, evaluations suggest that substance abuse prevention programs of the social resistance type are effective. Most of these evaluations have concentrated on the impact of social resistance programs on cigarette smoking rather than drug use,[44] though some research documents effectiveness with respect to alcohol and marijuana use. For example, evaluations of the STAR program, largely conducted by the designers of the program, have shown that students in the program have improved social skills, better grades, and less drug use.[45] Initial evaluations of Project DARE suggest that the program has a positive impact on students' work habits and grades and on abstinence from alcohol, cigarettes, and drugs.[46]

Although the effectiveness studies to date leave us with the conclusion that social resistance programs are the most promising, there are important problems with such programs as well. These include problems of complexity (the programs focus on too many different social skills and expect more different kinds of behavioral change than is realistic), problems of cost (the programs take a substantial amount of school time and typically come in the form of relatively expensive packages of manuals, films, guides, and consulting fees), problems of dissemination (because of the programs' complexity and sophistication, it may be impossible to train instructors adequately across the nation to deliver the programs in schools), and problems of relevancy (the programs are designed around the values and cultural assumptions of white, middle-class populations and may not be readily applicable to other target groups).[47]

CONCLUSIONS

In many ways, drug abuse prevention is at a crossroads in the United States. Burdened with a history of ineffective and disappointing programs, the drug prevention field has recently turned to a new approach involving resistance skills, which is showing promising signs of impact. And a number of other innovations, such as deterrence-based approaches, are being attempted.

Several important challenges still lie in the path of drug prevention. One is the evaluation challenge. Because traditional approaches have been so disappointing, newer approaches will be asked to carefully document evidence of results. This pressure for evaluation is evident in calls from the federal government for drug prevention funding to be linked to evidence of program success. John Walters, a special assistant to the secretary of education, has explained:

> We would like to require local school districts to assess the scope of their problem and report it to State authorities on a yearly basis as they receive money under the Act, to show progress in reducing student drug use and to show they have effective policies and effective programs based on what we know works from our own research. And we want that continued funding to the local school district contingent on demonstrating results or willingness to change programs that are not efficient.[48]

Although the demand for documented results seems reasonable, it does pose some dilemmas. An approach that emphasizes documented results can interfere with the impulse to innovate and with the decentralization and local control that are central values in the American educational system. Congressman Edolphus Towns of New York points out problems:

> It seems the Education Department wants strict accountability on one hand, but, on the other hand, wants States to take the initiative to find solutions. I'm afraid you cannot have it both ways. Either the Federal Government will provide strong oversight and an effective plan or 50 different States will use 50 different approaches. Let's face it, solutions will not be found unless there is a common plan capable of alterations which will accommodate individual differences. The Federal Government must provide the blueprint for the local schools.[49]

Note, however, that this can run afoul of the strong tradition in this country of local control of schools and local autonomy in what is taught in them. While a number of states have curriculum requirements of various kinds, the notion of going beyond a federal mandate to have an antidrug curriculum to a mandate that specifies the content of the curriculum is problematic.

Furthermore, the demand for evaluation to demonstrate which drug prevention programs are effective runs up against some thorny problems. Presumably, what we really want to know about these programs is whether they reduce the uptake of drugs by members of the target group. However, as documented in Chapter 1, it is impossible to assess the level of drug use and abuse with any precision; and because most drugs are used by only a very small fraction of the American public, accurate estimates of change in use levels would be needed in order to begin to assess the impact of prevention programs.[50] Even with such information, it would be impossible, without carefully constructed experimental and control groups, to know how much observed change in drug use is attributable to prevention programs rather than other factors. Such experimental designs require more care, financing, and autonomy from political pressures than most educational and mass media campaigns can muster. Even if such experimental designs were in place, timing of the evaluation poses a problem, as Kleiman argues:

> [Six] years must pass before we can start to measure the effects of a program aimed at sixth-graders on their drug-use status at graduation from high school. Six years is a long time to wait between the first trial and the first results, and a long time in the history of schools and drugs. The knowledge that Program X was a good program six years ago is only mildly helpful in determining its usefulness today; the kids have changed, the schools have changed, and the drug scene has changed.[51]

Another challenge facing drug abuse prevention is the likelihood that ongoing conflict over the nature of the drug problem will cause conflict over the content of drug abuse prevention curricula and messages. There is a substantial consensus in this country that prevention is a crucial point of attack on the drug problem. A Gallup poll conducted in January 1990 asked which of various activities in the government's fight against drugs deserves the most money and effort. The largest share of votes, 40 percent, went to "teaching young people about the dangers of drugs." (The next most popular priority, chosen by 28 percent of respondents, was "working with foreign governments to stop the exporting of drugs to this country.")[52] But despite the consensus over the importance of preventing drug abuse, there is far from a consensus over what should be said in prevention campaigns. This lack of consensus stems not so much from the disappointing results of many drug abuse prevention programs, as documented in this chapter, but from ideological differences in people's orientation to the drug problem generally. As Franklin Zimring and

Gordon Hawkins[53] note, those with a legalistic approach to the problem distrust informational strategies and wish to emphasize a moralistic message about the evils of drugs; those who strongly believe that some drugs are more dangerous than others want to emphasize precision and accuracy of information. These people want to avoid trivializing warnings about heroin, for example, which could occur in a mixed campaign that exaggerates the dangers of substances such as marijuana. Because such a "specifist" approach does not offer across-the-board preaching against drug use, however, it raises the ire of those with a legalistic orientation. In short, even while drug prevention programmers struggle to develop and evaluate educational campaigns that can show an impact on the attitudes and behavior of their target audience, their efforts are likely to become embroiled in broader conflicts over the drug issue.

But perhaps the most daunting challenge facing the drug prevention field is how to counter the flood of positive drug-oriented messages in American society. Steven Jonas argues that America has a highly drug-oriented culture and that this interferes with efforts to prevent drug abuse through education. As evidence for America's drug culture, Jonas notes that legal drugs, such as alcohol, cigarettes, and over-the-counter medicines, are heavily promoted through advertising. The third-highest category of magazine advertising expenditure is for smoking-related products, and the ninth-highest is for beer, wine, and liquor. A total of $428 million is spent annually for advertising of beer and wine on network television—the fifth-highest category of television advertising expenditures. The fourth-highest category of spending on network advertising is over-the-counter medication. Taken together, all this advertising of recreational drugs and medications feeds what Jonas calls "America's drug culture." The result, he argues, is the undermining of efforts to prevent illegal drug abuse:

> Most present prevention efforts for all drugs focus on public education. But what impact can a "Don't do cocaine" ad, delivered during a football game telecast by a serious, active football player, have when it is followed a few minutes later by a "Do do alcohol" ad, delivered by a group of jolly ex-football players? ... The fundamental inconsistency of the negative message dooms it to failure for most beholders. Young people, especially ... cannot be expected to readily say no to crack when they are bombarded with messages imploring them to say yes to alcohol and tobacco.[54]

Despite these many challenges, prevention represents a promising arena for drug policy. It offers the potential for dealing with the drug problem in ways that are less coercive, less expensive, and of more enduring value than the outcomes of either drug abuse treatment or drug rehabilitation. However, designing prevention programs that have a substantial impact while dodging the pitfalls of political controversy over the moral appropriateness of their content will be a daunting balancing act for the foreseeable future.

NOTES

1. Steven E. Rhoads, *The Economist's View of the World* (Cambridge: Cambridge University Press, 1985).
2. William Bukoski, "The Federal Approach to Primary Drug Abuse Prevention and Education," in James Inciardi, ed., *Handbook of Drug Control in the United States* (New York: Greenwood Press, 1990), p. 94.
3. Bukoski, 1990, pp. 96–97.
4. Bukoski, 1990, pp. 100–104.
5. Bukoski, 1990, p. 108.
6. U.S. House of Representatives, Select Committee on Narcotics Abuse and Control, *Educating America's Youth Against Drugs: Federal Drug Abuse Education Strategy* (Washington, DC: U.S. Government Printing Office, 1989c), p. 77.
7. White House, *National Drug Control Strategy: Budget Summary* (Washington, DC: Office of National Drug Control Policy, 1992), p. 30.
8. Select Committee on Narcotics Abuse and Control, 1989c, p. 42.
9. National Institute of Justice, *Searching for Answers: Research and Evaluation on Drugs and Crime* (Washington, DC: U.S. Department of Justice, 1990), pp. 24–25.
10. Jean E. Rhodes and Leonard A. Jason, *Preventing Substance Abuse Among Children and Adolescents* (New York: Pergamon, 1988), p. 21.
11. J. D. Swisher, J. L. Crawford, R. Goldstein, and M. Yura, "Drug Education: Pushing or Preventing?" *Peabody Journal of Education* 49 (1971), pp. 68–75; N. P. Gordon and A. L. McAlister, "Adolescent Drinking: Issues and Research," in T. J. Coates, A. C. Petersen, and C. Perry, eds., *Promoting Adolescent Health: A Dialog on Research and Practice* (New York: Academic Press, 1982).
12. Gilbert J. Botvin, "Substance Abuse Prevention: Theory, Practice, and Effectiveness," in Michael Tonry and James Q. Wilson, eds., *Drugs and Crime* (Chicago: University of Chicago Press, 1990), p. 465. © 1990 The University of Chicago. All rights reserved.
13. Donald Ian Macdonald, *Drugs, Drinking and Adolescents*, 2nd ed. (Chicago: Year Book Medical Publishers, 1990), p. 87.
14. National Institute of Justice, 1990, p. 25.
15. Botvin, 1990, p. 478.
16. J. D. Swisher and T. W. Hu, "Alternatives to Drug Abuse: Some Are and Some Are Not," in T. J. Glynn, C. G. Leukefeld, and J. P. Ludford, eds., *Preventing Adolescent Drug Abuse: Intervention Strategies* (Washington, DC: DHHS Publication no. [ADM] 83–1280, National Institute on Drug Abuse, 1983).
17. Botvin, 1990, pp. 489–490.
18. William DeJong, *Arresting the Demand for Drugs: Police and School Partnerships to Prevent Drug Abuse* (Washington, DC: National Institute of Justice, 1987), p. 4.
19. DeJong, 1987, p. 5.
20. Rick Aniskiewicz and Earl Wysong, "Evaluating DARE: Drug Education and the Multiple Meanings of Success," *Policy Studies Review* 9 (Summer 1990), p. 728.
21. Rhodes and Jason, 1988, 24.
22. Botvin, 1990, p. 496.

23. Select Committee on Narcotics Abuse and Control, 1989c, pp. 42–43.
24. U.S. House of Representatives, Select Committee on Narcotics Abuse and Control, *Drug Abuse Education* (Washington, DC: U.S. Government Printing Office, 1986), p. 23.
25. U.S. House of Representatives, Select Committee on Narcotics Abuse and Control, *Drug Abuse Prevention in America's Schools* (Washington, DC: U.S. Government Printing Office, 1987), p. 22.
26. Select Committee on Narcotics Abuse and Control, 1987, p. 35.
27. U.S. House of Representatives, Select Committee on Narcotics Abuse and Control, *Federal Strategy for Drug Abuse Education* (Washington, DC: U.S. Government Printing Office, 1990c), p. 64.
28. Select Committee on Narcotics Abuse and Control, 1987, p. 23.
29. Jan Chaiken, Marcia Chaiken, and Clifford Karchmer, *Multijurisdictional Drug Law Enforcement Strategies: Reducing Supply and Demand* (Washington, DC: National Institute of Justice, 1990), pp. 7–9.
30. Chaiken et al., 1990, p. 9.
31. White House, *National Drug Control Strategy* (Washington, DC: U.S. Government Printing Office, 1992), p. 36.
32. Avraham Forman and Susan B. Lachter, "The National Institute on Drug Abuse Cocaine Prevention Campaign," in Pamela Shoemaker, ed., *Communication Campaigns About Drugs* (Hillsdale, NJ: Erlbaum, 1989), pp. 16–17.
33. Mark Kleiman, *Against Excess: Drug Policy for Results* (New York: Basic Books, 1992), p. 176.
34. Select Committee on Narcotics Abuse and Control, 1987, p. 7.
35. National Institute of Justice, 1990, p. 25.
36. Botvin, 1990, p. 487.
37. Rhodes and Jason, 1988, p. 22.
38. Botvin, 1990, p. 487.
39. Kleiman, 1992, p. 176.
40. B. R. Flay and S. Sobel, "The Role of Mass Media in Preventing Adolescent Substance Abuse," in T. J. Glynn, C. G. Leukefeld, and J. P. Ludford, eds., *Preventing Adolescent Drug Abuse: Intervention Strategies* (Washington, DC: National Institute on Drug Abuse, Research Monograph 47, 1983).
41. Garrett J. O'Keefe and Kathaleen Reid, "The Uses and Effects of Public Service Advertising," in Larissa Grunig and James Grunig, eds., *Public Relations Research Annual*, vol. 2 (Hillsdale, NJ: Erlbaum, 1990), p. 68.
42. Botvin, 1990, p. 503.
43. O'Keefe and Reid, 1990, p. 83.
44. Botvin, 1990, p. 493.
45. Rhodes and Jason, 1988, p. 24.
46. DeJong, 1987, p. 4.
47. Rhodes and Jason, 1988, 27.
48. Select Committee on Narcotics Abuse and Control, 1987, p. 11.
49. Select Committee on Narcotics Abuse and Control, 1989c, p. 29.
50. Kleiman, 1992, p. 174.
51. Kleiman, 1992, p. 174.
52. Diane Colasanto, "Widespread Opposition to Drug Legalization," *Gallup Poll News Service* (Princeton, NJ: Gallup Organization, 1990), p. 4.
53. Franklin Zimring and Gordon Hawkins, *The Search for Rational Drug Control* (Cambridge: Cambridge University Press, 1992), pp. 12–13.
54. Steven Jonas, "The U.S. Drug Problem and the U.S. Drug Culture: A Public

Health Solution," in James Inciardi, ed., *The Drug Legalization Debate* (Newbury Park, CA: Sage, 1991), pp. 176–177.

Chapter
7

Domestic Drug-Law Enforcement

INTRODUCTION

The scene is familiar to anyone who watches television or films in the United States. A team of specialized police officers, clad in bulletproof vests and carrying a battering ram, swoop down on the home of a suspected drug dealer, announce their presence, and, after quickly gaining entry with the ram, rush in with guns drawn. Or a pair of undercover narcotics agents, dressed in stylish clothing and posing as drug dealers, sweat through their initial meeting with the drug supplier whose trust they hope to gain. These are the popular images of drug-law enforcement in the United States. Drug-law enforcement evokes yet other images as well—of U.S. government agents, along with their counterparts from Latin American countries, raiding clandestine laboratories in remote areas of the Andes. Because the nondomestic aspects of U.S. drug policy involve a host of complex foreign policy issues that are beyond the scope of this book, this chapter focuses primarily on domestic drug-law enforcement (including efforts to seal the nation's borders against the inflow of drugs).

The Scope of Drug-Law Enforcement

The familiarity of the images just mentioned suggests that drug-law enforcement is part of the fabric of American society. Official figures show that drug-law enforcement is indeed a substantial enterprise in this country. The budget of the federal Drug Enforcement Administration (DEA) alone was more than $750 million in 1991.[1] Across all agencies, the federal government devoted $3.47 billion to domestic drug-law enforcement in fiscal 1991, plus another $2.03 billion for interdiction of drugs at the border and an additional $1 billion for enforcement assistance to state and local governments.[2] Local public funds spent on drug-law enforcement by the thousands of police departments and sheriffs' offices in this country are not officially compiled, but the amount has been estimated to be nearly triple that spent by the federal government.[3] For example, the city of Houston devoted $171 million in local tax dollars to drug-law enforcement in 1989;[4] a single drug crackdown program in Manhattan cost $12 million annually in police salary costs alone.[5]

The magnitude of drug-law enforcement is also evident in the reported activities that these resources fund and in their spillover consequences for the courts and correctional institutions. In 1990, 869,000 arrests were made for drug law violations.[6] That same year, the DEA seized 549 clandestine drug laboratories.[7] A total of 19,271 defendants were processed in U.S. District Court in 1990 in cases involving the federal Drug Abuse, Prevention, and Control Act; 13,838 received prison sentences.[8]

Intergovernmental Features of Drug-Law Enforcement

Drug-law enforcement in the United States involves police agencies at the federal, state, and local levels. At the federal level, drug enforcement is the responsibility of the DEA, a unit of the federal Department of Justice. The DEA was created in 1973 through a reorganization of several competing drug enforcement units. Its responsibilities include the following:

- Investigation of major narcotics violators who operate at interstate and international levels;
- Enforcement of regulations governing the legal manufacture, distribution, and dispensing of controlled substances;
- Collection, development, analysis, and maintenance of intelligence information to support Federal, State, and local law enforcement;
- Coordination with Federal, State, and local law enforcement authorities and cooperation with counterpart agencies abroad;
- Training, research, and information exchange with other law enforcement agencies in support of drug traffic prevention and control, including development of new technology and scientific support to operational elements of DEA.[9]

Despite this apparently comprehensive role in drug-law enforcement, other federal agencies are also involved. The U.S. Customs Bureau is responsible for the interdiction of drug trafficking at all ports of entry, and the U.S. Marshals Service, the FBI, the Internal Revenue Service, and various U.S. attorneys within the Justice Department have become involved; a multiagency approach was instituted in 12 regional task forces in 1982–1983.

In addition, each of the 50 states has some agency charged with drug-law enforcement, such as the Oklahoma Bureau of Narcotics and Dangerous Drugs Control or the Missouri Bureau of Narcotics and Dangerous Drugs. Finally, local police agencies (police departments, county sheriffs' offices) are involved in drug-law enforcement, often through a specialized unit such as a vice squad or a narcotics team.

In Chapter 5, we saw that the key criterion in assessing the value of drug treatment is effectiveness—that is, does the treatment program generate the desired impacts on drug users? With respect to drug-law enforcement, effectiveness is also an important question. However, as this chapter will show, even when drug-law enforcement is effective at achieving one or another of its intended goals, it often creates issues in the form of undesirable, unintended consequences. Those unintended negative consequences may be viewed as nonmonetary costs, which are at least as important as the dollar costs of financing drug enforcement operations.

The first section of this chapter outlines the various strategies and tactics of drug-law enforcement. The second section focuses on the effectiveness of these law enforcement approaches in attaining desired goals. The final section discusses important negative consequences that must be balanced against the positive results of drug-law enforcement.

STRATEGIES AND TACTICS OF DRUG-LAW ENFORCEMENT

Because of differences in their powers and jurisdictional scope, drug-law enforcement programs at the federal level differ somewhat from state and local enforcement agencies. For example, activities such as interdiction of drugs at the border are the exclusive preserve of the federal government; state and local governments have no equivalent "border control" function. Despite such obvious differences, there are important commonalities between drug-law enforcement at different levels of government, and some enforcement activities involve agents from both the federal and local levels. For this reason, this section discusses enforcement strategies and tactics generically, though some uniquely local or uniquely federal strategies and tactics are included.

In general, available strategies for drug enforcement include (1) stakeouts, or surreptitious observation of drug trafficking in public places; (2) screening methods involving the discovery of drugs through routine searches of individuals or vessels, for example, at border crossings; (3) "buy-and-bust" methods, in which undercover agents make one or more purchases of drugs from suspects, then arrest and prosecute, using documentation of drug trafficking from the instigated drug buy; and (4) intensive investigatory approaches, which rely upon some combination of informants with high-level knowledge of an entire drug-trafficking organization, long-term wiretap surveillance, investigation of financial and other records, and often the building of a case using conspiracy statutes.[10] To this basic menu, we might add (5) eradication, which involves efforts to destroy illicit drugs at their point of origin. This menu of strategies has remained virtually unchanged over the long history of drug enforcement, though variants of each strategy have developed.

Each of the five strategies is an important tool in drug-law enforcement. Some, like the stakeout, tend to be used more episodically by general-purpose local police departments, while others, such as buy-and-bust or screening at border entry points, are part of the daily routine of specialized drug-law enforcement agencies. As the following sections show, each of these strategies involves important difficulties and limitations.

The Stakeout Strategy

Stakeouts are subject to an important limitation—namely, that the drug dealing that can be observed in public places typically involves only the lowest-level dealers.[11] Residents and officials in many cities complain about the existence of locations that are virtual drug bazaars, where drugs are openly bought and sold on the street and innocent passers-by are horrified at being approached by dealers. However, police efforts to make wholesale arrests of such drug dealers and buyers, by "sweeping the streets," typically net large numbers of relatively unimportant drug dealers who are easily replaced in the illicit drug market.[12] "Sweeping the streets" can overwhelm the criminal justice system with the sheer volume of cases it generates, without substantially affecting the drug market.[13]

Nevertheless, arrest sweeps occasionally become a popular tactic among law enforcement agencies. Chapter 4 details the zero-tolerance policy implemented by the Reagan administration in the late 1980s. Under this policy, individuals were arrested (and their vehicles or vessels seized) for possession of even very small amounts of drugs. Such a policy, which amounts to a national-level version of street sweeping, was quickly copied by at least one state—New Jersey. In hearings before the House Select Committee on Narcotics Abuse and Control, Peter Perretti, Jr., the attorney general for New Jersey, described this policy:

> The Action Plan further requires police officers to arrest all drug offenders, including juveniles, regardless of the quantity of drugs involved. No drug offense, in other words, is considered "too minor" to warrant an arrest. This

has become known throughout the country as New Jersey's version of "zero tolerance."[14]

Not surprisingly, New Jersey's zero-tolerance policy, like all street-sweeping tactics, netted a large number of individuals who were not major drug traffickers, and this clogged the arteries in the New Jersey criminal justice system. Figures presented by New Jersey state officials show that nearly 48,000 of the 65,317 drug-related arrests made in 1988 were in fact not for drug trafficking at all, but for simple possession and use of drugs; only 27 percent of drug-related arrests in that year were for sale or manufacturing of drugs.[15] Meanwhile, state officials acknowledged that this flood of new cases had adversely affected the court system:

> New Jersey's speedy trial goals, set by the New Jersey Supreme Court, cannot be met with existing resources; the backlog of defendants whose cases have failed to meet the goal of a 4-month period between indictment and disposition has grown to 12,400, and the backlog of cases awaiting indictment for more than the goal of 2 months has increased to more than 17,000 . . . . the magnitude of the drug problem is such that the criminal backlog continues to worsen.[16]

An important variant of the stakeout strategy, however, gained considerable attention in law enforcement circles. Focused crackdowns use a version of the stakeout strategy, but in limited, geographically targeted locations. One of the most visible examples was Operation Pressure Point I, a crackdown in a section of Manhattan instituted by Police Chief Benjamin Ward in 1984. Characteristic of crackdowns generally, Operation Pressure Point I was conceived as a temporary program, to last only two months. The temporary character of crackdowns is demanded by their relatively high costs. For local or state police departments, they involve temporary hiring or redeployment of personnel at costs that cannot be sustained indefinitely. In the initial weeks, Operation Pressure Point I yielded 65 arrests daily and made use of raids, an anonymous hot line, and intensified enforcement of traffic and parking regulations as ways of visibly affecting the drug market that was disrupting life in the target area.[17]

This crackdown and a similar one in Lynn, Massachusetts, have been studied carefully by Mark Kleiman, who suggests that the crackdown strategy can, in principle, be expected to have several desirable results. By disrupting drug marketing, even temporarily, crackdowns make access to drugs more difficult and presumably have some deterrent effect on drug use, especially for less experienced users who have fewer alternative sources of supply and who may be more intimidated by the threat of arrest. In addition, crackdowns occasionally uncover intelligence that can be used in higher-level investigations of drug-trafficking organizations. But perhaps most important, crackdowns are touted as a way of providing relief to neighborhoods that have been virtually destroyed by the traffic, noise, disruption, and violent behavior that accompany open drug dealing.[18]

Screening Methods: The Interdiction of Drugs

In the contemporary war on drugs, interdiction through enhanced screening methods has been a focal point of increased effort. In particular, the Reagan administration moved to more aggressively interdict illicit drug shipments by drawing upon the personnel and the technology of the military to detect and seize drug shipments as they were being floated or flown into the country. For example, in the period immediately following the Anti–Drug Abuse Act of 1986, the Defense Department provided about $360 million in mobile radar and ground sensor equipment; 17,000 hours of aerial surveillance to detect traffickers before they reached the border; over 28,000 hours of aerial support; and numerous other contributions of technology, technological training, and support for drug interdiction efforts.[19] In 1991, the federal government spent approximately $2.5 billion for various drug-related international and border control activities. Nearly $500 million was specifically for the U.S. Customs Bureau's interdiction program. For 1992, that program aimed, among other things, to examine about 20 percent of the containers entering the United States from drug source countries, or 4 percent of all containers entering the country; to fly nearly 50,000 hours of air interception time; and to operate 340 canine enforcement teams to examine cargo and passengers at ports of entry known to be susceptible to drug smuggling.[20]

The Buy-and-Bust Strategy

The buy-and-bust strategy involves the use of law enforcement officers, posing as drug buyers, to stage one or more drug purchases from traffickers who have been identified by surveillance, informants, or other means of intelligence. The buy-and-bust strategy has advantages over screening methods: police officers do not have to waste resources monitoring sites that do not yield observable drug transactions, and because officers are involved in the actual transaction, evidence can be secured more easily and direct testimony about the transaction can be had.[21]

On the other hand, the buy-and-bust strategy involves some dilemmas and drawbacks. Cases based on the strategy are vulnerable to defendants' claims of entrapment—the argument that the police created a crime that would not otherwise have occurred. In addition, each "bust" reveals the identity of an undercover officer, who may thereafter not be usable for the purpose, at least in the locale in which the bust was made; in this sense, the buy-and-bust strategy uses up a lot of police resources. The only way to deal with these problems is to modify the buy-and-bust strategy into somewhat longer-term covert operations, culminating in a bust only after a number of transactions. This has the virtue of providing ammunition against claims of entrapment, because the undercover buyer will have established the seller's willingness to engage in ongoing drug dealing. Other leads and information about participants in drug trafficking are likely to be picked up during the more extended operation, so the eventual bust will yield results that are more worthy of the "using up" of someone's cover.[22] As the next section shows, however, the more extended an undercover operation becomes, the more it is subject to a variety of other problems.

Intensive Investigation Strategy

The intensive investigation strategy, or what Mark Kleiman and Kerry Smith call "getting Mr. Big," involves long-term, elaborate case making targeted at major drug dealers. It differs from the buy-and-bust strategy in the extensiveness of the case development that precedes arrests. Such a strategy involves a variety of specific tactics, by now made familiar by dramatized versions of the drug enforcement scenario:

> Getting Mr. Big relies on . . . long-term, high-level undercover operations; developing informants, often by making cases against low-level dealers that can then be bargained away in return for their help against their suppliers ("working up the chain"); searching through police files, financial records, telephone logs, and the like to demonstrate connections; and, most powerful but most expensive, electronic surveillance (wiretaps and, less frequently, bugs).[23]

These long-term undercover operations pose a number of challenges and dilemmas, however. Law enforcement officers engaged in them are involved for a long period of time with drug dealers; they are entrusted with substantial amounts of money for drug purchases as they work their way up the ladder; and they must function in this environment without supervision and with limited accountability. Under these circumstances, the potential for corruption is high. The risk level is quite high as well. The longer the officer is under cover and the closer the officer gets to Mr. Big, the greater are the chances that the officer's identity will be discovered, with potentially fatal results. In addition, there are vexing legal and ethical issues, such as the amount of criminal activity that an undercover officer can rightfully be involved in during undercover work. Finally, such operations are resource-intensive, in that they involve highly specialized law enforcement officers who are tied up for long periods of time.[24] A number of splashy cases have been made through long-term undercover operations, and the entertainment industry has fixated on this approach in fictionalized accounts of drug enforcement; long-term undercover operations are not the standard, however, either for the federal DEA or local law enforcement agencies.[25]

There are other versions of the intensive investigation strategy. One enforcement method tracks money via monitoring of bank records and prosecutions of banking and income tax violations. An important tool for this is the Bank Secrecy Act of 1970, which requires that banks report currency transactions of more than $10,000 and that individuals report international transport of currency, bonds, and other financial instruments worth more than $10,000. In addition, the law demands that individuals under U.S. jurisdiction must report their involvement in financial accounts in foreign countries. An example of successful use of this approach to nab high-level drug traffickers was Operation Greenback, which began with the Treasury Department's discovery that the Miami branch of the Federal Reserve System had a huge excess of cash. The tracking of cash flow and assets of reputed drug-trafficking organizations in the area led to indictments against 51 defendants within a year and a half, and the government seized $20 million in currency.[26]

Ironically, the very lucrativeness of drug trafficking makes it susceptible to this form of investigation. Tremendous amounts of cash are generated, and the cash must either be physically smuggled out of the country or deposited in accounts at financial institutions. Smuggling the cash out involves obvious risks of being detected by authorities or "ripped off" by the courier. But managing large volumes of cash through financial institutions in this country without calling attention to oneself is difficult. If the transaction is detected, the monetary assets can be seized and forfeited through the provisions of the Bank Secrecy Act itself or through the asset forfeiture provisions of the Crime Control Act of 1984 (see Chapter 4). Individual traffickers can be subject to criminal prosecution based on violations of the Bank Secrecy Act or tax laws. Even if individual traffickers escape arrest, this strategy appears to be attractive because it can have a major financial impact on trafficking networks.

But, as Steven Wisotsky explains, drug traffickers use a number of methods to neutralize the effectiveness of this approach. For example, they can make deposits to phony accounts and then quickly wire them to accounts at foreign banks; they can divide huge sums into many different deposits of no more than $10,000; they can bribe bank employees to destroy the crucial reports that provide a paper trail to the depositor; or they can purchase entire banks for the sole purpose of money laundering. Furthermore, the sheer volume of reported transactions over $10,000 makes it difficult to discern drug money from legitimate transactions, unless authorities can link particular deposits to suspected drug-trafficking organizations on the basis of intelligence gained in other ways, such as undercover operations and informants.[27]

The Eradication Strategy

Eradication involves systematic efforts to choke off the supply of drugs by literally destroying the drugs at their source—the places where they are cultivated. For heroin and cocaine, this means the destruction of the opium poppy and coca plants in countries such as Laos, Thailand, Peru, and Bolivia, where they are grown for export; for marijuana, major countries of origin include Mexico, Colombia, and Jamaica. In these cases, eradication is obviously a matter of international agreement and joint activity. However, not all illicit substances are grown abroad. In recent years, the domestic cultivation of marijuana has expanded considerably; at least one-fourth of the marijuana sold in this country is now domestically produced.[28] Under these circumstances, campaigns to eradicate marijuana where it is cultivated constitute a domestic version of eradication strategy. The DEA, in collaboration with state and local law enforcement agencies that it assists, has engaged in this strategy.

For a number of years, the United States has relied primarily upon aerial spraying as the key element in its eradication campaigns. Beginning in 1990, however, the Bush administration signaled that aerial eradication was no longer its key focus,[29] presumably because such spraying programs display U.S. presence in countries where such a presence may be controversial and because spraying raises a number of environmental concerns. Other versions of eradication campaigns involve the use of satellite imaging technology and other intelligence efforts to locate clandestine crops, the sharing of such information with foreign governments, the provision of financial and other assistance for on-the-ground attempts to destroy crops in other countries, and high-level diplomacy focused on methods for replacing coca and poppy crops with other forms of economic activity.

THE EFFECTIVENESS OF DRUG-LAW ENFORCEMENT

There are several obstacles to easy assessment of drug-law enforcement. First is the lack of clarity about the goals of enforcement. In contrast with drug abuse treatment, where abstinence from use and increases in socially productive behaviors such as job holding are clear-cut and mutually compatible goals, law enforcement agencies confront a series of potentially conflicting goals: (1) minimizing the number of people using dangerous drugs and minimizing the drug-induced harms to these users (the goal of *drug abuse control*); (2) limiting the violence associated with drug trafficking (the goal of *crime control*); (3) disrupting the emergence of criminal organizations that profit from drugs (the goal of *organized-crime control*); and (4) protecting neighborhoods from threats to quality of life arising from drug dealing (the goal of *neighborhood protection*).[30] A strategy that effectively disrupts large, established criminal organizations, for example, might actually be counterproductive to the goal of limiting the violence associated with drug trafficking. The removal of a large criminal organization can effectively introduce competition into what was once a monopolistic drug market, bringing with it the violence that accompanies the struggle for market share. Similarly, strategies that focus on limiting the amount of drugs available to users may be counter-productive in regard to the goal of disrupting criminal organizations that profit from the drug trade. This is because effective drug-law enforcement against common traffickers will "eliminate those drug dealers who are least resistant to law-enforcement efforts and leave in place those drug traffickers who are most resistant, thereby exacerbating the organized-crime aspects of the drug problem."[31] In short, assessing effectiveness of drug enforcement begins with the question, Effective for what?

The sheer number and diversity of organizations involved in drug-law enforcement is another complicating factor. The absence of high-quality data on the intended impacts of drug-law enforcement is another. As noted in Chapter 1, various estimates of drug abuse, of quantities of drugs available, and of drug-related crime are available, but each has important weaknesses. And few estimates are available in a consistent, over-time series or in a comparable jurisdiction-by-jurisdiction form that would allow for evaluation of enforcement impact. These challenges to evaluation are amplified within individual law enforcement organizations—professionals in such organizations tend to dislike paperwork and record keeping and prefer tacit, informal evaluations of performance rather than the formal evidentiary evaluations of social and management science.[32]

Finally, evaluation of drug-law enforcement may not really be desired, either by enforcement practitioners or by the publics that they serve. Manning argues, "Drug police, like priests, are more important for what they symbolize and stand for than for what they do."[33] As we will see in Chapter 8, this symbolic importance is crucial to the long-term continuity in U.S. commitment to a law enforcement response to the drug issue, and we must acknowledge it if we are to understand why evaluative information about drug enforcement effectiveness is so limited and why there is so little consensus about the matter.

The Effectiveness of Interdiction

In principle, there are important problems and limitations with interdiction as a strategy for reducing the supply of drugs. On the one hand, the sheer volume of persons, parcels, and vessels to be screened and the number of miles of coastline and airspace to be monitored are overwhelming. Wisotksy, for example, notes that in a single year, U.S. Customs processed "more than 25 million entries of merchandise, 96.4 million carriers (vessels, aircraft, trucks, buses, cars, and trains), over 314 million passengers, 400 million pieces of luggage, and 84.4 million items of letter class mail."[34] Interdiction systems that screen only a small portion of this overwhelming volume will occasionally uncover a shipment of drugs. Use of intelligence to enhance information about where and when to search can enhance the odds of detection, as can the enhanced use of military resources. These stepped-up tactics of interdiction may be responsible for the relatively large numbers of successful interdictions in recent years and for the impressive size of many of the drug shipments seized.

The problem is that even these enhanced levels of interdiction are unlikely to be effective in stemming the drug supply or disrupting drug markets. The effects of any given seizure on any given drug trafficker are likely to be small, particularly since traffickers divide their shipments so that the loss of any one will not be so damaging. Even seizures that seem very large when publicized by drug-law enforcement authorities are likely to be only a small portion of the drug trafficker's total inventory.[35] Kleiman has also argued forcefully about the limitations of interdiction, when the logic of drug marketing is taken into account:

> But an economic analysis suggests that "interdiction"—seizures of bulk drugs—is of only limited usefulness, since the drugs that are cheap for the government to seize are also cheap for the dealers to replace. At an apparent ratio of several enforcement dollars spent per dollar of cost imposed on the illicit drug industry, interdiction does not appear to be a winning strategy.[36]

Stated another way, drug interdiction is easily seen to be no more than a cost of doing business for drug traffickers rather than a serious disruption of drug operations.

Effectiveness of the Stakeout, Buy-and-Bust, and Intensive Investigation Strategies

Although there is a surprising amount of agreement about the ineffectiveness of interdiction, there is no consensus about the appropriate emphasis to give to high-level investigations versus individual street-level busts versus arrest sweeps that net large numbers of low-level dealers and buyers. The lack of consensus stems partly from the fact that drug enforcement has multiple, conflicting goals and partly from lack of compelling evidence about the cost-effectiveness of any one strategy. However, on the basis of the logic of the situation, Mark Kleiman has argued that focusing resources on lower-level dealing, or "retail" sales, is more effective than going for Mr. Big.[37] His argument is based in part on the observation that "all of the money that feeds the illicit industry" stems from such retail sales. More important, he argues that going after major drug dealers deters drug use only to the extent that drug supplies are made more scarce and hence more expensive. But the profits of the remaining dealers are scarcely affected, and drug trafficking continues to thrive with a somewhat different cast of players. Furthermore, deterring drug use through tactics that raise prices carries with it undesirable side effects. Those who continue to use drugs are more likely to resort to crime to sustain their habit, for example. Kleiman argues that focusing enforcement resources on street-level sales discourages drug buying by making it riskier and more difficult for buyers to locate an appropriate seller. This has the potential to disrupt drug trafficking from below, without increasing drug prices.

However, Kleiman acknowledges that there is a different but important argument for going after Mr. Big—one based not on effectiveness but on justice. According to this view, "wealthy high-level drug dealers are obviously more important wrong-doers than street-level dealers," and hence they should be the primary target of our enforcement energy.[38]

Furthermore, there is a major drawback to an enforcement approach that emphasizes arrest sweeps at the retail level: the volume of arrests so generated creates an overload for the criminal justice system that must process those arrests.[39] The FBI's compilation of data from local law enforcement agencies across the country shows that in 1990, 869,000 individuals were arrested for drug violations.[40] In New York City, the proportion of arrests for drug offenses increased from 11 percent of the total in 1980 to 30 percent in 1988. This high volume of drug arrests "has placed tremendous burdens on already overloaded urban court systems, leading to severe overcrowding of detention facilities, increased prosecutor and public defender caseloads, case delay, and the need for substantial additional court resources."[41]

In practice, the choice of emphasis among these various strategies is likely to involve a complex array of political, organizational, and jurisdictional considerations. Local law enforcement agencies, for example, typically do not have the resources or the jurisdictional scope for truly high-level intensive investigations. "Complex, larger cases, as important as they might be for the attempt to control market movements and structure, are risky, [are] expensive for the organization and individual, and require skills and patience not possessed by most members" of typical law enforcement organizations.[42] On the other hand, drug enforcement officers at all levels presumably would find street sweeps to be much less glamorous and professionally interesting than undercover operations leading to busts of dealers somewhat higher up the trafficking hierarchy. Local enforcement agencies will periodically be under intense political pressure to engage in a visible action like a focused street sweep to respond to the complaints of citizens in neighborhoods disrupted by drug trafficking. And the DEA, while professionally inclined to go after Mr. Big, will also be inclined to devote resources to simpler buy-and-bust operations aimed at lower-level dealers whenever there is pressure to show immediate results.

Apart from these political and organizational imperatives, there are reasons to believe that the choice among these enforcement strategies should be contingent upon the type of drug targeted for enforcement. Crack, for example, is trafficked in many highly decentralized distribution networks. In order to have a noticeable impact on distribution of crack, officials must go through the expensive and dangerous process of infiltrating each of the subsidiary trafficking organizations. Hence, going after the crack version of Mr. Big is especially problematic. Heroin, in contrast, has traditionally been handled through "larger, well-integrated supply and distribution networks," which are more susceptible to a single operation that works its way up to Mr. Big.[43]

The Effectiveness of Eradication Programs

Eradication has not been an effective strategy in the war on drugs. For one thing, most eradication programs are complicated by the fact that they must be implemented by another country, whose internal politics and external relations with the United States may make drug eradication a difficult and frustrating venture. Furthermore, the supply of drugs to the United States will be only temporarily disrupted by a successful eradication program in a single country. Other sources of supply will quickly emerge to fill the gap. For example, when the supply of heroin from Turkey was interrupted in 1973–1974, a shortage of heroin developed in the United States, but within two years, Mexico and Southeast Asia had emerged as replacement sources of heroin.[44] And when imports of Mexican marijuana were disrupted in the early 1970s by a program that sprayed the crop with paraquat, a defoliant that frightened would-be users of the marijuana, Colombia simply took over as a supply source—a substitution that took only a few months.[45] The magnitude of the replacement problem is highlighted when one considers that the yearly consumption of heroin in the United States can be sustained by a poppy crop grown on only 25 square miles of land—a mere postage stamp of area compared to the acreage throughout the world that is suitable for cultivating the opium poppy.[46]

In short, the success of the eradication strategy is limited by two factors: (1) the unwillingness of some countries to readily cooperate with such efforts, especially if drugs represent an important source of export earnings in an otherwise impoverished economy or if drug eradication pits government authorities against powerful and wealthy drug cartels that can generate violent reprisals; and (2) the impossibility, within limited budgets, of finding and eradicating opium poppies, coca bushes, and marijuana plants simultaneously in the many and varied geographical locations where they can be grown.

Furthermore, even the limited successes and temporary disruptions yielded by foreign eradication (and interdiction) programs can lead to substitution with domestic supply sources—hardly a desirable outcome. With respect to marijuana, for example, efforts to choke off foreign supplies have simply fueled efforts to develop domestic cultivation programs. As a result, domestic cultivation now accounts for 25 percent of marijuana consumption in the United States.[47] Coca plants and opium poppies cannot as readily be cultivated in the United States. However, domestic alternatives to "harder" drugs such as cocaine and heroin can be produced domestically in clandestine laboratories. In particular, there is already a laboratory-produced alternative to cocaine—methamphetamine hydrochloride, or methedrine, a powerful stimulant. A smokable form of methamphetamine ("crystal meth" or "ice") has also been developed.[48]

When domestic production develops as a substitute for foreign production, eradication programs can, of course, be refocused on domestic supplies. However, domestic eradication programs have not been notably successful either. California's Campaign Against Marijuana Planting, or CAMP, is a visible example of this. National Drug Enforcement Policy Board figures show that the CAMP program cost $9.20 for each plant eradicated in 1984. This is not typical—eradication programs nationally averaged $1.33 per plant in 1984—but the figure suggests that commitment of resources to an eradication program may not yield cost-effective results. In addition, there is evidence that rather than eliminating marijuana cultivation, the CAMP program simply displaced it, or at least some portion of it, to the neighboring state of Oregon; and there is no evidence that eradication programs nationwide have had a discernible effect on the availability of marijuana in this country.[49] Even after years of drug enforcement and eradication efforts, the U.S. Forest Service reported in 1989 that extensive areas of federal land were being used to grow marijuana, and there is evidence as well that marijuana is increasingly being cultivated indoors in the United States.[50]

The Effectiveness of Enforcement: General Observations

Apart from the many challenges and difficulties already outlined, all enforcement-oriented strategies confront one major limitation: the drug-related arrest is only the first step in a long criminal justice process. Drug-law enforcement, in the largest sense, means not only drug arrests but the successful prosecution of those arrested and, presumably, the meting out of adequately stiff sentences. However, recent escalations in the war on drugs have not necessarily netted satisfactory results throughout the criminal justice process. For example, Reuter reports that in a sample of five states, "the percent of felony drug convictions resulting in some incarceration (prison or jail) rose from 71 percent in 1983 to 83 percent in 1986"; in California, the likelihood of serving prison time for a felony drug conviction increased from 5 percent in 1979 to only 17 percent in 1988.[51] While figures such as these are often touted as showing increasing toughness, the absolute levels reflected in these figures suggest that there is not as much toughness in drug sentencing as drug warriors in general and arresting officials in particular might like to see. What they tell us is that even at the height of drug war enthusiasm in the late 1980s, nearly one-fifth of those convicted on a felony drug violation did not spend so much as a single day in jail; and even in one of the tougher states, only a minority (17%) of those convicted of felony drug laws will spend more than 12 months in incarceration. Furthermore, at the national level, a dramatic increase in the *number* of people convicted on drug charges in the late 1980s was accompanied by a "modest decline in the expected time served for those who were convicted of drug trafficking (from 22 months to 20 months)."[52]

Because of the many difficulties and unresolvable dilemmas, it is often assumed that drug-law enforcement is, at bottom, ineffective—that it is simply an ongoing process of narcotics agents chasing traffickers, with no real impact on drug use in the United States. However, some systematic evidence has been marshaled to suggest that drug-law enforcement can be successful—and has, in some periods and for some drugs, met the core goal of reduction of the supply of drugs available. Using data on the street price of drugs at various times (as determined by federal drug agencies) and on the extent of drug consumption (as determined by the national surveys described in Chapter 1), Mark Moore isolated several periods in which drug prices increased even while consumption was on the decline. This is, of course, the opposite of what would be expected if supply and demand were unaffected by enforcement efforts.[53] A decline in consumption normally generates a corresponding decline in prices in a competitive market. If there is less and less demand for widgets, competing widget makers will by necessity have to drop the price, and other things being equal, the same is true of drug suppliers. When the opposite occurred, Moore inferred that fewer drugs were being supplied relative to price because of the impact of law enforcement efforts. This scenario, which arguably shows that law enforcement is effective, occurred in the latter 1970s with respect to heroin and from 1979 to the present with respect to marijuana. However, Moore could find no period during which, by this inferential method, law enforcement could be shown to have had an impact on cocaine supply.

UNINTENDED CONSEQUENCES OF DRUG-LAW ENFORCEMENT

Apart from the issue of its effectiveness, drug-law enforcement has been subject to some scathing critiques concerning its unintended negative consequences. Some of these side effects have to do with increases in crime stemming from the fact that the law forces drugs into a high-priced black market. This argument is considered further in Chapter 9. Here, we consider two unintended consequences that are more directly traceable to the actual dynamics of drug-law enforcement: corruption, and encroachments on civil liberties.

Corruption

That corruption of law enforcement agencies is an offshoot of drug-law enforcement should be no surprise to anyone attentive to the many recent instances of the problem. As the drug war has escalated, the newspapers have correspondingly been filled with stories of drug-related corruption: law enforcement personnel accepting bribes from drug dealers in exchange for nonenforcement, the extorting of such bribes, theft of drugs from police property rooms and labs, seizure of drugs from traffickers for conversion to personal use or for sale, and theft of monies from drug dealers.[54]

Given Miami's central position in the war on drugs, it is not surprising that charges of drug-related police corruption have emerged in that area. In January 1990, for example, 3 police officers were charged in a federal indictment with conspiracy to steal $1 million in cash, 110 pounds of cocaine, and a ton of marijuana from drug dealers. A fourth police officer was charged with attempted distribution of cocaine. These arrests evoked memories of the 15 Miami police officers charged with robbing drug dealers in 1984 and 1985.[55] But Miami is by no means the only site for drug-related police corruption. For example, several cases involved New York City police officers, including the arrest in one year of 12 officers on drug-related corruption charges. Several DEA agents have been convicted on such charges.[56] Nor is drug-related police corruption confined to highly urbanized areas. In rural Mingo County, West Virginia, investigators found police collusion with a drug distribution ring in 1988;[57] and the Georgia Bureau of Investigation reported in 1988 that sheriffs in a dozen of the state's 159 counties had been implicated in drug-smuggling cases.[58]

Initially, it is tempting to argue that corruption is not really an unintended consequence of drug-law enforcement—that if enforcement agencies were only professional enough, or managed well enough, corruption could be rooted out. However, a strong case can be made that corruption is *inevitably* a result of the enforcement of laws against victimless crimes, which is to say crimes for which there is no complainant and hence no witness.[59] The structure of the situation in such cases creates incentives for police corruption of two sorts. On the one hand, since there is no complainant to serve as a witness to alleged events, police agents who are under real or imagined pressure to deliver results are relatively free to use illegal searches or other unconstitutional methods and to lie about them as the case proceeds through the criminal justice system. On the other hand, and again because there is no complainant to serve as a witness to alleged events, police agents have the discretion to overlook drug-law violations they discover, especially if a substantial financial inducement is provided to them in exchange. And because drug dealing is so highly profitable, it is easy for dealers to offer financial inducements of a size that cannot fail to corrupt at least some, if not many, law enforcement agents. One investigator of drug-related police corruption indicated that $100,000 would be considered a modest bribe from a small to medium-sized drug-trafficking operation.[60]

Still other features of the drug-law enforcement setting make it vulnerable to corruption. Many forms of drug-related corruption involve police theft of drugs or drug money from traffickers, and the occupational culture of policing makes it possible to rationalize this behavior as more excusable than the theft of legally earned money. Corrupt behavior is also encouraged by the sense of invulnerability that comes from police officers' perceptions that their word will be believed over that of addicts and drug dealers. Invulnerability is also enhanced by the code of secrecy that governs police conduct—a code that makes it highly inappropriate for officers to divulge the secrets of their fellow officers.[61]

Encroachments on Civil Liberties

Especially if it is conducted in the context of a high-profile war on drugs, drug-law enforcement involves activities that can be construed as encroachments on civil liberties. Perhaps the most egregious of these involve threats to constitutional protections against unwarranted searches and seizures and against arrests without probable cause. One of the more controversial enforcement practices in this regard is the use of "profiles," or descriptions of otherwise innocuous physical characteristics and behaviors, as a means of determining who to stop on suspicion of drug-law violations. Drug enforcement agents can and do detain and search individuals at airports, at borders, and at other transit points if they fit such profiles.

For those who are caught in such a net because they happen to be traveling to or from a city or country known for drug smuggling, or who because of personal circumstances have purchased only a one-way ticket or carry on their baggage, or whose skin color places them in a suspect ethnic group, such a detention can be far worse than a minor annoyance. Consider, for example, the case of Ade Adedokian, a legal resident of the United States who is of Nigerian ancestry. Ade was detained at the Houston airport when he returned from a visit to his native country. In the ensuing eight hours, his luggage was searched and he was subjected to detailed questioning for over an hour and to a physical search of his person. In addition, he was told that unless he had an X-ray exam to determine whether he had swallowed pouches of drugs, he would not be allowed into the country. After being handcuffed and driven to a hospital, and having waited to be given the X-ray, Ade was finally freed when the X-ray found no drugs.[62]

While many are detained for much shorter and simpler questioning processes, the practice of using drug profiles to detain individuals causes large numbers of innocent individuals to be embarrassed and inconvenienced. The Supreme Court ruled in April 1989 that any airline passenger can be detained on the basis of such profiles because they constitute reasonable grounds for an investigatory stop.[63] Such detentions are not, therefore, literally a violation of constitutional rights. However, civil libertarians, along with growing numbers of aggravated individuals who have been subjected to such detentions, argue that the practice certainly violates their sense of a right to freedom from unreasonable search and arrest without probable cause.

Still other enforcement activities have led to criticism that innocent citizens are not necessarily safe from police intrusion even in their own homes. Because drug dealers can quickly destroy evidence or organize a violent response when police officers come to the door, narcotics agents have long argued for tactics that allow them to gain immediate access to the premises that are being raided. As noted in Chapter 2, this led during the Nixon administration to provisions officially authorizing police to enter premises without first knocking and identifying themselves. Use of these no-knock searches led to cases of officers mistakenly barging in on and terrorizing innocent citizens at the wrong address. Even without formal no-knock authority, drug raids can yield the same results if officers swoop down on an address and batter down the front door after only a cursory pause for identification. And drug raids on mistaken addresses are yielding tragic consequences. Not surprisingly, official statistics on the number of these incidents are not available. However, a number of such cases have been documented in the popular media:

> Jeffery Miles, age twenty-four, died on March 26, 1987, after a Jeffersontown, Kentucky, police officer shot and killed him. The officer had been sent to the wrong house looking for a suspected drug dealer. On March 12, 1988, Tommy C. Dubose, age fifty-six, was shot and killed by a San Diego police officer who had burst into Dubose's living room looking for drugs. The police had obtained a search warrant based on a tip. As it turned out, Dubose was a civilian instructor at a nearby naval station and was, according to his friends, strongly opposed to drugs. No drugs were found at his apartment after his death.[64]

The drug war has also led to increases in the number of authorized wiretaps in use;[65] to aggressive use of expanded powers of seizure and forfeiture of property without a charge, let alone a conviction, on drug-law violations (see Chapter 4); to restrictions on bail (see Chapter 4) that make the Eighth Amendment seem a distant memory; and to a variety of other aggressive tactics that have caused civil libertarians to shudder. There is at least anecdotal evidence that these "evictions, raids, curfews, random searches and the summary forfeiture of property" have extensive public support across the nation.[66] And "public officials ranging from politicians to high school principals believe that intrusive practices such as these are justified—as long as they are conducted on behalf of the war on drugs."[67] It is precisely such a climate that makes the threat to constitutional rights and civil liberties so substantial.

CONCLUSIONS

Law enforcement officers have long been on the front line of the nation's various wars on drugs. Supply reduction efforts, ranging from interdiction to the most routine buy-and-bust cases by local police departments, continue to consume the greatest share of resources devoted to antidrug policy. This chapter shows that in practice, these resources support a repertoire of traditional tactics, including arrest sweeps in targeted areas, screening at ports of entry, buy-and-bust cases, more sophisticated surveillance cases, and eradication of crops. Many of these tactics are inherently limited in effectiveness. And the choice of tactics appears to be driven as much by tradition, professional imperatives, and political pressures as by strategic planning or careful assessment of effectiveness trade-offs.

Not surprisingly, there is little hard evidence about the actual impact of enforcement efforts. What evidence there is suggests that drug-law enforcement can be viewed as successful only in the narrowest and most limited of senses—in particular time periods, enforcement has affected the availability (relative to price) of heroin and marijuana. Against this modest success, the unintended negative consequences of drug-law enforcement loom especially large. The substantial corruption and encroachments on civil liberties that seem to inevitably accompany drug-law enforcement are especially troubling. As Chapter 8 shows, these disappointing results and troubling side effects play an important role in an ongoing debate over the wisdom of drug legalization.

NOTES

1. White House, *National Drug Control Strategy: Budget Summary* (Washington, DC: Office of National Drug Control Policy, 1992), p. 91.
2. White House, 1992, p. 213.
3. Peter Reuter, "Can the Borders Be Sealed?" in Ralph Weisheit, ed., *Drugs, Crime and the Criminal Justice System* (Cincinnati: Anderson, 1990), p. 13.
4. U.S. House of Representatives, Select Committee on Narcotics Abuse and Control, *The Drug Enforcement Crisis at the Local Level* (Washington, DC: U.S. Government Printing Office, 1989b), p. 7.
5. Mark Kleiman, "Crackdowns: The Effects of Intensive Enforcement on Retail Heroin Dealing," in Marcia Chaiken, ed., *Street-Level Drug Enforcement: Examining the Issues* (Washington, DC: National Institute of Justice, 1988), p. 15.
6. U.S. Bureau of the Census, *Statistical Abstract of the United States 1992*, 112th ed. (Washington, DC: U.S. Government Printing Office, 1992), p. 187.
7. U.S. Bureau of the Census, 1992, p. 188.
8. U.S. Bureau of the Census, 1992, p. 194.
9. White House, 1992, p. 91.

10. James Q. Wilson, *The Investigators* (New York: Basic Books, 1978), pp. 40–46; see also Mark Moore, *Buy and Bust* (Lexington, MA: Heath, 1977), pp. 130–149.
11. Wilson, 1978, p. 40.
12. Mark Kleiman and Kerry Smith, "State and Local Drug Enforcement: In Search of a Strategy," in Michael Tonry and James Q. Wilson, eds., *Drugs and Crime* (Chicago: University of Chicago Press, 1990), p. 84. © 1990 The University of Chicago. All rights reserved.
13. Kleiman and Smith, 1990, p. 87.
14. U.S. House of Representatives, Select Committee on Narcotics Abuse and Control, *The Federal Drug Strategy* (Washington, DC: U.S. Government Printing Office, 1990d), p. 101.
15. Select Committee on Narcotics Abuse and Control, 1990d, pp. 108–109.
16. Select Committee on Narcotics Abuse and Control, 1990d, p. 104.
17. Kleiman, 1988, p. 15.
18. Kleiman, 1988, pp. 10–12.
19. Mary Cooper, *The Business of Drugs* (Washington, DC: Congressional Quarterly, 1990), p. 115.
20. White House, 1992, pp. 172–175.
21. Moore, 1977, p. 141.
22. Moore, 1977, pp. 140–146.
23. Kleiman and Smith, 1990, pp. 82–83.
24. Moore, 1977, pp. 144–147.
25. Steven Wisotsky, *Beyond the War on Drugs* (Buffalo: Prometheus Books, 1990), p. 74.
26. Wisotsky, 1990, pp. 81–82.
27. Wisotsky, 1990, pp. 83–86.
28. Cooper, 1990, p. 117.
29. Elaine Sciolino, "World Drug Crop Up Sharply in 1989 Despite U.S. Effort," *New York Times*, March 2, 1990, p. 1.
30. Kleiman and Smith, 1990, p. 71.
31. Mark Moore, "Supply Reduction and Drug Law Enforcement," in Michael Tonry and James Q. Wilson, eds., *Drugs and Crime* (Chicago: University of Chicago Press, 1990), p. 117.
32. Peter K. Manning, *The Narc's Game: Organizational and Informational Limits on Drug Law Enforcement* (Cambridge: MIT Press, 1980), pp. 220–231.
33. Manning, 1980, p. 253.
34. Wisotsky, 1990, p. 63.
35. Moore, 1990, p. 142.
36. Mark Kleiman, *Against Excess: Drug Policy for Results* (New York: Basic Books, 1992), p. 134.
37. Kleiman, 1992, pp. 136–137.
38. Kleiman, 1992, p. 138.
39. Steven Belenko, "The Impact of Drug Offenders on the Criminal Justice System," in Ralph Weisheit, ed., *Drugs, Crime and the Criminal Justice System* (Cincinnati: Anderson, 1990), p. 29.
40. U.S. Bureau of the Census, 1992, p. 187.
41. Belenko, 1990, pp. 28, 35.
42. Manning, 1980, p. 255.

43. Steven Holmes, "Fewer Turf Battles, More Drug Arrests," *New York Times*, January 21, 1990, sec. 4, p. 22.
44. Moore, 1990, p. 136.
45. Kleiman, 1992, p. 132.
46. Daniel K. Benjamin and Roger L. Miller, *Undoing Drugs* (New York: Basic Books, 1992), pp. 31–32.
47. Benjamin and Miller, 1992, p. 43.
48. Benjamin and Miller, 1992, p. 43.
49. Cooper, 1990, p. 118.
50. White House, *National Drug Control Strategy* (Washington, DC: U.S. Government Printing Office, 1990), p. 18.
51. Peter Reuter, "On the Consequences of Toughness," in Melvyn B. Krauss and Edward P. Lazear, eds., *Searching for Alternatives: Drug Control Policy in the United States* (Stanford, CA: Hoover Institution, 1991), pp. 142–143.
52. Reuter, 1991, p. 143.
53. Moore, 1990, pp. 125–126.
54. David L. Carter, "An Overview of Drug-Related Misconduct of Police Officers: Drug Abuse and Narcotic Corruption," in Ralph Weisheit, ed., *Drugs, Crime and the Criminal Justice System* (Cincinnati: Anderson, 1990), pp. 90–91.
55. "Three Officers Are Charged in Thefts of Cash and Drugs," *New York Times*, January 25, 1990, p. A18, col. 1.
56. Benjamin and Miller, 1992, p. 69.
57. B. Drummond Ayres, "Corruption Inquiry Brings Hope to 'Bloody Mingo,'" *New York Times*, March 25, 1988, p. A7.
58. Philip Shenon, "Enemy Within: Drug Money Is Corrupting the Enforcers," *New York Times*, April 11, 1988, p. 1.
59. Randy Barnett, "Curing the Drug-Law Addiction: The Harmful Side Effects of Legal Prohibition," in Ronald Hamowy, ed., *Dealing with Drugs: Consequences of Government Control* (Lexington, MA: Heath, 1987), p. 95.
60. Carter, 1990, p. 94.
61. Carter, 1990, pp. 95–96.
62. Lisa Belkin, "Airport Anti-Drug Nets Snare Many People Fitting 'Profiles,'" *New York Times*, March 20, 1990, p. 1.
63. Belkin, 1990, p. 1.
64. Benjamin and Miller, 1992, p. 137.
65. Wisotsky, 1990, p. 126.
66. Seth Mydans, "Powerful Arms of Drug War Arousing Concern for Rights," *New York Times*, October 16, 1989, p. 1.
67. Benjamin and Miller, 1992, p. 139.

Chapter
8

Limits of Policy Change

INTRODUCTION

Preceding chapters have shown that there is substantial continuity and limited change in American drug policy. There have been some new developments in the fields of drug-law enforcement, treatment, and prevention. Law enforcement personnel have sometimes emphasized dramatic sweeps of lower-level dealers and sometimes turned to more sophisticated efforts at long-term surveillance and building cases against high-level drug dealers. Treatment professionals have developed new techniques of psychotherapeutic drug counseling. And in the drug prevention field, new techniques of resistance skills training have been introduced. However, despite these innovations, the traditional methods from each field—buy-and-bust techniques, group counseling, and straightforward drug information programs—are still widely used. More important, despite some dramatic turns, such as the brief period of emphasis on drug treatment during the Nixon administration, American drug policy has been characterized for virtually all of its history by emphasis on supply-side efforts, such as law enforcement and interdiction, rather than demand-side efforts, such as treatment and prevention.

To many observers, then, the drug policy field may seem to be one in which the same tired approaches are constantly being recycled, with at best some small modifications at the tactical level. And this is so despite much evidence of disappointing results. Many of the disappointments and policy failures are more fully documented in Chapter 9, which takes up the arguments of drug legalization proponents. Here, one need only acknowledge that years, and indeed decades, of drug-fighting policies have brought us to a point at which cocaine is still obtained easily and relatively cheaply, heroin use and availability may be on the upswing, and many U.S. cities are struggling with street violence linked to drug trafficking. Yet drug policy exhibits the continuity that it always had, despite these manifestations of failure. How might we account for this?

From the perspective of *incrementalism*, there is nothing surprising, or for that matter inappropriate, about the continuity of drug policy. In Charles Lindblom's classic formulation of this theory, policy-making

Put in paper

cannot be anything other than a process of piecemeal adjustment leading to minor remedial change.[1] This is because of two major obstacles to comprehensive, radical change: cognitive limits and lack of value consensus. Cognitive limits have to do with the obstacles to comprehensive, theory-based information processing on the part of individuals and institutions. Given limits on time, theoretical knowledge, and ability to gather and make good use of massive amounts of data, policymakers must inevitably simplify decision making. And the key method of simplification, according to Charles Lindblom, is to consider only those proposals that involve minimal change from the status quo. "Such a limitation immediately reduces the number of alternatives to be investigated and also drastically simplifies the character of the investigation of each" because policymakers can make heavy use of the knowledge gained from experience with policy that is in effect.[2]

Lack of consensus on values is another obstacle to comprehensive, radical policy reform, according to Lindblom. Even individual decision makers cannot generate rankings of the weight to be accorded to each of their own values in the abstract; and determining what is or should be valued most is even more complicated in public-choice settings involving multiple participants whose value orderings presumably differ and whose intensities of preference are difficult to judge. Under these circumstances, decision making focuses instead on a limited number of policy alternatives, differing only modestly from current practice, because current practice reflects the best compromise that can be had in the face of competing values.

Lindblom's analysis suggests that policy change is inevitably incremental because of this combination of cognitive limitation and lack of consensus. Policy continuity can be attributed to other causes as well. Michael Hayes, for example, suggests that institutional features of decision making in the United States, such as the separation of powers and federalism, are at least as relevant:

> We can now see that incrementalism is only partly the result of inherent limits on rational decision making. Contrary to Lindblom's expectations, proposals for major policy change frequently receive consideration from policy makers, and at least some of the time they are enacted into law. More often, however, the need to construct concurrent majorities distributed across a series of veto points makes bargaining and compromise imperative, leading to incremental policy outcomes.[3]

Another possible explanation for policy continuity lies in the character of interest group involvement in the policy process. In a number of fields of public policy, such as energy and agriculture, analysts have depicted the existence of powerful organized interests, which have been able to develop insulated spheres of influence within the legislative and administrative venues dealing with their policy specialty. These "subgovernments" have been characterized as being highly specialized, nonaccessible to alternative interests, invisible to the general public, and capable of shaping policy to meet the needs of those inside the subgovernment. Not surprisingly, such subgovernments have also been characterized as "highly resistant to change."[4]

Through its development of the concept of subgovernments, interest group theory offers a potentially important explanation for policy continuity in the drug area. If organized groups with stakes in the continuation of a national war on drugs have entrenched themselves in a powerful subgovernment, then it is no wonder that strong challenges to existing approaches and radical policy change are not to be found.

This chapter explores the possibility that an entrenched set of interest groups is responsible for drug policy continuity. As we will see, however, there is one major problem with this explanation: the drug policy subgovernment that once existed has been transformed into a much more diverse and competitive network of interests. This change in the drug policy area is, in fact, consistent with what scholars have found in a number of other policy domains.[5] Especially in the 1970s, "policy subsystems relating to tobacco, pesticides, air and water pollution, airlines, trucking, telecommunications, and nuclear power were all destroyed or radically altered"[6] as organized interests with different stakes and alternative policy views challenged the interests that had dominated the discussion. The drug policy domain has experienced just such a transformation away from a powerful subgovernment to a more diversified set of organized interests. Because this is so, the continuity of drug policy cannot as easily be attributed to a monolithic, conservative drug policy subgovernment. Instead, the story of interest groups and drug policy leaves us with a puzzle. Why has the breakdown of the drug policy subgovernment *not* had the policy consequences, in terms of challenge and nonincremental change, that might have been predicted?

The concluding section of the chapter turns to a set of ideas about political symbolism and accountability avoidance that help explain policy continuity despite change in the character of the interest groups active in the drug policy area, and despite the failings of drug policy to date.

ORGANIZED INTERESTS IN DRUG POLICY

Portrait of a Subgovernment

Throughout the 32-year-period ending in 1962, during which Harry Anslinger was director of the Federal Bureau of Narcotics (FBN), the drug policy domain could be characterized as having a subgovernment. Referring to this period as the Harrison-Anslinger era, Arnold Trebach argues that drug policy was locked into a conservative, even repressive enforcement-oriented posture, largely because of Anslinger's ability to dominate drug policy-making discussions and to thwart the voices of alternative drug policy interests.[7] Similarly, John McWilliams argues that drug policy in this period was under the control of Anslinger, who regularly mobilized a constellation of agencies and organizations, dubbed Anslinger's army, to speak for legislation favored by the FBN and to undermine any legislative proposal opposed by Anslinger. This army of organized interests included a variety of state and local criminal justice officials. When they were necessary for particular purposes, Anslinger could also mobilize a variety of other groups, such as the General Federation of Women's Clubs and the National Women's Christian Temperance Union, the American Drug Manufacturers, the Federal Wholesale Druggists, and the National Hotel Druggists' Association.[8]

To provide a more precise description of the enforcement-oriented subgovernment that once dominated the drug policy domain (and then to show the transformation of that subgovernment), this chapter considers the interest groups and organizations that have testified at drug-related congressional hearings in various periods. Giving testimony at congressional hearings is, of course, only one of the many activities of organized interests in the policy formation process. Organized interests also engage in direct lobbying and informal contacts with legislators and other public officials, relations with the media, and many other activities. However, a focus on testimony at congressional hearings is a useful way of constructing a portrait of the subgovernment. Testifying at hearings is a method of influence used virtually universally by organized interests; it is one of the activities that consume the largest share of the time and resources of such groups.[9] The importance and unusually widespread use of formal testimony stems from the multifaceted usefulness of hearings as an avenue of influence:

> Foremost, of course, is that hearings are an opportunity for interest groups to present carefully reasoned arguments and technical information. . . . Interests also get involved in Congressional hearings in order to shape the legislative record in ways that may work to their advantage . . . when executive agencies or the federal courts are scrutinizing the record to gain a better understanding of congressional intent. Testifying at hearings may also provide organizations with access to key legislators whom they may not have been able to contact in more private and direct ways. . . . In addition, Congressional hearings sometimes offer organized interests a propaganda forum that is virtually unparalleled in Washington.[10]

Congressional staffers are responsible for determining who should be invited to testify; they make their choices on the basis of knowledge of organized interests from lobbying activity, trying also to provide a balanced cross section of opinion on the issue at hand.[11] This means that the staging of hearings will tend to reflect who is active in the policy domain in other ways. Congressional hearings therefore provide a historical record of the activity of organized interests in particular policy domains.

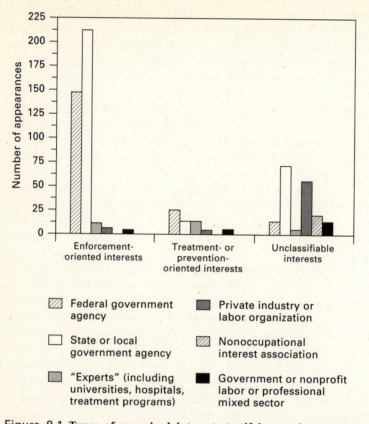

Figure 8.1 **Types of organized interests testifying at drug-related congressional hearings, by role orientation, 1950–1955.** Organizations and individuals appearing at the hearings were coded by the author as oriented either toward the law enforcement approach to drugs or toward drug treatment and prevention, on the basis of their occupational role and not the subjective tenor of their testimony. Organized interests without a clear and consistent occupational stake in either the enforcement or the treatment and prevention side of the drug issue were treated as unclassifiable. (*Source:* Original coding of entities testifying at all congressional hearings on drug abuse or narcotics enforcement topics, 1950–1955.)

An analysis of organized interests appearing at drug-related congressional hearings in the period from 1950 to 1955 provides a snapshot of the subgovernment that dominated the drug policy field throughout the Harrison-Anslinger era. Figure 8.1 shows that this subgovernment was dominated by law enforcement interests, which appeared much more often than treatment- or prevention-oriented interests. These law enforcement interests included federal, state, and local government agencies ranging from the FBN, the Customs Bureau, and the Justice Department to local police departments, sheriffs' offices, and prosecuting attorneys. The comparatively small number of treatment- and prevention-oriented interests that testified before Congress in the 1950s included an assortment of nongovernment or mixed-sector professional associations, such as the American Medical Association; university-, hospital-, or treatment program–based experts; state and local departments of public health; and, at the federal level, the Public Health Service and the National Institute of Mental Health.

The groups and individuals shown as unclassifiable in Figure 8.1 are ones that do not have clear *occupational* stakes in either the criminal or the medical side of the drug issue. In the 1950s, these included several religious or moralist groups, such as the Catholic Youth Organization, the national Women's Christian Temperance Union, and the General Federation of Women's Clubs. A number of business groups are also included, such as the National Association of Retail Druggists, several state pharmacy boards, and private pharmaceutical companies like the New York Quinine Company. As McWilliams notes, many of these organizations were enlisted into Anslinger's army and mobilized to testify on behalf of policy positions favored by the FBN.[12]

Indeed, the FBN was the hub of the drug policy subgovernment. At least one individual from the FBN testified in 23 of the 30 drug-related hearings held in this period, and Anslinger himself was the FBN representative in 9 hearings. In hearings where the FBN did not testify, state or local criminal justice officials were invariably present to carry the flag for the enforcement-oriented approach to the drug problem. In two of the six years in this period (1950 and 1952), no treatment- or prevention-oriented interests were represented among those testifying at congressional hearings; by contrast, enforcement-oriented interests were present each year, in substantial magnitude.

Furthermore, drug-related hearings were held by a relatively small number of congressional committees during this period—committees largely sympathetic to the criminal justice model of the drug problem. All but 6 of the 30 drug-related hearings from 1950 to 1955 were held by the Senate Judiciary Committee's Subcommittee on Improvements in the Federal Criminal Code, the Senate Special Committee to Investigate Organized Crime in Interstate Commerce, the subcommittees on narcotics of the House Ways and Means Committee or the Senate Judiciary Committee, and the House and Senate Committees on the District of Columbia.

In sum, drug policy-making in the 1950s exemplified the operation of a powerful subgovernment that dominated during Anslinger's tenure as director of the FBN. Enforcement-oriented interests were dominant in terms of sheer frequency of appearance; there was continuity of representation of these interests across time; and the venues for congressional attention to drug policy were largely limited to committees with a substantive stake in criminal justice rather than health and medical affairs. It should not be surprising, then, that federal drug policy throughout the Anslinger era of subgovernment hegemony showed an emphasis on a criminal rather than a medical model of the drug problem.

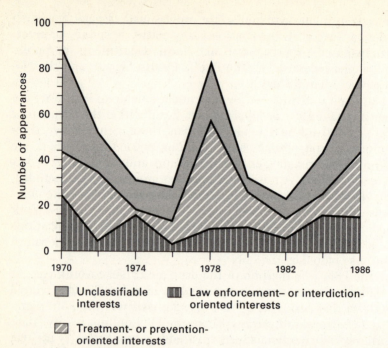

Figure 8.2 **Appearances of organized interests at drug-related congressional hearings, by role orientation, 1970–1986. A random sampling is used because of the large volume of hearings in many of the years. (*Source:* Original coding of entities testifying at a 25 percent random sampling of congressional hearings on drug-related topics in each of the even-numbered years from 1970 to 1986.)**

Drug Policy Interests After Subgovernment Transformation

The dominance of the drug-law enforcement subgovernment had crumbled by the time of the Nixon administration, and a newer, more diverse issue network was in its place. Drug policy-making for all three episodes considered in Chapters 2 through 4 was conducted within the framework of this more diversified issue network. The character of this issue network can be seen in Figure 8.2. It shows that organized interests representing the enforcement side of the drug policy debate were eclipsed, in terms of sheer frequency of appearance, by treatment- or prevention-oriented interests at many crucial points during the period from 1970 to 1986. Treatment and prevention interests appeared much more frequently at congressional hearings than did enforcement-oriented interests in 1972, at the height of Nixon's war on drugs; in 1978, the high point of drug policy attention during the Carter administration; and in 1986, a year of frenzied attention in the contemporary war on drugs. These interests dramatically reversed the portrait of organizational activity that had characterized the old subgovernment in this policy domain. Congressional discussions of drug policy now were very likely to include drug therapy experts from university medical schools and drug treatment programs; professional associations, such as the American Public Health Association, the National Education Association, the National Association of State Drug Abuse Coordinators, the National Association of Prevention Professionals, and the National Association of City Drug Coordinators; and administrators from NIDA, the Office of Education, the National Institute of Mental Health, and various counterpart agencies at the state and local levels.

Enforcement-oriented interests were by no means dormant, of course. They were relatively active in 1974, when the drug issue was not at the forefront of public attention, and they competed with the treatment and prevention groups for appearance frequency in the drug war initiated in the Reagan administration. But enforcement-oriented interests no longer overwhelm treatment and prevention interests at congressional hearings, as they did during Harry Anslinger's reign as FBN chief.

The transformation from a homogeneous, closed subgovernment to a more diversified issue network is also evident in the increasing number of venues for congressional attention to the drug policy issue. In contrast with the Anslinger era, a diverse array of congressional committees and subcommittees are now engaged in drug policy–related hearings. In 1978, for example, hearings were held by the House Select Committee on Narcotics Abuse and Control, the Senate Committee on Labor and Human Resources, and the House Committee on Interstate and Foreign Commerce, as well as the House Committee on the Judiciary. Although the sample of hearings for Figure 8.2 did not include all of them, drug-related hearings were held in 1986 by the Subcommittee on Judiciary and Education and the Subcommittee on Fiscal Affairs and Health of the House Committee on the District of Columbia; by the House Education and Labor Committee's Subcommittee on Human Resources; by the House Energy and Commerce Committee's Subcommittee on Health and Environment; by the House Committee on Interior and Insular Affairs; by the House Committee of the Judiciary's Subcommittee on Crime; by the House Select Committee on Narcotics Abuse and Control; by the House Select Committee on Children, Youth, and Families; and others as well.

What led to the transformation of the drug policy subgovernment to a much more diversified issue network? One key was surely the subgovernment's loss of its central leadership figure. In 1962, in a move that some analysts believe was orchestrated by President Kennedy and Attorney General Robert Kennedy,[13] Harry Anslinger resigned from his long tenure as head of the FBN. Anslinger's departure may have energized drug treatment experts and professionals, who had been active at the state and local level but whose interests had been blocked at the federal level by the dominating presence of Anslinger.

The important matter here, however, is not *how* the drug policymaking process diversified to incorporate a greater variety of interests; rather, it is the *limited policy change* stemming from this diversification. As Chapters 5 and 6 show, U.S. federal drug policy includes resources for a variety of drug treatment, rehabilitation, and prevention

programs. The institutionalization of these programs and the incorpora-
tion of treatment and prevention interests in the drug policy-making issue network may be viewed as going hand in hand. However, as Chapters
2 through 4 show, there has been substantial continuity in the nation's
drug policy approach. With one exception, policy enacted since 1970 has
sustained the dominance of the criminal law, or supply-side, approach
over the treatment- and prevention-oriented, or demand-side, approach
to the drug problem. The exception is the extraordinary but brief federal
commitment to treatment initiatives during the Nixon administration, a
commitment that increased demand-side drug policy spending to a level
considerably above supply-side spending, for perhaps the first time in
U.S. history.[14] But, as noted in Chapter 2, this was a brief reversal of for-
tunes. During the Carter administration, funding for the two sides of the
drug policy issue evened out; and throughout the Reagan-Bush era, the
national drug control budget was apportioned at about 70 percent for
drug-law enforcement and interdiction and about 30 percent for treatment and prevention.[15] Given the disappointing results of the nation's
war on drugs and the existence of competing claimants for resources,
this sustained emphasis on the enforcement side is truly remarkable.

In short, U.S. drug policy has maintained a consistent emphasis on
criminal-model interpretations and law enforcement spending rather
than a medical-model interpretation and treatment and prevention
spending. And this consistency persists despite dramatic change in the
character and activities of organized interests in the drug policy-making
process. The consistency of drug policy in the period from 1914 to the
late 1960s can perhaps be attributed to the power of entrenched enforcement-oriented interest groups. But the continuation of that same emphasis in drug policy throughout the contemporary period is not so easily explained by simplistic models of interest group power. What else, then,
accounts for the continuity in U.S. drug policy?

OTHER EXPLANATIONS FOR POLICY CONTINUITY

If we are concerned about continuity in drug policy despite evidence of
policy failure, we must investigate other interpretations that can account for this failure of development or lack of "policy learning." One
important reason for a lack of policy learning is that the mechanisms by
which the general public detects policy shortcomings and holds politicians accountable for them are seriously flawed. Rather than assuming
that public officials can be held responsible for policy failure, many analysts emphasize the numerous mechanisms that public officials can use
to avoid blame. These blame avoidance devices can be grouped into two
categories: (1) those that interfere with citizens' capacity to clearly see
and appreciate what policy results really are (blurred policy outcomes)
and (2) those that interfere with citizens' ability to link recognizably

problematic policy outcomes to the actions of particular politicians (blurred policy responsibility).

Blurred Policy Outcomes

The results of public policies and the functioning of government programs can be obscured so that disappointing and counterproductive outcomes are not clear to citizens. One way to short-circuit information about program failure is to use institutional bureaucratic arrangements to shield performance from scrutiny by political masters. As Jeffrey Berry shows in his study of the food stamp program, this is possible even when a program is badly in need of reform, especially if the program has no politically powerful clients to galvanize congressional scrutiny of the program. For years after its inception, the food stamp program was hobbled by a set of purchase requirements that systematically served as a disincentive for program participation. This was clear from data showing that "participation in food stamp programs in most states was 30 to 60 percent lower than that in the earlier commodity programs."[16] But program administrators led Congress to believe (and perhaps even fooled themselves into believing) that the low participation rate was not a real problem—that it reflected undue laxness in the earlier commodity distribution program, a temporary glitch as individuals got used to the new program, or some other minor matter.

More generally, scholars have acknowledged the existence of a number of "permanently failing organizations"—organizations whose performance is, by all objective standards, highly disappointing and yet which manage to go on indefinitely, using the same failing practices.[17] Permanently failing organizations survive because organizations, and the policies and programs that they implement, involve two kinds of stakeholders: those who benefit from organizational effectiveness (who have a stake in organizational *performance*) and those who depend upon the organization for benefits that are derivable whether or not the organization performs well (who have a stake in organizational *maintenance*). The latter includes, for example, managers, other individuals employed by the organization, and suppliers. Because they value organizational permanence over changes designed for performance enhancement, stakeholders of the latter type are motivated to use all the power resources at their disposal for continuity rather than change.[18]

These resources are considerable. Most particularly, those with a stake in organizational permanence tend to have more information than those who have a stake in enhanced performance. The very things that make these people highly dependent upon the organization—their specialized knowledge and skills in the function to which the organization is dedicated—provide one such advantage. In addition to this "expertise" advantage, managers and other employees of permanently failing organizations have an advantage in that they typically control information about the operations and outputs of the organization.

With these advantages in expertise and information, it is not surprising that organizations such as the DEA are relatively impervious to encroachments on agency continuity stemming from the efforts of performance-oriented stakeholders. General criticisms of the drug war by academics, journalists, and elected officials who are not specialists in drug policy can be rebuffed by agents who speak with the authority of having "been there" on the front lines of the drug war; disappointing performance can be hidden in an avalanche of agency statistics on arrests, seizures, and the like. Meanwhile, congressional oversight, which might in theory seem the perfect venue for close scrutiny of performance, tends in fact to involve those with stakes in organizational maintenance rather than performance. Joel Aberbach explains the situation:

> Many in Congress who look like opponents to the naive observer because they denounce programs and the officials who implement them are actually program advocates. They gain credit from unhappy constituents through rectifying problems connected to the programs but need the programs in operation to gain the credit. They therefore work to preserve and even enhance programs while sounding the alarm about an agency's faults.[19]

Congressional oversight, then, tends to be more a matter of program advocacy, limited to incremental problem solving, rather than full-scale evaluation of performance with the real possibility of radical revision.

But the blurring of disappointing policy results is not simply a matter of the power of the bureaucracy to shield itself from Congress. Elected officials, as well as administrators, wish to avoid blame for failed policy, and they have important resources for doing so. One of the simplest yet most powerful is the use of rhetoric to offer false reassurances to the public. Murray Edelman, an insightful commentator on the use of political symbolism and myths, argues that symbolic evocation of threats and reassurances deters the acknowledgement of government failure:

> Knowing that they are often helpless to control their own fate, people resort to religion and to government to cope with anxieties they cannot otherwise ward off.... Eagerness to believe that government will ward off evils and threats renders us susceptible to political language that both intensifies and eases anxiety at least as powerfully as the language of religion does.[20]

As an example, Edelman refers to the Defense Department's historic pattern of first frightening Americans about the magnitude of the security threat from the Soviet Union, then offering reassurances about the capability of the U.S. defense establishment to meet that threat. In short, political symbols and myths are potent devices for disguising the real failings of government action, in part because people are so motivated to believe that government is effectively taking care of problems, and in part because government officials can use a cycle of symbolic threat in-

tensification followed by reassurance to keep the citizenry psychologi-
cally dependent upon government action. The threat-reassurance dy-
namic was exemplified in President Bush's pronouncement in December
1990 that on the one hand, the administration was "fully committed to
fighting this [the drug] problem and stopping this scourge" and on the
other hand, there was "some very encouraging news" with respect to the
drug war (declines in survey-reported drug use).[21]

The political use of symbols to disguise the failings of government
action is, according to Edelman, a widespread phenomenon, observable
across many types of policy areas. However, it is presumably even more
potent with respect to phenomena like the drug issue, which allow
politicians to play upon deep-seated public fears—fears of loss of control
of one's children, of random violence, or of the actions of alien elements
and dangerous classes. Symbolic manipulation is presumably also particularly powerful when the magnitude of the problem to which the policy
is directed is gauged by ambiguous statistics and assessments that cannot be readily discounted by personal experience. With respect to the
government's macroeconomic policy, by contrast, official pronouncements that we have "turned the corner" on a recession can quickly and
decisively be rebutted either by contradictory readings from authoritative government statistics or by individual experience to the contrary, as
in perceptions of the continuing misfortunes of local businesses and the
unemployment of family members, friends, and neighbors. By contrast,
Nixon's speech claiming that the country had "turned the corner" on the
drug problem in 1973 could not as readily be subjected to empirical veri-
fication, even if citizens had been inclined to challenge this symbolic reassurance. Although the institutionalization of multiple official indicators of drug use (see Chapter 1) and the institutionalization of partisan
dueling over drug issues (see Chapter 4) have made claims about the drug
problem somewhat more subject to challenge, politicians' attempts to offer symbolic reassurances about drugs, as in President Bush's pronouncement, can still be effective with the mass public.

Of course, not all politicians and bureaucrats are equally prone to use
such myths and symbols, nor are they equally skillful and effective in
their choice of symbols. This may be one important reason for the continuing success of law enforcement interests and their criminal model of
the drug problem, in contrast to interests with a stake in redefining drug
policy toward a medical model and toward greater emphasis on reducing
demand.

The first section of this chapter showed that organized interests involved with drug treatment, rehabilitation, and prevention have become
much more active and prominent in drug policy deliberations. These interests have gained at least as much access to congressional drug policy
arenas as drug-law enforcement interests have long had, but the content
and character of the messages they bring to that policy-making venue
are not the same. A content analysis of the testimony of law enforcement–oriented and demand reduction–oriented interests shows that the

former are much more likely to use politically effective symbolic themes.

Consider, for example, the following three themes, each of which is relevant to debates over drug policy: (1) the existence of coordination problems that can threaten the effectiveness of drug-law enforcement, drug abuse treatment, or drug abuse prevention; (2) the existence of questions and uncertainty about what kinds of programs work; and (3) claims of success with respect to existing programs. Two of these themes—coordination problems and uncertainty about what works—are symbolically problematic and presumably counterproductive to interests wishing to have their programs extended. Raising the theme of coordination problems is damaging because it is an admission that turf battles, jurisdictional confusion, and programmatic overlap threaten the effectiveness of policy implementation. Acknowledgement of uncertainty about which programs work is damaging because it is an admission that there is a lack of consensus, even among the experts and professionals within the field, about what should be done. By contrast, the success-claiming theme is a positive one, perfectly suited to politicians' needs to claim credit and to the sort of symbolic reassurance that diverts the public from critical appraisal of government policy.

Not surprisingly, the success-claiming theme is the most commonly voiced of the three themes in the congressional testimony examined for this analysis. A little over half (51.7%) of those appearing before Congress were found to voice success claims of some sort. For example, an assistant U.S. attorney for the Southern District of New York testified before the House Select Committee on Crime in 1970:

> But in the area of narcotics prosecution, we of the Southern District of New York have been eminently successful, if I may blow my own horn or our own horn . . . . the list of those who have been successfully prosecuted in our district in the past 13 years literally reads like a "Who's Who" of organized crime. Our percentile of success is somewhere between 95 and 100 percent.[22]

Similarly, an administrator at Beth Israel Hospital made strong claims of success for the institution's drug treatment program:

> We have managed to keep 80 percent of all the patients who have ever come in the program . . . and . . . this is a phenomenal retention rate. . . . We make employable citizens out of most of them. The arrest records are phenomenal . . . . In the methadone program, they almost disappear, so here we take hard bitten heroin addicts, make productive citizens out of them, take them off welfare, keep them out of jail, put families together and do it at a very nominal cost.[23]

Table 8.1   THEMES OFFERED IN CONGRESSIONAL TESTIMONY,
BY TYPE OF ORGANIZED INTEREST, 1970–1986

	Percentage using theme			
	Enforcement interests	Treatment interests	Tau B	Significance
Coordination problems	20.2%	17.0%	−.04	.25
Success claims	33.0	21.2	−.11	.03
Uncertainty about program effectiveness	6.4	23.6	.23	.00
N	109	165		

ªData based on analysis of organized interests appearing at randomly sampled drug-related congressional hearings in each of the even-numbered years from 1970 to 1986.

The two politically problematic themes are much less commonly voiced. However, nearly one-fifth (17.2%) of those giving testimony introduced the theme of coordination problems; even the most damaging theme, uncertainty over what works, was introduced by 15 percent of those giving testimony at drug-related congressional hearings.

Most important, however, are the *differences* between enforcement-oriented and treatment-oriented agencies in their use of these themes. As Table 8.1 shows, treatment interests are less likely than enforcement interests to make strong claims of success, and they are *much* more likely to acknowledge uncertainties over what works.

Why are organized interests on the demand side of the drug policy issue less likely to engage in success claiming and, perhaps more important, so much more likely than law enforcement interests to express uncertainties about what works? The answer presumably lies in the professional imperatives of the treatment, rehabilitation, and preventive agencies and organizations that comprise demand-side drug policy. These organizations and agencies are based in the medical and psychological professions, where the norm of experimentation and documentation of effectiveness is very strong. Professionals in the field of demand reduction expect that treatment programs will be carefully evaluated to determine their effectiveness.[24] The professional paradigm guiding treatment- and prevention-oriented interests is such that questioning what works and maintaining scientific skepticism about the effectiveness of particular programs is a standard mode of operation. The key point is that such a mode of operation can be damaging to organized interests in settings where the politics of symbolic reassurance are critical to success.

It is also true that claims of success and similar uses of symbolic rhetoric can allow organizations implementing drug programs to escape categorization as failing enterprises conducting "impossible jobs." According to Erwin Hargrove and John Glidewell, a public agency has an impossible job (1) if it must deal with "clients" whose legitimacy is questionable because of their irresponsible or strange behavior; (2) if it is based upon a profession that is *not* authoritative and respected; (3) if it must deal with multiple constituencies (political masters, client groups, opponents of client groups, etc.) that are in conflict between and among themselves over the agency's mandate; and (4) if the agency myth is weak—that is, if public support for the organization is not sustained by widespread belief that the organization's goals are reassuring and worth pursuing without close attention to actual goal attainment.[25] Correctional institutions, welfare agencies, and mental health facilities are prime examples of organizations with impossible jobs. Drug treatment and drug-law enforcement agencies are also prime candidates for such a classification. But, as Hargrove and Glidewell explain, an organization that would otherwise sink into the category of impossible jobs can be saved from that fate by skillful managers who can use rhetoric and symbolism to strengthen the agency's myth. When this tactic works, an organization is largely excused from the expectation that it will produce results or the need to demonstrate effectiveness:

> Strong and stable myths define altruistic, impossible goals. The goals are maintained as reassuring and sustaining guides, but no one expects actual attainment and anyone who demanded it would have little public support. Commissioners . . . [of such organizations] have goals that are such altruistic public goods that all constituencies fully understand actual attainment is not expected.[26]

Drug-law enforcement agencies have been singularly successful in sustaining the agency myth that "fighting the good fight" against drugs is such an important ideal that close inquiry into results and cynicism about effectiveness are not appropriate. By contrast, drug treatment organizations have not been able to sustain an idealistic agency myth. The preceding analysis of themes offered in congressional testimony suggests that in fact, spokespersons for these agencies are likely to introduce themes that invite a pragmatic rather than an idealistic view of their agencies' mission. Organizations dealing with drug treatment thus have a weak agency myth; they have clients with negligible legitimacy because of their drug-taking behavior; they are based on counseling and related professions that are not viewed as highly authoritative; and they have competing constituencies (including legislative oversight bodies, communities where facilities are sited, professional credentialling bodies, and clients). All this means that those running drug treatment agencies have truly impossible jobs. Hence, it is not surprising that policymakers are not inclined to radically redirect drug policy in the direction of an emphasis on this sector.

Blurred Policy Responsibility

As in other domains, policy improvement with respect to drugs is also hampered because even when citizens do recognize shortcomings in existing policies and programs, many devices prevent them from holding particular officials accountable for the shortcomings. Because they are protected from that accountability link, politicians are less motivated for policy reform. Only to the extent that they have "good policy" motivations are politicians inclined to search for better solutions to the drug problem; their electoral motivations cannot be counted upon to give urgency to the matter.[27]

The devices that prevent citizens from linking the actions of particular government officials to perceived policy shortcomings are numerous and powerful, as Kent Weaver explains:

> They [politicians] often try to redefine a blame-generating issue or make their own position on it more obscure. Legislators, for example, often provide themselves with a series of votes to soften (or obfuscate) their position on controversial issues. In public statements on such issues, politicians tend to be ambiguous.... Alternatively, the politician may be able to find a scapegoat for their positions or actions.[28]

Charlotte Twight offers a theory of "transaction-cost augmentation" that further explains how politicians can blur responsibility for policy failure. "Transaction costs are costs of reaching and enforcing agreements.... [They] include both information costs and other costs of negotiating and policing agreements."[29] Government action is often viewed as a solution to high transaction costs in certain kinds of market exchanges. For example, labor laws stipulating the rights and obligations of management and unions and defining processes for mediation in labor disputes are justifiable in part because it may be too difficult for private firms and workers to come to agreement without such externally imposed ground rules. However, government decisions also involve transaction costs. More importantly, government officials have "the capability and incentive to alter in self-serving ways the transaction costs facing private citizens and other political actors—both information costs and other costs of taking political action.... Typically, transaction-cost-increasing measures 'raise the threshold required to provoke political change.'"[30]

The transaction-cost-increasing arrangements that allow politicians to avoid blame are many and varied. They include devices such as the automatic indexing of benefits,[31] which obscures the involvement of members of Congress in program cost increases; off-budget financing mechanisms,[32] which obscure the magnitude of public resource commitments being made to various programs; and "ex post alteration of legislators' comments in the Congressional Record,"[33] which gives legislators the opportunity to make their stand on issues appear in a more favorable light. All of these are forms of transaction-cost augmentation because they systematically "benefit a dominant coalition of government office-holders by raising the costs to private individuals of perceiving and react-ing politically to particular governmental actions."[34]

While tendencies toward transaction-cost augmentation are univer-sal in U.S. politics, pressures to engage in such practices and opportuni-ties for the strategic manipulation of information imbalances are greater in some contexts than others. Twight argues that transaction-cost aug-mentation is more likely for complex technical issues than for simpler ones and less likely when politicians are dealing with a matter that is highly salient to constituents.[35] Those generalizations are based upon her study of government performance in a regulatory policy area, the case of asbestos regulation, in which politicians hid their inaction be-hind the technical nature of the health and safety questions involved un-til the media sensitized the mass public to the health threats. The basic idea is that government officials can more readily protect themselves from citizens' scrutiny on matters that can be made to seem too complex and technical for the average citizen; and they can more readily evade public scrutiny on matters that are not particularly interesting and im-portant to the average citizen.

However, the American experience with the drug issue seems to sug-gest that the reverse pattern holds for such symbolic issues. That is, transaction-cost augmentation is more possible for these issues to the extent that they *are* highly salient to the mass public and to the extent that they are cast as *nontechnical* issues. Under these circumstances, transaction-cost augmentation may not take the same form as it does for complex regulatory issues—politicians are not, for example, insulated by a wall of citizen indifference or willingness to defer to the experts. How-ever, such issues allow politicians to manipulate citizen's emotional re-sponses. Rhetoric and political symbolism then become the effective de-vices for keeping citizens' uninformed and politically inert.

It is likely that ideological and political dynamics have exacerbated these tendencies toward blurring of policy responsibility and mainte-nance of a continuous emphasis on law enforcement responses in Amer-ican drug policy. During much of the period covered in this book, Repub-lican administrations were in office, and Republicans, more than Democrats, have typically staked out an emphasis on law enforcement approaches to drug abuse. Democrats, despite their dominance in Con-gress, were constrained from aggressively pursuing a wholesale reorien-tation because they would have deadlocked with Republican presidents. Those attempting to undo the law enforcement emphasis would have been "taking a major political risk because law enforcement advocates may label them as 'soft on drugs'"[36]—a label as damaging as being "soft on crime." Hence, political symbols and the dynamics of blame avoid-ance have stood in the way of any radical revision of U.S. drug policy.

CONCLUSIONS

We have explored a variety of possible explanations for the substantial continuity that can be observed in U.S. drug policy. An explanation focused on the power of entrenched interest groups is problematic, because, as the chapter shows, diverse interest groups in the drug policy domain bring a variety of treatment- and prevention-oriented approaches into the policy-making process. The introduction of these groups has not led to a substantial reorientation of drug policy, perhaps because treatment- and prevention-oriented groups have not been as capable as law enforcement interests in making convincing use of the themes in the symbolic politics of threat and reassurance. In general, drug policy reform has been constrained by devices that subvert the flow of information about policy shortcomings and insulate politicians from accountability for policy failure. Although ideological currents that support a law enforcement approach to drugs are obviously important as well, the devices for blurring policy outcomes and responsibility are crucial in helping to account for drug policy continuity. They also help us to understand politicians' tendency to stoke the fires of public concern about drugs, despite the fact that no truly effective solution to drug use and abuse has yet been implemented in this country. As this chapter suggests, an effective solution is not really needed if politicians are skillful in offering symbolic reassurances and if agency administrators are skillful in building an "agency myth" that discourages close inquiry about results.

NOTES

1. Charles Lindblom, "The Science of 'Muddling Through,'" *Public Administration Review* 19 (Spring 1959), pp. 79–88.
2. Lindblom, 1959, p. 84.
3. Michael Hayes, *Incrementalism and Public Policy* (New York: Longman, 1992), p. 39.
4. Frank R. Baumgartner and Bryan D. Jones, "Agenda Dynamics and Policy Subsystems," *Journal of Politics* 53 (November 1991), p. 1045.
5. See Christopher Bosso, *Pesticides and Politics: The Life Cycle of a Policy Issue* (Pittsburgh: University of Pittsburgh Press, 1987); William P. Browne, *Private Interests, Public Policy, and American Agriculture* (Lawrence: University Press of Kansas, 1987); and Robert H. Salisbury, John P. Heinz, Edward O. Laumann, and Robert Nelson, "Who Works with Whom? Interest Group Alliances and Opposition," *American Political Science Review* 81 (December 1987), pp. 1217–1234.
6. Baumgartner and Jones, 1991, p. 1045.
7. Arnold Trebach, *The Heroin Solution* (New Haven: Yale University Press, 1982), pp. 160–168.
8. John McWilliams, *The Protectors: Harry J. Anslinger and the Federal Bu-*

reau of Narcotics, 1930–1962 (Newark: University of Delaware Press, 1990), p. 90.

9. Kay Lehman Schlozman and John Tierney, *Organized Interests and American Democracy* (New York: HarperCollins, 1986).
10. Schlozman and Tierney, 1986, p. 296.
11. Kevin Leyden, "Organized Interests and the Use of Congressional Hearings: The Rationale Behind Public Lobbying," paper presented at the Annual Meeting of the Midwest Political Science Association, Chicago, April 18–20, 1991.
12. McWilliams, 1990, p. 90.
13. Trebach, 1982, pp. 228–229.
14. Peter Goldberg, "The Federal Government's Response to Illicit Drugs, 1969–1978," in Drug Abuse Council, *The Facts About "Drug Abuse"* (New York: Free Press, 1980), p. 57.
15. White House, *National Drug Control Strategy* (Washington, DC: U.S. Government Printing Office, 1991), p. 134.
16. Jeffrey Berry, *Feeding Hungry People* (New Brunswick, NJ: Rutgers University Press, 1984), p. 41.
17. Marshall W. Meyer and Lynne G. Zucker, *Permanently Failing Organizations* (Newbury Park, CA: Sage, 1989).
18. Meyer and Zucker, 1989, pp. 91–92.
19. Joel Aberbach, *Keeping a Watchful Eye: The Politics of Congressional Oversight* (Washington, DC: Brookings, 1990), p. 177.
20. Murray Edelman, *Political Language: Words That Succeed and Policies That Fail* (New York: Academic Press, 1977), p. 4.
21. Joseph B. Treaster, "Bush Hails Decline in Drug Abuse But Critics Say Survey Is Flawed," *New York Times,* December 20, 1990, p. A12.
22. U.S. House of Representatives, Select Committee on Crime, *Crime in America—Heroin Importation, Distribution, Packaging and Paraphernalia* (Washington, DC: U.S. Government Printing Office, 1970), p. 53.
23. Select Committee on Crime, 1970, p. 268.
24. Barry Brown, "The Growth of Drug Abuse Treatment Systems," in James Inciardi, ed., *Handbook of Drug Control in the United States* (New York: Greenwood Press, 1990), p. 54.
25. Erwin C. Hargrove and John C. Glidewell, *Impossible Jobs in Public Management* (Lawrence: University Press of Kansas, 1990), pp. 5–8.
26. Hargrove and Glidewell, 1990, pp. 7–8.
27. R. Kent Weaver, *Automatic Government* (Washington, DC: Brookings, 1988), p. 19.
28. Weaver, 1988, pp. 26–27.
29. Charlotte Twight, "Regulation of Asbestos: The Microanalytics of Government Failure," *Policy Studies Review* 10 (Fall 1990), p. 10.
30. Twight, 1990, pp. 10–11.
31. Weaver, 1988.
32. Herman Leonard, *Checks Unbalanced: The Quiet Side of Public Spending* (New York: Basic Books, 1986).
33. Twight, 1990, p. 11.
34. Twight, 1990, p. 11.
35. Twight, 1990, p. 27.
36. Kenneth Meier, "The Politics of Drug Abuse: Laws, Implementation, and Consequences," *Western Political Quarterly* 45 (March 1992), p. 43.

Chapter
9

Possibilities for Drug Policy

INTRODUCTION

So far, this book has been devoted to a description of the content of U.S. drug policy through several episodes and to an analysis of why we do what we do with respect to drug policy. Inevitably, however, we are left with the question, What next? In this chapter we examine the prospects for domestic drug policy in the United States in the foreseeable future. In doing so, we naturally focus attention on one drug policy alternative that has generated extended debate in recent years—the legalization of heretofore illicit drugs. As the following sections show, the legalization debate, while interesting and instructive in several respects, is largely a futile exercise; in addition to their other weaknesses, legalization proposals fail the most important public policy test of all—the test of political feasibility. We therefore move on to a consideration of other alternatives, all less radical than legalization, which have the potential to ameliorate some of the most serious flaws of existing drug policy.

LEGALIZATION

The Case for Legalization

One of the foremost proponents of legalization, Ethan Nadelmann, provides a comprehensive overview of the arguments for legalization:

> There are three reasons why it is important to think about legalization. . . . First, current drug-control policies have failed . . . because they are fundamentally flawed. Second, many drug-control efforts are not only failing, but

also proving highly costly and counterproductive. . . . Third, there is good reason to believe that repealing many of the drug laws would not lead . . . to a dramatic rise in drug abuse.[1]

In shorthand form, these three arguments for legalization might be referred to as the *failure-of-control argument,* the *costs and unintended consequences argument,* and the *safety of legalization argument.* To these three might be added a fourth, the *libertarian argument,* which is based on objections in principle to government restrictions on individual behaviors in a free society. As the following sections show, supporters of each argument raise a variety of points.

Failure of Control Proponents of legalization typically launch their argument with a discussion of the failures of existing drug-control policy. As earlier chapters have shown, the U.S. approach to drugs has been multifaceted, with policies and programs devoted to treatment and prevention as well as to law enforcement and interdiction. Proponents of legalization typically do not raise the issue of limitations and problems in treatment and prevention policies. Rather, they emphasize the difficulties of the enforcement side, which, as we have seen, has generally consumed the majority of U.S. drug policy resources. And it is not difficult to find evidence of the failure of drug-law enforcement.

The key failure of law enforcement is its apparent inability to consistently and noticeably decrease the supply of drugs available on the streets of America. Surveying data on the various indicators outlined in Chapter 1, David Courtwright concludes, "Price and purity levels, treatment and emergency-room admissions, urinalyses, and most other indices of drug availability showed a worsening of the problem during the 1980s."[2] Although there was some improvement in these indicators at the end of the decade, the good news quickly turned to bad again. For example, in May 1992, the federal government reported that the number of hospital emergencies attributable to cocaine and heroin abuse had increased by at least 10 percent in the previous three-month period; furthermore, this was the third consecutive three-month period in which the number of drug-related hospital emergencies had increased.[3]

Defenders of the law enforcement approach might be tempted to claim that drugs would be even more readily available (at lower costs and greater purity levels) were it not for enforcement efforts. While such claiming of credit is understandable, it does not constitute a compelling counterargument. For one thing, any difference between actual supply of drugs and what the supply "would have been" could equally well be attributed to diminished demand for drugs, stemming from prevention efforts, generational changes, or other sources of shifting preferences in American society. In any case, it is difficult to call enforcement a success: the National Institute on Drug Abuse (NIDA) estimates that over 850,000 Americans use cocaine frequently (about once a week); in one six-month period, at least 47,000 people sought emergency-room help after using cocaine; and in one three-month period, over 9,000 people were seen in emergency rooms with crises over heroin use.[4]

Costs and Unintended Consequences If the failure of drug-law enforcement and interdiction to achieve intended goals helps to provide a case for legalization, an even more powerful case derives from acknowledgement of the substantial costs and, worse still, the unintended negative consequences of drug-law enforcement. As earlier chapters have shown, the majority of the federal drug budget, as much as 70 percent in recent years, is devoted to drug-law enforcement and interdiction rather than treatment or prevention. In 1991, this amounted to over $7 billion.[5] In addition, substantial state and local resources are devoted to drug-law enforcement.

In addition to these direct costs, law enforcement has a variety of indirect costs. The most obvious of these are the costs associated with a criminal justice system that is overwhelmed with drug-related cases. Overcrowded jails, backlogged court dockets, and similar problems and pressures are costly results of enforcement-oriented wars on drugs. In 1990, the number of people incarcerated in America swelled to over 1 million, almost half of them drug offenders. Critics of the drug war use such statistics as evidence of an important set of costs: "The next time someone complains about unsolved murders, rapes or robberies, or complains about the inefficiency of our court system or about prisons being overcrowded, you will know the culprit—overzealous enforcement of drug laws."[6]

But the most powerful arguments of proponents of drug legalization involve allegations of a perverse set of unintended consequences, all having to do with unintentional *stimulation* of crime. Drug prohibition is alleged to increase crime in a variety of ways. For example, prohibition means that drugs are trafficked on a black market, in which the price of drugs is by definition higher than it would otherwise be. One result is that many drug users are forced into crime as a means of financing their drug use. Another result is that many are lured into dealing drugs because it is so profitable. In addition, drug users who are caught end up with criminal records that short-circuit possibilities for a normal life with legitimate employment. This further encourages individuals into a life of drug dealing. Because drug dealing is conducted outside legitimate channels of commerce, disputes are handled extralegally, thus increasing the level of violent crime.[7] Critics of drug prohibition point to the fact that *violent* drug-related crime stems almost completely from the illegal status of drugs rather than from drug use itself. Ira Glasser, for example, refers to a 1989 study by Narcotic and Drug Research, Inc., which examined each of the 218 drug-related homicide cases that occurred in four of New York City's high-crime zones. Two-thirds of these homicides involved individuals killed as a result of cocaine dealing. Only 14 percent of the homicides could be classified as "psychopharmacological"—that is, ones in which usage of a substance caused the perpetrator's violent action—and in most of these cases, the substance at issue was alcohol rather than an illicit drug. Viewing results like these, critics of drug prohibition conclude that "the 'drug problem,' by which most people mean the drug-related crime and violence problem, is almost entirely a function of our bankrupt drug policy—prohibition."[8]

As Chapter 7 shows, critics of drug prohibition can point to other unintended consequences of drug-law enforcement as well. These include real and potential encroachments on civil liberties and substantial problems of corruption in law enforcement agencies.

Finally, legalization proponents typically make reference to yet another kind of cost of drug prohibition—the foregone benefits of tax revenue from legal drug sales. When drugs are illicit, their sales on the black market generate no tax revenues to be used for desirable societal purposes. If illicit drugs were legalized, however, they could be taxed, just as liquor, cigarettes, and many other substances are. Some suggest that taxes on legalized drugs must be moderate so that taxation does not amount to a de facto effort to destroy drug marketing, but that such taxes could be high enough to theoretically compensate for any harms to society that the drugs cause.[9] More specifically, many proponents suggest that the revenues derived from taxing drug sales could and should be used to fund drug abuse treatment and prevention programs. Estimating the likely volume of tax revenues available for such purposes is fraught with difficulty. There are uncertainties over the magnitude of current drug use, and calculation of the tax take from legalization requires still more difficult and distant estimates of the magnitude of drug use after legalization and the amount of tax revenue that would be used up in the oversight of a legalized drug industry. However, it has been estimated that the legalization of marijuana alone might generate $11 billion annually in tax revenues.[10] The prospect of tax revenues, in contrast to the tremendous out-of-pocket costs of the current war on drugs, is clearly a most enticing carrot that proponents of drug legalization can dangle before the noses of skeptics.

The Safety of Legalization Proponents of legalization argue that legalization would offer relief from the costs and failures of drug-law enforcement and it would *not* result in substantially increased use of drugs, nor would it leave in place an unacceptably large public health problem. Ethan Nadelmann, for example, argues this point of view:

> Like tobacco, many of the illicit substances are highly addictive, but can be consumed on a regular basis for decades without any demonstrable harm. Like alcohol, most of the substances can be, and are, used by most consumers in moderation, with little in the way of harmful effects.[11]

While acknowledging that some drug users die of overdoses, that drug addiction is a curse to those afflicted with it, and that other drug use carries with it a variety of health implications, legalization proponents such as Nadelmann suggest that the most severe health consequences from drugs affect only a very small percentage of drug users and that the more moderate health consequences are no more dramatic than those stemming from use of legal substances such as alcohol and tobacco. And while those more "moderate" health consequences of alcohol and tobacco use are far from trivial, proponents of legalization argue that if society is willing to tolerate them for alcohol and tobacco use, it should do the same for currently illicit drugs.

The legalization alternative would not be viable if nontrivial numbers of new users could be expected to turn to drugs in the wake of legalization. Consequently, proponents of legalization have also marshaled evidence to suggest that this uptake level would be negligible. Assessments of the impact legalization would have on drug consumption are often based upon evidence concerning the impact repeal of prohibition had on alcohol consumption. Using such information, Jeffrey Miron suggests that increased consumption after legalization would be minimal:

> At the beginning of prohibition, consumption declined significantly, to approximately 30 percent of its preprohibition level. Beginning in the early 1920s however, alcohol consumption increased sharply, to about 60–70 percent of the preprohibition value. Most important, alcohol consumption immediately after the repeal of prohibition remained virtually the same as during the latter part of prohibition, although consumption increased to approximately its preprohibition level during the subsequent decade.[12]

Stated another way, legalization proponents suggest that because drug prohibition is ineffective, the vast majority of individuals who are inclined to take drugs are already doing so; thus, they expect removing sanctions against the use of drugs to yield trivial change in the number of people taking drugs.

Yet another aspect of the safety argument has to do with allegations that legalized drugs would be safer for those who do use them. Proponents of drug legalization argue that there are no mechanisms to ensure that black-market drugs are not adulterated with other substances and that purity levels are standardized to prevent overdoses. Furthermore, when drugs are illicit, it is claimed, drug use is more likely to occur in an underground context replete with the most dangerous of practices, such as the sharing of dirty needles. By contrast, according to legalization proponents, legal drugs could be subject to regulations, including health warnings, purity standardization, potency labeling, and the like.[13]

The Libertarian Argument For those frustrated with the lack of incontrovertible evidence to support or refute claims about the extent of prohibition failures, the magnitude of unintended consequences of prohibition, and the degree of safety to be expected from legalization, legalization proponents offer yet another argument. It is based upon philosophical principles rather than an instrumental critique of the utility of drug prohibition. As a number of analysts note, this argument derives from John Stuart Mill's concerns, expressed in his 1859 treatise *On Liberty*, about the inappropriate encroachment of the state on individual freedom when it attempts to prevent intemperance.[14] Recognition of these libertarian roots helps to explain what might otherwise seem to be an anomaly—support for legalization by some notable conservatives, such as William F. Buckley and Milton Friedman. They embrace the concept of drug legalization because drug prohibition, in their view, constitutes an inappropriate extension of the coercive machinery of the state into private realms, an extension which can, in the process, delegitimize the institutions of government.

But perhaps the most fiery spokesperson for this point of view is Thomas Szasz, who argues forcefully that citizens in a free society have a fundamental right to choose what they wish to ingest and that a society that attempts to control those choices quickly becomes something other than a free society:

> The argument that people need the protection of the state from dangerous drugs but not from dangerous ideas is unpersuasive. No one has to ingest any drug he does not want, just as no one has to read a book he does not want. Insofar as the state assumes control over such matters, it can only be in order to subjugate its citizens—by protecting them from temptation, as befits children, and by preventing them from assuming self-determination over their lives, as befits an enslaved population.[15]

As this passage suggests, the libertarian argument may not be the most compelling and pragmatic of those proffered by drug legalization proponents. But it is by far the most passionately articulated.

Limits of the Legalization Argument

One important problem with the legalization argument is its lack of specificity. As a number of critics have pointed out, it is one thing to discuss drug legalization in the abstract; it is quite another to offer a specific set of legalization proposals, covering such important matters as which drugs should be legalized; what the allowable potency level should be for legal drugs; what age limits, if any, there should be for legal access to drugs; where we should allow drugs to be sold; what kinds of advertising, if any, should be allowed; what restrictions, if any, should apply to those working at jobs where impairment of performance would be dangerous; whether drug sales and use should be permitted in public accommodations; and much more.[16] Others castigate participants on all sides of the current debate over drug legalization for their lack of specificity and charge that "the propensity to avoid questions of detail is the major intellectual vice of the decriminalization debaters."[17]

Because the legalization debate has largely been conducted without much specification of details, criticisms of the legalization concept are always subject to deflection on the grounds that some alternative vision of the concept would not have the problems stipulated. For example, many qualms about safety and some of the critique of political feasibility are obviated if legalization is taken to mean no more than decriminalization of possession of marijuana or more permissive, prescription use of heroin for addicts. Most proponents of legalization presumably are advocating something more than this; but they often are advocating something less radical than complete availability of any and all psychoactive substances to any and all potential users, regardless of age or medical status and without restriction as to place of use.

For purposes of this discussion, we might take legalization to mean something like the proposal offered by Richard Karel, who has attempted to provide at least some detail. Karel suggests, for example, that because of their different health risks, coca leaves and powdered cocaine should be legalized while crack should be legalized only if a substantial black market in it persists after legalization of cocaine in its other forms;[18] cultivation of marijuana, coca leaves, and opium poppies for personal use would be allowed in his scheme, but a "more restrictive clinical/prescription system" would be used to provide controlled access to heroin, methadone, and other narcotics.[19] Because phencyclidine (PCP) appears to create violent, psychotic behavior, Karel suggests that it not be legalized; however, he would make natural and synthetic psychedelic drugs, such as peyote and lysergic acid diethylamide (LSD), legally available to individuals who can demonstrate, through an examination, screening test, and interview, that they are aware of the effects of these drugs. Karel goes on to stipulate that legal drugs would be available only to adults; that milder forms, such as "cocaine chewing gum, and smoking and edible opium," could be distributed by profit-making pharmaceutical companies while controlled access to narcotics would be handled by licensed physicians, clinics, and distribution centers; that government would tax, at a moderate level, and regulate the purity of legally available drugs; that advertising of drugs should be largely prohibited; and that limitations on use of drugs by those in certain occupations, such as public transport, should be in place.[20]

While Karel's proposal presumably has some elements that would be objectionable to some legalization proponents, it has the key feature of legalization—dramatically more legal access to a variety of psychoactive substances, toward the purpose of eliminating black markets for such substances. If something like Karel's proposal is what legalization really means, what, then, are the limits of this drug policy alternative?

One problem with the legalization alternative is that despite claims to the contrary by proponents, there is *not* compelling evidence that increased uptake of drugs could be avoided. For one thing, the evidence from the nation's experience with alcohol prohibition and repeal can be interpreted as showing the dangers of enhanced availability. Having given up on alcohol prohibition, the nation returned within a decade to levels of consumption that were as high as they had been before prohibition temporarily depressed them,[21] and the United States has been awash in alcohol since. In congressional testimony on the drug legalization issue, John Lawn, administrator of the DEA, argued that as a nation we have not handled the easy availability of alcohol very well:

> In 1985, nearly 100,000 10 and 11 year olds reported getting drunk at least once a week. We can attribute over 100,000 deaths a year in the United States to alcoholism. . . . History has shown us time and again that when addictive drugs are socially accepted and easily available, their use is associated with a high incidence of individual and social damage.[22]

Others, such as Herbert Kleber, argue that the lessons from alcohol underestimate what the uptake of illicit drugs would be after legalization because drugs such as cocaine and heroin have much greater addictive potential than alcohol. Kleber notes that ready availability of such drugs in some Southeast Asian countries and in the medical profession is associated with high levels of addiction. On the basis of his research, Kleber expects the creation of at least 12 million and as many as 55 million addicted users if narcotics were legalized.[23]

The legalization argument can also be criticized for a failing of logic at its most central purpose—defining a drug policy that would largely eliminate the evils of black markets. This is so because most legalization proponents advocate both taxation of legally available drugs and some limits on availability, such as prohibition of sales to minors. These features would open up substantial opportunities for continuing black markets, as drug traffickers would have incentives to smuggle drugs to avoid taxes and to maintain black markets to supply juveniles, prisoners, and others barred from access to otherwise legal drugs.[24]

The legalization proposal fails perhaps most dramatically with respect to political feasibility. Despite the apparent surge in articles and books on the topic, it is simply not an "idea in good currency" and is unlikely to become so. Robert E. Peterson argues this point:

> There is no groundswell of ranks to legalize drugs, the concept is opposed by a six-to-one margin, politically it is a dead issue, and the nation's recognized leaders in drug prevention, education, treatment, and law enforcement

adamantly oppose it . . . . the drug legalization discussion is more a pseudo-academic and entertainment exercise than a policy debate.[25]

Peterson is not exaggerating in his claim that legalization is opposed by a six-to-one margin, at least in mass public opinion. In a Gallup poll conducted on January 17, 1990, a national sample of citizens was asked the following question: "Some people feel that current drug laws haven't worked and that drugs like marijuana, cocaine and heroin should be legalized and subject to government taxation and regulation like alcohol and tobacco. Do you think drug legalization is a good idea or a bad idea?" In response, 80 percent of the people asked indicated that drug legalization is a bad idea, and only 14 percent called it a good idea. What is more, these attitudes toward legalization are strongly held. In a follow-up question on the same Gallup poll, 72 percent of respondents said that they felt "very strongly" about drug legalization, and another 21 percent said that they felt "fairly strong" in their opinion.[26] It is possible, of course, that public opinion might not be this dramatically opposed to legalization if the question were worded differently—for example, if the question referred only to the legalization of marijuana and heroin but not cocaine, or if it referred to possible taxation and regulation methods more stringent than those associated with alcohol and tobacco. But the question as worded provides a good statement of what many proponents of legalization appear to mean by the term, and it is difficult to see the response as anything other than a wholesale rejection by the American public.

There is another reason why legalization scores low on political feasibility: government agencies and professional groups have important stakes in the continuation of drug-control policy. As Chapter 8 shows, these organized interests do not necessarily occupy the same position in debates over drug policy, and they are not all equally effective in promoting their interests. But the most durable and effective of these organizations and groups, those on the law enforcement side, have important ideological and self-interest stakes in the maintenance of a criminal-law approach to the drug problem. Jerald Vaughn, executive director of the International Association of Chiefs of Police, testified in congressional hearings on the topic of drug legalization:

I can say without any hesitation that the law enforcement executives in the United States and other nations are unequivocally opposed to the legalization of drugs and, in fact, are quite concerned even about the ongoing debate on this topic. The debate appears to provide legitimacy to a cause that ultimately is detrimental to the health, welfare, and safety of all American citizens.[27]

The low political feasibility of the legalization concept is damaging to this alternative both directly and indirectly. In a direct sense, because it is still viewed as an idea outside the mainstream, legalization is kept from serious attention on the institutional agenda of government. The congressional hearings on drug legalization held in 1988 may seem to be an exception to this, but in fact, rather than legitimizing the concept, the hearings appear to have served the purpose of authoritatively undermining the legalization arguments that had been circulating among intellectuals and in the media for some time. In an indirect sense, political feasibility hinders the legalization alternative by forcing legalization proponents to take responsibility for providing incontrovertible evidence about relative costs, benefits, and risks. And, given what might be called the problem of magnitude, this burden of evidence is virtually insurmountable.

The problem of magnitude hinges on the fact that a cost-benefit analysis of drug prohibition versus legalization would have to consider several kinds of costs and benefits. Drug control is intended to prevent not simply the harms that drug users do to themselves but also the harms they do to others, that is, the external costs. Joel Hay provides an excellent summary of these external costs of drug use:

> The external costs of drug use include: (a) drug-addiction treatment and additional health-care costs caused by drug abuse that are borne by the taxpayer or the nondrug-using health insurance beneficiary; (b) the damage done by drug-abusing parents to their offspring; (c) the accidental deaths, injuries, and property losses imposed by drug abusers on third parties due to drug-induced violence, incapacity, misjudgment, irresponsibility, neglect, and other behavioral impairments . . . and (e) the pain, suffering, distress, and anxiety imposed by drug abusers on their friends and relatives.[28]

In addition to these various *costs of drug use,* the legalization debate, as we have seen, revolves around the various *costs of drug control,* such as the higher prices of substances when they are made illegal and the incentives that this creates for illegal and violent markets for drugs. While proponents of legalization emphasize the external costs of drug control, opponents of legalization emphasize the costs of drug use. Legalization proponents would have a compelling argument if the costs of drug control could be shown to vastly exceed the costs of actual and expected drug use itself. However, a definitive assessment of the magnitude of both types of costs is well beyond anyone's grasp. Many of the harms at issue cannot be reliably measured or easily expressed in dollar terms; and uncertainty over the levels of drug uptake to be expected under legalization further complicates the picture.

Objectively documenting the relative magnitude of the costs of drug abuse and the costs of drug control is, however, the responsibility of legalization proponents. Acknowledging this reality, the congressional Select Committee on Narcotics Abuse and Control noted, in its summary of findings from legalization hearings, that "the burden of proof regarding the benefits of drug legalization must be placed on the advocates of such a policy. Until the proponents of drug legalization can demonstrate that the benefits of such a policy outweigh the risks to health and drug-related violence, drug legalization should be rejected."[29]

Finally, legalization falters because it is too much premised on the instrumental side of government policy and misses the important expressive purpose of policy. Viewed from the instrumental side, the purpose of government is problem solving, in response to articulated needs of the citizenry and in line with the preferences of the public. Viewed from the expressive side, government also has a role in shaping values and perceptions by articulating standards of what is socially desirable and what preferences are legitimate.[30] Proposals to legalize drugs are heavily based upon a critique of the instrumental failures of drug prohibition—that is, the high costs, unintended consequences, and low effectiveness of current antidrug policy. Despite its instrumental failures, public policy can serve an important expressive function that involves the articulation of important values. The expressive function is what officials have in mind when they claim that tough drug laws send a message about the undesirability of drugs. This function is obviously undermined if drugs are legalized.

To the extent that legalization proponents recognize this expressive function at all, they tend to reject it on the libertarian grounds outlined earlier. However, that argument, with its roots in Mill's utilitarianism, does not carry the day. There are equally deep and compelling philosophical arguments that establish an important role for democratic governments in restraining the vices toward which people are inclined.[31] It is true that "the distinctive nature of the American system has led many of its supporters (to say nothing of its critics) to argue that it should be indifferent to character formation."[32] And it is also true that because economic conceptions of consumer sovereignty are relatively powerful in our society, Americans have a philosophical predisposition to believe that personal tastes should be beyond government manipulation.[33] However, like prostitution, drinking and driving, and many other behaviors that are authoritatively prohibited, drug use involves important harms to others as well as harms to the individual user. Given this reality, government in a free society presumably has a legitimate role in authoritatively sanctioning such behavior (the expressive function) even if it has difficulty in implementing those sanctions in a cost-effective manner (the instrumental function).

There are, however, problems with the expressive side of public policy. It may tend to generate more divisiveness than does the discussion of policy in the instrumental mode. This is because in its expressive function, government is by definition engaging in a process of defining dominant values, and this can lead to a zealousness among participants in the dialogue.[34] Over the history of drug policy, one particular version of this danger has often been observed—the justification of strong policy responses to drugs on the basis of their symbolic association with undesirable groups of one sort or another. Another important problem is the possibility that the powerful but simple symbols of expressive politics will generate simplistic responses to complex social problems that deserve more sophisticated answers.[35] All these problems of expressive policy indicate that drug policy alternatives must emphasize balance and moderation and must derive more from careful thought about consequences than from simplistic zealousness. The following section considers suggestions of this sort and the prospects for their realization.

OTHER SUGGESTIONS

If legalization is neither appropriate nor politically likely, what alternatives to current drug policy might be worthy of consideration? This section considers a number of related suggestions, all involving the theme of moderation in the drug policy area.

One possibility is to accept that there are limits to what we can reasonably accomplish with drug policy and, recognizing this, to develop more thoughtful alternatives for how we spend scarce dollars to deal with the drug problem. In this vein, Steven Wisotsky suggests that drug policy could be considerably improved if priorities were set more realistically:

> It is not possible to do everything. It is therefore both logical and necessary to make distinctions among things that are more or less important. Consider these differences in priority: (a) drug use by children (top priority) versus drug use by adults (low priority); (b) marijuana smoking (low priority) versus use of harder drugs (higher priority); (c) public use of drugs (high priority) versus private use of drugs at home (low priority); (d) drug consumption (no priority) versus drug impairment (high priority); (e) occasional use (low priority) versus chronic or dependent use (higher priority).[36]

Perhaps the most interesting and useful suggestions with regard to priority setting come from Mark Kleiman, whose recent work on the subject (*Against Excess*) might be considered a manifesto for those interested in replacing all-or-nothing thinking with more careful consideration of the many improvements in drug policy that could be made through simple adjustments and trade-offs within the current legal framework. For example, Kleiman suggests that the allocation of drug enforcement resources ought to be more sensitive to the possibilities presented by different illicit drugs. Because the heroin market is so much smaller than the cocaine market, comparatively modest enforcement resources might be expected to seriously disrupt heroin trafficking while even large amounts of resources hardly make a dent on cocaine trafficking. Given these contingencies, Kleiman argues for changing priorities:

Prosecutors making plea bargains or sentencing recommendations, judges handing out prison time, and legislators and sentencing commissions adjusting the statutes and guidelines governing who does how much time should consider the possible value of reallocating some prison cells from cocaine dealers to heroin dealers.[37]

Similarly, Kleiman argues that because heavy cocaine users cause the bulk of the problems of the cocaine epidemic, policies such as workplace drug testing and the "user accountability" measures stressed in the 1988 drug legislation (see Chapter 4) should have low priority. Such measures concentrate too many resources on casual users relative to heavy users and thus are not effective.

Others argue that such prioritizing, while seemingly obvious on logical grounds, will be resisted by those who approach the drug problem with an ideology of legalism, emphasizing the absolute immorality of all drug use:

> The current *National Drug Control Strategy* refused to assign priority candidates for public effort among the wide spectrum of illicit drugs. The problem, we are repeatedly told, is all drugs, all drug users, and in no particular order. . . . If the central harm in drug taking is the moral and political nature of the act, this immoral defiance is spread evenly across the range of currently prohibited substances.[38]

Apart from the ideological obstacles to priority setting, there are likely to be other complications. In 1991, for example, a district court ruled against a Minnesota law that provided more severe penalties for possession of crack than for possession of powdered cocaine. The majority of states had already enacted or were about to enact such laws, based upon judgments that cocaine in its smokable form—crack—is more addictive, is more easily trafficked to children because it is cheap, and is more likely to be the focus of violent competition among traffickers. However, in large part because it is cheaper, crack is preferred to powdered cocaine by black users while powdered cocaine is predominantly used by whites. Judge Alexander of Hennepin County District Court ruled the Minnesota law unconstitutional. It stipulated a four-year jail term for those convicted for the first time of possessing 3 grams of crack but only probation for those convicted for the first time of possessing the same amount of powdered cocaine.[39] The judge explained her decision:

> There had better be a good reason for any law that has the practical effect of disproportionately punishing members of one racial group. If crack was significantly more deadly or harmful than cocaine, that might be a good enough reason. But there just isn't enough evidence that they're different enough to justify the radical difference in penalties.[40]

The judge's comments point out the challenge to those who would legislate drug policy that treats different drugs, drug users, and drug use occasions differently. It will be difficult to ensure that priority setting is based upon reasoned evidence about comparable harms rather than upon myths, half-truths, and scare tactics. An unreasoned set of priorities is likely to be at least as bad as an undifferentiated "war on drugs." As we saw in Chapter 2, there is a historic tendency for U.S. drug policy to be driven by the fears derived from the linkage of drug use to "dangerous classes," especially minority groups. Drug policy differentiations that tap into such long-standing fears are not likely to be useful.

Most important, drug policy would be improved if it were less frenzied. As much of this book has shown, the drug issue is susceptible to policy-making based upon politically opportunistic use of fear. The result has been a histrionic approach to the drug issue. Drugs do create serious problems for American society, ranging from the miseries of addicts to the lost productivity of many workers to the dysfunctional families of drug abusers to the tragedies of crack babies and much more. But the seriousness of these problems does not relieve us from keeping a sense of proportion in our policy responses. As Mark Kleiman has noted, "making drug policy has something in common with taking drugs: both are activities prone to excess, and the key to avoiding problems with either one is knowing when to stop."[41]

Stated another way, we would do better to subject our drug policy-making to an important principle of economics—the principle of marginalism. As Steven Rhoads argues, the simple principle of marginalism is the opposite of extremism. It suggests that even the most valued of activities are subject to decreasing marginal utility and increasing marginal cost.[42] This being the case, it is not appropriate to wage drug wars that do not weigh the benefits (if any) to be gained from additional units of effort against the costs of that effort, including the costs of forgoing other valued activities:

> Yet most of the debate concerning drug control in the 1980s has treated prohibition policy as a package deal, a take-it-or-leave-it $25 billion proposition in which $5 billion nuances of program level or component mix are insignificant. An emphasis on drug control policy at the margin would be a welcome reform in the planning process for individual programs and an important paradigm shift in thinking about the scale of the entire drug control effort.[43]

The advantages of balance can be seen both within and across the various categories of U.S. drug policy. Looking across the categories, the principle of balance suggests that law enforcement and interdiction efforts, which have been absorbing about 70 percent of the federal drug budget, should be scaled back in favor of a better balance of effort with respect to drug prevention, treatment, and rehabilitation. This is so not only because of the many disappointments of a supply-side war on drugs but also because even those working on the enforcement side have begun to realize that supply-side efforts can never be very successful without corresponding efforts at demand reduction.

Within the various categories of drug policy activity, the principles of marginalism and balance can also be useful. Within the field of drug treatment, for example, many individuals have called for expansion of drug treatment slots to the point that there are no waiting lists and treatment can be had on demand. Meanwhile, others have pressed for mandatory or at least coerced treatment of drug abusers in the form of drug programs for prisoners and compulsory involvement in employee assistance programs for workers who test positive for drug use. All this would require a level of treatment capacity that many would find excessive; and there is reason to question whether compulsory drug treatment can be effective. However, some expansion of treatment capacity, particularly in the areas with the largest verifiable waiting lists, is called for, along with continuing research and experimentation on forms of treatment that are an improvement over existing methods.

Similarly, prevention of drug abuse may deserve expanded support. However, dramatic expansion of this activity is probably not warranted as long as prevention programs yield only the minimal behavioral changes in their audiences that have been observed to date. And the available evidence suggests that scarce prevention dollars might much better be allocated to organized, in-school education programs rather than dramatic but apparently ineffective mass media campaigns.

Finally, the principles of marginalism and balance suggest that within the supply-side effort, more effort should go to enforcement relative to interdiction. Although we cannot and should not throw our borders wide open to drug traffickers, the evidence suggests that there are high marginal costs and very limited marginal benefits from pressing the war on drugs at the border. In addition, the principles of marginalism and balance are consistent with the enforcement priorities proposed by Arnold Trebach in congressional testimony on the issue of legalization. Trebach suggests that enforcement funds be targeted primarily against "violent criminal syndicates that traffic in drugs and other illegal commodities" and that "less law enforcement attention should be paid to small dealers and simple users, who should be virtually ignored by the police unless they commit other crimes, such as robbery or burglary, or create public nuisances by interfering with normal street traffic."[44]

Some might argue that this is the functional equivalent of legalizing drugs, at least for a certain category of users and purveyors, and hence subject to all the problems, including lack of political acceptability, that have been attributed to legalization proposals. But in the ways that count, this is not the equivalent of legalization. Drug use and dealing would *not* be openly and authoritatively declared to be acceptable, and efforts to disrupt drug trafficking higher up the ladder would continue.

By largely ignoring small dealers and users, however, drug-law enforcement would require fewer resources, and agents would encounter fewer temptations for the corruption and abuse of civil liberties that have tainted current approaches to drug-law enforcement.

A balanced drug policy is not only one that eschews disproportionate effort in any area of antidrug activity; it is also one that is based upon realistic goals. America's various wars on drugs have often been waged with claims that drug trafficking can be totally disrupted, that the scourge of drugs can be removed from American society, and other such hyperbole. There has been some evidence in recent years of a tempering of this. For example, the Bush administration's first drug policy plan had very modest goals—so modest, in fact, that some critics in Congress argued that a more decisive commitment was needed. But in his response, William Bennett, then drug policy director, urged realism over rhetoric:

> I think the American people have been overpromised too many times about winning the war on drugs. It's important that we give a sober assessment, recognizing that the situation in some communities is close to being out of control, and then saying, these are the reasonable objectives. . . . If in ten years, Congressman, if in ten years, it is, in fact, the case that we have reduced the number of crack users by 50 percent, I think we can say that we have managed a significant victory.[45]

It is possible, of course, that this more realistic rhetoric was more the result of budget stalemate than of enhanced respect for the intelligence of the American public on the part of politicians. If there has been any policy learning on the part of the American public and political officials, however, it may lead to a more limited and realistic set of goals. Such a perspective will include what Franklin Zimring and Gordon Hawkins call the "chronic-disease perspective"—"a view that the appetite for licit and illicit mood-altering substances is a permanent part of American life insusceptible by its nature to a complete cure."[46]

From a political scientist's perspective, these various suggestions for policy reasonableness—that is, setting priorities, balancing costs and benefits, marginal costing, and setting reasonable goals—are far from easy to realize. They constitute, as it were, a major change from much contemporary practice and make a sharp break with the historical pattern of manipulating the drug issue and the policy excesses that result. As Chapter 3 shows, the main exception to this, President Carter's efforts to defuse the drug issue and to rationalize drug policy, was a notable failure. And if a drug policy of reasonableness constitutes a major policy innovation, then the prospects for it would not seem to be good. As Chapter 8 explains, inertial forces in American political life stand in the way of policy innovation, and a movement toward reasonableness in drug policy may not be in the immediate interests of some powerful organized interests in the drug policy domain.

Nevertheless, several considerations suggest that a move to a more balanced and reasonable drug policy is a possibility. Frank Baumgartner and Bryan Jones explain that in fact, policy history is marked by sharp shifts in policy as well as long periods limited to incremental change. Dramatic reversals in policy can occur during periods when changes in either policy venue or policy image create a self-reinforcing system of change.[47] By *policy venue*, Baumgartner and Jones refer to the institutions that have jurisdiction over particular issues. As Chapter 8 shows, there has already been change in the drug policy venue. In particular, drug policy is now being debated in congressional committees and subcommittees with differing levels of receptivity to law enforcement, treatment, and prevention interests.

Perhaps more important, there is accumulating evidence that the image of the drug issue has begun to change. By *policy image*, Baumgartner and Jones mean the "public and elite understandings of public policy problems" that influence beliefs about appropriate policy solutions.[48] In the drug issue, the most important image change is the gradually accumulating awareness that drug policy itself is part of the problem rather than part of the solution. This image is, of course, heavily promoted by proponents of drug legalization. But if change in policy image were confined to the intellectual circles where legalization is being debated, it would have limited impact. Instead, negative images of contemporary drug policy are also increasingly evident in popular magazines, movies, and the like. For example, general acknowledgement that drug-law enforcement entails corruption of law enforcement agencies is manifested in popular movies that feature corrupt agents and compromised agencies. And in recent years a flurry of critical articles have appeared in popular magazines; for example, *Newsweek* reported on the failures of the drug war in Washington, D.C. ("A Failed 'Test Case': Washington's Drug War," January 29, 1990) and on drug-war tactics that threaten constitutional rights ("Uncivil Liberties," April 23, 1990). These and many other popular articles, television shows, and radio talk-shows are presumably changing the image of the drug problem and the nation's war on drugs.

CONCLUSIONS

There is a certain irony in the proposal for policy reasonableness. Conventional wisdom holds that public policy in the United States is typically *not* radical, drastic, or immoderate, but rather the bland outcome of political compromise. Under these circumstances, policies are criticized for being too timid and too partial, and policy innovation is envisioned as a fresh wind of vigorous government effort, albeit in a new direction. We have seen that in contrast with this conventional wisdom, U.S. drug policy is flawed primarily in its extremism. A long-standing tradition of immoderate, unbalanced policy is the problem; and policy innovation is needed *not* in the sense of an explosion of new energy directed at the problem but in the sense of a major standing down from vociferous approaches to the problem. As in so many policy issues in the public health area, from abortion to the AIDS epidemic, it will be difficult for policy-makers to hold to a new and moderate policy approach. However, if the policy history traced in this book has suggested anything, it is that government officials tend to create the public hysteria over drugs rather than simply to respond to it. The power and the responsibility to demobilize that hysteria are in the hands of public officials as well.

NOTES

1. Ethan Nadelmann, "The Case for Legalization," in James Inciardi, ed., *The Drug Legalization Debate* (Newbury Park, CA: Sage, 1991), pp. 19–20. Reprinted by permission of Sage Publications, Inc.
2. David T. Courtwright, "Drug Legalization, the Drug War, and Drug Treatment in Historical Perspective," *Journal of Policy History* 3 (1991), p. 394.
3. Joseph B. Treaster, "Hospital Visits Show Abuse of Drugs Is Still on the Rise," *New York Times*, May 14, 1992, p. 8.
4. Joseph B. Treaster, "Use of Cocaine and Heroin Rises Among Urban Youth," *New York Times*, December 19, 1991, p. A18.
5. White House, *National Drug Control Strategy: Budget Summary* (Washington, DC: Office of National Drug Control Policy, 1992), p. 3.
6. Kevin B. Zeese, "Drug War Forever?" in Melvyn B. Krauss and Edward P. Lazear, eds., *Searching for Alternatives: Drug Policy in the United States* (Stanford, CA: Hoover Institution, 1991), p. 260.
7. James Ostrowski, "Answering the Critics of Drug Legalization," in Melvyn B. Krauss and Edward P. Lazear, eds., *Searching for Alternatives: Drug Control Policy in the United States* (Stanford, CA: Hoover Institution, 1991), pp. 304–305.
8. Ira Glasser, "Drug Prohibition: An Engine for Crime," in Melvyn B. Krauss and Edward P. Lazear, eds., *Searching for Alternatives: Drug Control Policy in the United States* (Stanford, CA: Hoover Institution, 1991), p. 274.
9. Zeese, 1991, p. 262.
10. Douglas McVay, "Marijuana Legalization: The Time Is Now," in James Inciardi, ed., *The Drug Legalization Debate* (Newbury Park, CA: Sage, 1991), p. 156.
11. Nadelmann, 1991, p. 41.
12. Jeffrey Miron, "Drug Legalization and the Consumption of Drugs: An Economist's Perspective," in Melvyn B. Krauss and Edward P. Lazear, eds., *Searching for Alternatives: Drug Control Policy in the United States* (Stanford, CA: Hoover Institution, 1991), p. 75.
13. Zeese, 1991, p. 262.
14. Franklin E. Zimring and Gordon Hawkins, *The Search for Rational Drug Control* (New York: Cambridge University Press, 1992), pp. 82–91; James B. Bakalar and Lester Grinspoon, *Drug Control in a Free Society* (Cambridge: Cambridge University Press, 1984).

15. Thomas Szasz, "The Morality of Drug Controls," in Ronald Hamowy, ed., *Dealing with Drugs: Consequences of Government Control* (Lexington, MA: Heath, 1987), p. 344.
16. James Inciardi and Duane McBride, "The Case Against Legalization," in J. Inciardi, ed., *The Drug Legalization Debate* (Newbury Park, CA: Sage, 1991), pp. 47–49.
17. Franklin E. Zimring and Gordon Hawkins, "The Wrong Question: Critical Notes on the Decriminalization Debate," in Melvyn B. Krauss and Edward P. Lazear, eds., *Searching for Alternatives: Drug Control Policy in the United States* (Stanford, CA: Hoover Institution, 1991), p. 30.
18. Richard B. Karel, "A Model Legalization Proposal," in James A. Inciardi, ed., *The Drug Legalization Debate* (Newbury Park, CA: Sage, 1991), pp. 81–82.
19. Karel, 1991, p. 86.
20. Karel, 1991, pp. 91–96.
21. Miron, 1991, p. 75.
22. U.S. House of Representatives, Select Committee on Narcotics Abuse and Control, *Legalization of Illicit Drugs: Impact and Feasibility, Part I* (Washington, DC: U.S. Government Printing Office, 1988c), p. 71.
23. Herbert Kleber, as cited in Courtwright, 1991, p. 396.
24. Courtwright, 1991, pp. 397–405.
25. Robert E. Peterson, "Legalization: The Myth Exposed," in Melvyn B. Krauss and Edward P. Lazear, eds., *Searching for Alternatives: Drug Control Policy in the United States* (Stanford, CA: Hoover Institution, 1991), p. 324.
26. Diane Colasanto, "Widespread Opposition to Drug Legalization," *Gallup Poll News Service* (Princeton, NJ: Gallup Organization, 1990), p. 5.
27. Select Committee on Narcotics Abuse and Control, 1988c, p. 76.
28. Joel W. Hay, "The Harm They Do to Others: A Primer on the External Costs of Drug Abuse," in Melvyn B. Krauss and Edward P. Lazear, eds., *Searching for Alternatives: Drug Control Policy in the United States* (Stanford, CA: Hoover Institution, 1991), p. 203.
29. U.S. House of Representatives, Select Committee on Narcotics Abuse and Control, *Legalization of Illicit Drugs: Impact and Feasibility (A Review of Recent Hearings)* (Washington, DC: U.S. Government Printing Office, 1989d), p. 4.
30. Philip Heymann, "How Government Expresses Public Ideas," in Robert Reich, ed., *The Power of Public Ideas* (Cambridge: Harvard University Press, 1988).
31. Zimring and Hawkins, 1991, pp. 9–12.
32. James Q. Wilson, *On Character* (Washington, DC: AEI Press, 1991), p. 22.
33. Steven E. Rhoads, *The Economist's View of the World* (Cambridge: Cambridge University Press, 1985), p. 62.
34. Heymann, 1988, pp. 101–102.
35. Heymann, 1988, p. 103.
36. Steven Wisotsky, "Beyond the War on Drugs," in James Inciardi, ed., *The Drug Legalization Debate* (Newbury Park, CA: Sage, 1991), p. 117. Reprinted by permission of Sage Publications, Inc.
37. Mark Kleiman, *Against Excess* (New York: Basic Books, 1992), p. 369.
38. Zimring and Hawkins, 1992, p. 179.
39. Robb London, "Judge's Overruling of Crack Law Brings Turmoil," *New York Times*, January 11, 1991, p. B5. Copyright © 1991 by The New York Times Company. Reprinted by permission.

40. London, 1991, p. B5. Copyright © 1991 by the The New York Times Company. Reprinted by permission.
41. Kleiman, 1992, p. 388.
42. Rhoads, 1985, pp. 11–38.
43. Zimring and Hawkins, 1992, p. 184.
44. Select Committee on Narcotics Abuse and Control, 1988c, p. 327.
45. U.S. House of Representatives, Select Committee on Narcotics Abuse and Control, *National Drug Control Strategy* (Washington, DC: U.S. Government Printing Office, 1990b), p. 15.
46. Zimring and Hawkins, 1992, p. 191.
47. Frank R. Baumgartner and Bryan D. Jones, "Agenda Dynamics and Policy Subsystems," *Journal of Politics* 53 (November 1991), pp. 1045–1051.
48. Baumgartner and Jones, 1991, p. 1046.

Works Cited

GOVERNMENT DOCUMENTS

Dodaro, Gene L. 1988. *Asset Forfeiture Programs: Corrective Actions Underway But Additional Improvements Needed.* Washington, DC: U.S. General Accounting Office.

Kleinman, Paula, George Woody, Thomas Todd, Robert Millman, Sung-Yeon Kang, Jack Kemp, and Douglas Lipton. 1990. "Crack and Cocaine Abusers in Outpatient Psychotherapy." *Psychotherapy and Counselling in the Treatment of Drug Abuse.* NIDA Research Monograph 104. Washington, DC: U.S. Government Printing Office, pp. 24–35.

National Institute of Justice. 1990. *Searching for Answers: Research and Evaluation on Drugs and Crime.* Washington, DC: U.S. Department of Justice.

National Institute on Drug Abuse and National Institute on Alcohol Abuse and Alcoholism. 1990. *National Drug and Alcoholism Treatment Unit Survey (NDATUS) 1989 Main Findings Report.* Rockville, MD: U.S. Department of Health and Human Services.

National Institute on Drug Abuse. 1991. *Drug Use Among American High School Seniors, College Students and Young Adults, 1975–1990.* Washington, DC: U.S. Government Printing Office.

National Institute on Drug Abuse. 1991. *National Household Survey on Drug Abuse: Main Findings 1990.* Washington, DC: U.S. Government Printing Office.

National Narcotics Intelligence Consumers Committee (NNICC). 1988. *The NNICC Report 1987: The Supply of Illicit Drugs to the United States.* Washington, DC: NNICC.

Public Papers of the Presidents of the United States. Richard Nixon, 1971. 1972. Washington, DC: U.S. Government Printing Office.

Public Papers of the Presidents of the United States. George Bush, Book II, 1989. 1990. Washington, DC: U.S. Government Printing Office.

Public Papers of the Presidents of the United States. Jimmy Carter, Book I, 1977. 1977. Washington, DC: U.S. Government Printing Office.

Public Papers of the Presidents of the United States. Ronald Reagan, Book I, 1988. 1990. Washington, DC: U.S. Government Printing Office.

U.S. Bureau of the Census. 1992. *Statistical Abstract of the United States 1992,* 112th ed. Washington, DC: U.S. Government Printing Office.

U.S. House of Representatives. Committee on Armed Services. Special Subcommittee on Alleged Drug Abuse in the Armed Services. 1971. *Alleged Drug Abuse in the Armed Services.* Washington, DC: U.S. Government Printing Office.

U.S. House of Representatives. Committee on Education and Labor. Subcommittee on Employment Opportunities. 1988. *Oversight Hearing on Drug Testing in the Work Force.* Washington, DC: U.S. Government Printing Office.

U.S. House of Representatives. Committee on the Judiciary. Subcommittee on Crime. 1986. *Forfeiture Issues.* Washington, DC: U.S. Government Printing Office.

U.S. House of Representatives. Committee on Merchant Marine and Fisheries. Subcommittee on Coast Guard and Navigation. 1988. *"Zero Tolerance" Drug Policy and Confiscation of Property.* Washington, DC: U.S. Government Printing Office.

U.S. House of Representatives. Select Committee on Crime. 1970. *Crime in America—Heroin Importation, Distribution, Packaging and Paraphernalia.* Washington, DC: U.S. Government Printing Office.

U.S. House of Representatives. Select Committee on Narcotics Abuse and Control. 1977. *Decriminalization of Marihuana.* Washington, DC: U.S. Government Printing Office.

U.S. House of Representatives. Select Committee on Narcotics Abuse and Control. 1978. *Oversight Hearings on Federal Drug Strategy.* Washington, DC: U.S. Government Printing Office.

U.S. House of Representatives. Select Committee on Narcotics Abuse and Control. 1986. *Drug Abuse Education.* Washington, DC: U.S. Government Printing Office.

U.S. House of Representatives. Select Committee on Narcotics Abuse and Control. 1987. *Drug Abuse Prevention in America's Schools.* Washington, DC: U.S. Government Printing Office.

U.S. House of Representatives. Select Committee on Narcotics Abuse and Control. 1988a. *Intravenous Drug Use and AIDS: The Impact on the Black Community.* Washington, DC: U.S. Government Printing Office.

U.S. House of Representatives. Select Committee on Narcotics Abuse and Control. 1988b. *Cocaine Babies.* Washington, DC: U.S. Government Printing Office.

U.S. House of Representatives. Select Committee on Narcotics Abuse and Control. 1988c. *Legalization of Illicit Drugs: Impact and Feasibility, Part I.* Washington, DC: U.S. Government Printing Office.

U.S. House of Representatives. Select Committee on Narcotics Abuse and Control. 1989a. *Efficacy of Drug Abuse Treatment Programs, Part I.* Washington, DC: U.S. Government Printing Office.

U.S. House of Representatives. Select Committee on Narcotics Abuse and Control. 1989b. *The Drug Enforcement Crisis at the Local Level.* Washington, DC: U.S. Government Printing Office.

U.S. House of Representatives. Select Committee on Narcotics Abuse and Control. 1989c. *Educating America's Youth Against Drugs: Federal Drug Abuse Education Strategy.* Washington, DC: U.S. Government Printing Office.

U.S. House of Representatives. Select Committee on Narcotics Abuse and Control. 1989d. *Legalization of Illicit Drugs: Impact and Feasibility (A Review of Recent Hearings).* Washington, DC: U.S. Government Printing Office.

U.S. House of Representatives. Select Committee on Narcotics Abuse and Control. 1990a. *Efficacy of Drug Abuse Treatment Programs, Part II.* Washington, DC: U.S. Government Printing Office.

U.S. House of Representatives. Select Committee on Narcotics Abuse and Control. 1990b. *National Drug Control Strategy.* Washington, DC: U.S. Government Printing Office.

U.S. House of Representatives. Select Committee on Narcotics Abuse and Control. 1990c. *Federal Strategy for Drug Abuse Education*. Washington, DC: U.S. Government Printing Office.

U.S. House of Representatives. Select Committee on Narcotics Abuse and Control. 1990d. *The Federal Drug Strategy*. Washington, DC: U.S. Government Printing Office.

U.S. House of Representatives. Select Committee on Narcotics Abuse and Control. 1991. *National Drug Control Strategy*. Washington, DC: U.S. Government Printing Office.

U.S. Senate. Committee on the Judiciary. Subcommittee on Criminal Law. 1984. *Comprehensive Crime Control Act of 1983*. Washington, DC: U.S. Government Printing Office.

White House. 1990. *National Drug Control Strategy*. Washington, DC: U.S. Government Printing Office.

White House. 1991. *National Drug Control Strategy*. Washington, DC: U.S. Government Printing Office.

White House. 1992. *National Drug Control Strategy*. Washington, DC: U.S. Government Printing Office.

White House. 1992. *National Drug Control Strategy: Budget Summary*. Washington, DC: Office of National Drug Control Policy.

SCHOLARLY BOOKS AND ARTICLES

Aberbach, Joel. 1990. *Keeping a Watchful Eye: The Politics of Congressional Oversight*. Washington, DC: Brookings.

Ackerman, Deborah L. 1991. "A History of Drug Testing." In Robert H. Coombs and Louis J. West, eds., *Drug Testing: Issues and Options*. New York: Oxford University Press, pp. 3–21.

Anderson, Patrick. 1981. *High in America: The True Story Behind NORML and the Politics of Marijuana*. New York: Viking Press.

Aniskiewicz, Rick, and Earl Wysong. 1990. "Evaluating DARE: Drug Education and the Multiple Meanings of Success." *Policy Studies Review* 9 (Summer): 727–747.

Anglin, M. Douglas. 1988. "The Efficacy of Civil Commitment in Treating Narcotics Addictions." *Journal of Drug Issues* 18 (Fall): 527–545.

Anglin, M. Douglas, and Yih-Ing Hser. 1990. "Treatment of Drug Abuse." In Michael Tonry and James Q. Wilson, eds., *Drugs and Crime*. Chicago: University of Chicago Press, pp. 393–460.

Axel, Helen. 1991. "Drug Testing in Private Industry." In Robert H. Coombs and Louis J. West, eds., *Drug Testing: Issues and Options*. New York: Oxford University Press, pp. 140–154.

Bakalar, James B., and Lester Grinspoon. 1984. *Drug Control in a Free Society*. Cambridge: Cambridge University Press.

Barber, James David. 1985. *The Presidential Character*, 3rd ed. Englewood Cliffs, NJ: Prentice-Hall.

Barnett, Randy. 1987. "Curing the Drug-Law Addiction: The Harmful Side Effects of Legal Prohibition." In Ronald Hamowy, ed., *Dealing with Drugs: Consequences of Government Control*. Lexington, MA: Heath, pp. 73–102.

Baumgartner, Frank R., and Bryan D. Jones. 1991. "Agenda Dynamics and Policy Subsystems." *Journal of Politics* 53 (November): 1044–1074.

Belenko, Steven. 1990. "The Impact of Drug Offenders on the Criminal Justice System." In Ralph Weisheit, ed., *Drugs, Crime and the Criminal Justice System*. Cincinnati: Anderson, pp. 27–78.

Bellis, David J. 1981. *Heroin and Politicians: The Failure of Public Policy to Control Addiction in America*. Westport, CT: Greenwood Press.

Benjamin, Daniel K., and Roger L. Miller. 1992. *Undoing Drugs*. New York: Basic Books.

Berry, Jeffrey. 1984. *Feeding Hungry People*. New Brunswick, NJ: Rutgers University Press.

Bosso, Christopher. 1987. *Pesticides and Politics: The Life Cycle of a Policy Issue*. Pittsburgh: University of Pittsburgh Press.

Botvin, Gilbert J. 1990. "Substance Abuse Prevention: Theory, Practice, and Effectiveness." In Michael Tonry and James Q. Wilson, eds., *Drugs and Crime*. Chicago: University of Chicago Press, pp. 461–520.

Brown, Barry. 1990. "The Growth of Drug Abuse Treatment Systems." In James Inciardi, ed., *Handbook of Drug Control in the United States*. New York: Greenwood Press, pp. 51–69.

Browne, William P. 1987. *Private Interests, Public Policy, and American Agriculture*. Lawrence: University Press of Kansas.

Bukoski, William. 1990. "The Federal Approach to Primary Drug Abuse Prevention and Education." In James Inciardi, ed., *Handbook of Drug Control in the United States*. New York: Greenwood Press, pp. 93–114.

Carter, David L. 1990. "An Overview of Drug-Related Misconduct of Police Officers: Drug Abuse and Narcotic Corruption." In Ralph Weisheit, ed., *Drugs, Crime and the Criminal Justice System*. Cincinnati: Anderson, pp. 79–110.

Chaiken, Jan, Marcia Chaiken, and Clifford Karchmer. 1990. *Multijurisdictional Drug Law Enforcement Strategies: Reducing Supply and Demand*. Washington, DC: National Institute of Justice.

Cobb, Roger, Jennie-Keith Ross, and Marc Ross. 1976. "Agenda Building as a Comparative Political Process." *American Political Science Review* 70 (March): 126–138.

Cook, Royer F. 1989. "Drug Use Among Working Adults: Prevalence Rates and Estimation Methods." In Steven Gust and J. Michael Walsh, eds., *Drugs in the Workplace: Research and Evaluation Data*. Washington, DC: U.S. Government Printing Office, pp. 17–32.

Cooper, Mary. 1990. *The Business of Drugs*. Washington, DC: Congressional Quarterly.

Cornish, Craig M. 1988. *Drugs and Alcohol in the Workplace: Testing and Privacy*. Wilmette, IL: Callaghan.

Courtwright, David T. 1991. "Drug Legalization, the Drug War, and Drug Treatment in Historical Perspective." *Journal of Policy History* 3(4): 393–412.

DeJong, William. 1987. *Arresting the Demand for Drugs: Police and School Partnerships to Prevent Drug Abuse*. Washington, DC: National Institute of Justice.

De Leon, George. 1990. "Treatment Strategies." In James Inciardi, ed., *Handbook of Drug Control in the United States*. New York: Greenwood Press, pp. 115–138.

Dombrink, John, James Meeker, and Julie Paik. 1988. "Fighting for Fees—Drug Trafficking and the Forfeiture of Attorney's Fees." *Journal of Drug Issues* 18:

421–436.

Downs, Anthony. 1973. "Up and Down with Ecology—the 'Issue-Attention Cycle.'" *The Public Interest* 32: 38–50.

Dye, Thomas R. 1992. *Understanding Public Policy*, 7th ed. Englewood Cliffs, NJ: Prentice-Hall.

Edelman, Murray. 1974. *The Symbolic Uses of Politics*. Urbana: University of Illinois Press.

Edelman, Murray. 1977. *Political Language: Words That Succeed and Policies That Fail*. New York: Academic Press.

Epstein, Jay. 1977. *Agency of Fear*. New York: Putnam.

Falco, Mathea. 1989. *Winning the Drug War: A National Strategy*. New York: Priority Press.

Flay, B. R., and S. Sobel. 1983. "The Role of Mass Media in Preventing Adolescent Substance Abuse." In T. J. Glynn, C. G. Leukefeld, and J. P. Ludford, eds., *Preventing Adolescent Drug Abuse: Intervention Strategies NIDA*. Washington, DC: U.S. Government Printing Office, Research Monograph 47, pp. 5–35.

Forman, Avraham, and Susan B. Lachter. 1989. "The National Institute on Drug Abuse Cocaine Prevention Campaign." In Pamela Shoemaker, ed., *Communication Campaigns About Drugs*. Hillsdale, NJ: Erlbaum, pp. 13–20.

Genovese, Michael A. 1990. *The Nixon Presidency: Power and Politics in Turbulent Times*. New York: Greenwood Press.

Glasser, Ira. 1991. "Drug Prohibition: An Engine for Crime." In Melvyn B. Krauss and Edward P. Lazear, eds., *Searching for Alternatives: Drug Control Policy in the United States*. Stanford, CA: Hoover Institution, pp. 271–282.

Goggin, Malcolm, Ann O'M. Bowman, James P. Lester, and Laurence J. O'Toole, Jr. 1990. *Implementation Theory and Practice*. Glenview, IL: Scott, Foresman.

Goldberg, Peter. 1980. "The Federal Government's Response to Illicit Drugs, 1969–1978." In Drug Abuse Council, *The Facts About "Drug Abuse."* New York: Free Press, pp. 20–62.

Goode, Erich. 1989. *Drugs in American Society*, 3rd ed. New York: McGraw-Hill.

Gordon, N. P., and A. L. McAlister. 1982. "Adolescent Drinking: Issues and Research." In T. J. Coates, A. C. Petersen, and C. Perry, eds., *Promoting Adolescent Health: A Dialog on Research and Practice*. New York: Academic Press, pp. 201–224.

Hargrove, Erwin C., and John C. Glidewell. 1990. *Impossible Jobs in Public Management*. Lawrence: University Press of Kansas.

Hay, Joel W. 1991. "The Harm They Do to Others: A Primer on the External Costs of Drug Abuse." In Melvyn B. Krauss and Edward P. Lazear, eds., *Searching for Alternatives: Drug Control Policy in the United States*. Stanford, CA: Hoover Institution, pp. 200–225.

Hayes, Michael. 1992. *Incrementalism and Public Policy*. New York: Longman.

Heymann, Philip. 1988. "How Government Expresses Public Ideas." In Robert Reich, ed., *The Power of Public Ideas*. Cambridge: Harvard University Press, pp. 85–108.

Hilgartner, Stephen, and Charles L. Bosk. 1988. "The Rise and Fall of Social Problems: A Public Arenas Model." *American Journal of Sociology* 94 (July): 53–78.

Himmelstein, Jerome. 1983. *The Strange Career of Marihuana.* Westport, CT: Greenwood Press.

Hubbard, Robert, J. Valley Rachal, S. Gail Craddock, and Elizabeth R. Cavanaugh. 1984. "Treatment Outcome Prospective Study (TOPS): Client Characteristics and Behaviors Before, During, and After Treatment." In Frank Tims and Jacqueline Ludford, eds., *Drug Abuse Treatment Evaluation: Strategies, Progress, and Prospects.* Rockville, MD: National Institute on Drug Abuse, pp. 42–68.

Hubbard, Robert, Mary Ellen Marsden, J. Valley Rachal, Henrick Harwood, Elizabeth Cavanaugh, and Harold Ginzburg. 1989. *Drug Abuse Treatment: A National Study of Effectiveness.* Chapel Hill: University of North Carolina Press.

Inciardi, James, and Duane McBride. 1991. "The Case Against Legalization." In James Inciardi, ed., *The Drug Legalization Debate.* Newbury Park, CA: Sage, pp. 45–79.

Jaffe, Jerome. 1984. "Evaluating Drug Abuse Treatment: A Comment on the State of the Art." In Frank Tims and Jacqueline Ludford, eds., *Drug Abuse Treatment Evaluation: Strategies, Progress, and Prospects.* Rockville, MD: National Institute on Drug Abuse, pp. 13–28.

Jonas, Steven. 1991. "The U.S. Drug Problem and the U.S. Drug Culture: A Public Health Solution." In James Inciardi, ed., *The Drug Legalization Debate.* Newbury Park, CA: Sage, pp. 161–182.

Karel, Richard B. 1991. "A Model Legalization Proposal." In James A. Inciardi, ed., *The Drug Legalization Debate.* Newbury Park, CA: Sage, pp. 80–102.

Kingdon, John. 1984. *Agendas, Alternatives, and Public Policies.* New York: HarperCollins.

Kleber, Herbert, and Frank H. Gawin. 1984. "Cocaine Abuse: A Review of Current and Experimental Treatments." In John Grabowski, ed., *Cocaine: Pharmacology, Effects, and Treatment of Abuse.* NIDA Research Monograph 50. Washington, DC: U.S. Government Printing Office, pp. 111–129.

Kleiman, Mark. 1988. "Crackdowns: The Effects of Intensive Enforcement on Retail Heroin Dealing." In Marcia Chaiken, ed., *Street-Level Drug Enforcement: Examining the Issues.* Washington, DC: National Institute of Justice, pp. 3–34.

Kleiman, Mark. 1992. *Against Excess: Drug Policy for Results.* New York: Basic Books.

Kleiman, Mark, and Kerry Smith. 1990. "State and Local Drug Enforcement: In Search of a Strategy." In Michael Tonry and James Q. Wilson, eds., *Drugs and Crime.* Chicago: University of Chicago Press, pp. 69–108.

Leonard, Herman. 1986. *Checks Unbalanced: The Quiet Side of Public Spending.* New York: Basic Books.

Leukefeld, Carl, and Frank Tims. 1988. "Compulsory Treatment: A Review of Findings." In Leukefeld and Tims, eds., *Compulsory Treatment of Drug Abuse: Research and Clinical Practice.* Washington, DC: National Institute on Drug Abuse, pp. 236–252.

Leyden, Kevin. 1991. "Organized Interests and the Use of Congressional Hearings: The Rationale Behind Public Lobbying." Paper presented at the Annual Meeting of the Midwest Political Science Association, Chicago, April 18–20.

Lindblad, Richard. 1988. "Civil Commitment Under the Federal Narcotics Act."

Journal of Drug Issues 18 (Fall): 599.

Lindblom, Charles. 1959. "The Science of 'Muddling Through.'" *Public Administration Review* 19 (Spring): 79–88.

Lund, Adrian, David Preusser, and Allan Williams. 1989. "Drug Use by Tractor-Trailer Drivers." In Steven Gust and J. Michael Walsh, eds., *Drugs in the Workplace: Research and Evaluation Data.* Washington, DC: U.S. Government Printing Office, pp. 47–68.

Lyman, Michael. 1989. *Practical Drug Enforcement.* New York: Elsevier.

Macdonald, Donald Ian. 1990. *Drugs, Drinking and Adolescents,* 2nd ed. Chicago: Year Book Medical Publishers.

McVay, Douglas. 1991. "Marijuana Legalization: The Time Is Now." In James Inciardi, ed., *The Drug Legalization Debate.* Newbury Park, CA: Sage, pp. 147–160.

McWilliams, John C. 1990. *The Protectors: Harry J. Anslinger and the Federal Bureau of Narcotics, 1930–1962.* Newark: University of Delaware Press.

Manning, Peter K. 1980. *The Narc's Game: Organizational and Informational Limits on Drug Law Enforcement.* Cambridge: MIT Press.

Meier, Kenneth. 1991. "Political Institutions and the Control of U.S. Drug Enforcement Policies." Paper presented at the Annual Meeting of the Midwest Political Science Association, Chicago, April 18–20.

Meier, Kenneth. 1992. "The Politics of Drug Abuse: Laws, Implementation, and Consequences." *Western Political Quarterly* 45 (March): 41–70.

Meyer, Marshall W., and Lynne G. Zucker. 1989. *Permanently Failing Organizations.* Newbury Park, CA: Sage.

Miron, Jeffrey. 1991. "Drug Legalization and the Consumption of Drugs: An Economist's Perspective." In Melvyn B. Krauss and Edward P. Lazear, eds., *Searching for Alternatives: Drug Control Policy in the United States.* Stanford, CA: Hoover Institution, pp. 68–76.

Moore, Mark. 1977. *Buy and Bust.* Lexington, MA: Heath.

Moore, Mark. 1990. "Supply Reduction and Drug Law Enforcement." In Michael Tonry and James Q. Wilson, eds., *Drugs and Crime.* Chicago: University of Chicago Press, pp. 109–158.

Musto, David F. 1973. *The American Disease: Origins of Narcotics Control.* New Haven: Yale University Press.

Nadelmann, Ethan. 1991. "The Case for Legalization." In James Inciardi, ed., *The Drug Legalization Debate.* Newbury Park, CA: Sage, pp. 17–44.

Nathan, Richard P. 1975. *The Plot That Failed: Nixon and the Administrative Presidency.* New York: Wiley.

O'Keefe, Garrett J., and Kathaleen Reid. 1990. "The Uses and Effects of Public Service Advertising." In Larissa Grunig and James Grunig, eds., *Public Relations Research Annual,* vol. 2. Hillsdale, NJ: Erlbaum, pp. 67–91.

Ostrowski, James. 1991. "Answering the Critics of Drug Legalization." In Melvyn B. Krauss and Edward P. Lazear, eds., *Searching for Alternatives: Drug Control Policy in the United States.* Stanford, CA: Hoover Institution, pp. 296–323.

Palumbo, Dennis. 1988. *Public Policy in America.* New York: Harcourt Brace Jovanovich.

Paolino, Ronald M. 1991. "Identifying, Treating, and Counseling Drug Abusers." In Robert H. Coombs and Louis J. West, eds., *Drug Testing: Issues and Options.* New York: Oxford University Press, pp. 215–234.

Peele, Stanton. 1989. *Diseasing of America: Addiction Treatment Out of Control.* Lexington, MA: Heath.

Peters, B. Guy. 1993. *American Public Policy: Promise and Performance,* 3rd ed. Chatham, NJ: Chatham House.

Peterson, Robert E. 1991. "Legalization: The Myth Exposed." In Melvyn B. Krauss and Edward P. Lazear, eds., *Searching for Alternatives: Drug Control Policy in the United States.* Stanford, CA: Hoover Institution, pp. 324–355.

Reuter, Peter. 1990. "Can the Borders Be Sealed?" In Ralph Weisheit, ed., *Drugs, Crime and the Criminal Justice System.* Cincinnati: Anderson, pp. 13–26.

Reuter, Peter. 1991. "On the Consequences of Toughness." In Melvyn B. Krauss and Edward P. Lazear, eds., *Searching for Alternatives: Drug Control Policy in the United States.* Stanford, CA: Hoover Institution, pp. 138–164.

Rhoads, Steven. 1985. *The Economist's View of the World.* Cambridge: Cambridge University Press.

Rhodes, Jean E., and Leonard A. Jason. 1988. *Preventing Substance Abuse Among Children and Adolescents.* New York: Pergamon.

Salamon, Lester M. 1979. "The Time Dimension in Policy Evaluation: The Case of New Deal Land Relief Programs." *Public Policy* (Spring): 129–183.

Salisbury, Robert H., John P. Heinz, Edward O. Laumann, and Robert Nelson. 1987. "Who Works with Whom? Interest Group Alliances and Opposition." *American Political Science Review* 81 (December): 1217–1234.

Schlozman, Kay Lehman, and John Tierney. 1986. *Organized Interests and American Democracy.* New York: HarperCollins.

Senary, Edward C. 1984. "Clinical Implications of Drug Abuse Treatment Outcome Research." In Frank Tims and Jacqueline Ludford, eds., *Drug Abuse Treatment Evaluation: Strategies, Progress, and Prospects.* Rockville, MD: National Institute on Drug Abuse, pp. 139–149.

Siegel, R. K. 1982. "Cocaine Smoking." *Journal of Psychoactive Drugs* 14: 271–359.

Simpson, D. Dwayne, and S. B. Sells. 1983. "Effectiveness of Treatment for Drug Abuse: An Overview of the DARP Research Program." In Barry Stimmel, ed., *Evaluation of Drug Treatment Programs.* New York: Haworth Press, pp. 7–29.

Stephens, Richard C. 1987. *Mind-Altering Drugs: Use, Abuse, and Treatment.* Newbury Park, CA: Sage.

Stone, Deborah. 1989. "Causal Stories and the Formation of Policy Agendas." *Political Science Quarterly* 104: 281–300.

Swisher, J. D., J. L. Crawford, R. Goldstein, and M. Yura. 1971. "Drug Education: Pushing or Preventing?" *Peabody Journal of Education* 49: 68–75.

Swisher, J. D., and T. W. Hu. 1983. "Alternatives to Drug Abuse: Some Are and Some Are Not." In T. J. Glynn, C. G. Leukefeld, and J. P. Ludford, eds., *Preventing Adolescent Drug Abuse: Intervention Strategies.* Washington, DC: DHHS Publication no. (ADM) 83-1280, National Institute on Drug Abuse, pp. 141–153.

Szasz, Thomas. 1987. "The Morality of Drug Controls." In Ronald Hamowy, ed., *Dealing with Drugs: Consequences of Government Control.* Lexington, MA: Heath, pp. 327–352.

Taggart, Robert. 1989. "Results of the Drug Testing Program at Southern Pacific Railroad." In Steven Gust and J. Michael Walsh, eds., *Drugs in the Work-*

place: Research and Evaluation Data. Washington, DC: U.S. Government Printing Office, pp. 97–110.

Thompson, Frank J., Norma M. Riccucci, and Carolyn Ban. 1991. "Drug Testing in the Federal Workplace: An Instrumental and Symbolic Assessment." *Public Administration Review* 51 (November/December): 515–525.

Tonry, Michael, and James Q. Wilson, eds. 1990. *Drugs and Crime.* Chicago: University of Chicago Press.

Trebach, Arnold. 1982. *The Heroin Solution.* New Haven: Yale University Press.

Twight, Charlotte. 1990. "Regulation of Asbestos: The Microanalytics of Government Failure." *Policy Studies Review* 10 (Fall): 9–39.

Walsh, J. Michael, and Jeanne G. Trumble. 1991. "The Politics of Drug Testing." In Robert H. Coombs and Louis J. West, eds., *Drug Testing: Issues and Options.* New York: Oxford University Press, pp. 22–49.

Weaver, R. Kent. 1988. *Automatic Government.* Washington, DC: Brookings.

Weir, Margaret. 1992. *Politics and Jobs: The Boundaries of Employment Policy in the United States.* Princeton, NJ: Princeton University Press.

Weiss, Carol H. 1977. "Research for Policy's Sake: The Enlightenment Function of Social Research." *Policy Analysis* 3: 531–545.

Wilson, James Q. 1978. *The Investigators.* New York: Basic Books.

Wilson, James Q. 1991. *On Character.* Washington, DC: AEI Press.

Wisotsky, Steven. 1990. *Beyond the War on Drugs.* Buffalo: Prometheus Books.

Wisotsky, Steven. 1991. "Beyond the War on Drugs." In James Inciardi, ed., *The Drug Legalization Debate.* Newbury Park, CA: Sage, pp. 103–129.

Zeese, Kevin B. 1991. "Drug War Forever?" In Melvyn B. Krauss and Edward P. Lazear, eds., *Searching for Alternatives: Drug Control Policy in the United States.* Stanford, CA: Hoover Institution, pp. 251–270.

Zimring, Franklin E., and Gordon Hawkins. 1991. "The Wrong Question: Critical Notes on the Decriminalization Debate." In Melvyn B. Krauss and Edward P. Lazear, eds., *Searching for Alternatives: Drug Control Policy in the United States.* Stanford, CA: Hoover Institution, pp. 3–32.

Zimring, Franklin E and Gordon Hawkins. 1992. *The Search for Rational Drug Control.* New York: Cambridge University Press.

NEWSPAPER ARTICLES AND OTHER JOURNALISTIC SOURCES

Ayres, B. Drummond. 1988. "Corruption Inquiry Brings Hope to 'Bloody Mingo.'" *New York Times,* March 25: A7.

Belkin, Lisa. 1990. "Airport Anti-Drug Nets Snare Many People Fitting 'Profiles.'" *New York Times,* March 20: 1.

Berke, Richard. 1989a. "A Record 14 Officers Killed in '88 in Drug Incidents, a Study Shows." *New York Times,* September 3: 11.

Berke, Richard. 1989b. "Public Enemy No. 1." *New York Times,* September 3: 1 (sec. 4).

Colasanto, Diane. 1990. "Widespread Opposition to Drug Legalization." *Gallup Poll News Service.* Princeton, NJ: Gallup Organization (microfiche).

"Comprehensive Drug Control Bill Cleared by Congress." 1970. *CQ Almanac,* vol. 26. Washington, DC: Congressional Quarterly, pp. 531–539.

"Congress Clears Comprehensive Drug Control Bill." 1970. *CQ Weekly Report.* October 16: 2539–2542.

"Election-Year Anti-Drug Bill Enacted." 1988. *CQ Almanac.* Washington, DC: Congressional Quarterly, pp. 85–112.

"Excerpts from President's Message on Drug Abuse Control." 1971. *New York Times,* June 18: 22.

"Excerpts from Speech on Halting Drug Abuse." 1986. *New York Times,* September 15: B10.

Gallup, George. 1977. *The Gallup Poll: Public Opinion 1972–1977,* vol. 2, 1976–1977. Wilmington, DE: Scholarly Resources.

Goldstein, Tom. 1977. "Backing Grows for Easing Marijuana Laws." *New York Times,* February 3: 14.

Greenhouse, Linda. 1986. "Congress Approves Anti-Drug Bill as Senate Bars a Death Provision." *New York Times,* October 18: 33.

Holmes, Steven. 1990. "Fewer Turf Battles, More Drug Arrests." *New York Times,* January 21: 22 (sec. 4).

Horsley, Lynn. 1989. "Case of Alleged Sale of Baby Cited as Proof of Drug Crisis." *Kansas City Times,* September 30: B4.

Johnston, David. 1989. "Democrats Claim Success in Drug Policy." *New York Times,* October 8: 14.

London, Robb. 1991. "Judge's Overruling of Crack Law Brings Turmoil." *New York Times,* January 11: B5.

"Major Crime Package Cleared by Congress." 1984. *CQ Almanac.* Washington, DC: Congressional Quarterly, pp. 215–229.

Martin, Douglas. 1991. "'Tough Love' for Those Most in Need." *New York Times,* June 5: A16.

McKinley, James. 1989. "In New York, New Drug Tests Set for Police." *New York Times,* September 6: 16.

Mydans, Seth. 1989. "Powerful Arms of Drug War Arousing Concern for Rights." *New York Times,* October 16: 1.

Nemy, Enid. 1982. "First Lady Finds a Cause." *New York Times,* February 19: B5.

New York Times Index, 1971. 1972. New York: New York Times Company.

New York Times Index, 1982. 1983. New York: New York Times Company.

Reinhold, Robert. 1977. "Smoking of Marijuana Wins Wider Acceptance." *New York Times,* May 23: 46.

Rosenbaum, David. 1989. "Cost Is Estimated on Bush Drug War." *New York Times,* September 6: 11.

Schmidt, Dana Adams. 1972. "U.S. Officials Report Progress in Stopping Drugs." *New York Times,* August 17: 16.

Schmidt, William E. 1989. "Drug War Funds Arouse Conflict." *New York Times,* November 12: 1.

Sciolino, Elaine. 1990. "World Drug Crop Up Sharply in 1989 Despite U.S. Effort." *New York Times,* March 2: 1.

Shelly, Barbara. 1990a. "Experts Debate Value of Therapy." *Kansas City Star,* April 18: A1, A16.

Shelly, Barbara. 1990b. "Insurers Tighten Controls." *Kansas City Star,* April 17: A6.

Shenon, Philip. 1988. "Enemy Within: Drug Money Is Corrupting the Enforcers." *New York Times,* April 11: 1.

Sloane, Todd. 1989. "States: Read Our Lips, Send More Money," *City & State,*

September 11–24: 30.

"Text of President's Speech on National Drug Control Strategy." 1989. *New York Times*, September 6:10.

"Three Officers Are Charged in Thefts of Cash and Drugs." 1990. *New York Times*, January 25: A18.

"Transcripts of the President's News Conference on Foreign and Domestic Matters." 1981. *New York Times*, March 7: 10.

Treaster, Joseph B. 1990. "Bush Hails Decline in Drug Abuse But Critics Say Survey Is Flawed." *New York Times*, December 20: A12.

Treaster, Joseph B. 1991. "Use of Cocaine and Heroin Rises Among Urban Youth." *New York Times*, December 19: A18.

Treaster, Joseph B. 1992. "Hospital Visits Show Abuse of Drugs Is Still on the Rise." *New York Times*, May 14: 8.

"U.S. Shifts Emphasis in New Drive on Drug Abuse." 1982. *New York Times*, October 6: 14.

Weinraub, Bernard. 1989. "States Would Pay Much of the Bill for the Drug War." *New York Times*, September 8: 1.

Index